P9-DMU-215

BURN DOWN THE GROUND

BURN DOWN THE GROUND

A Memoir

KAMBRI CREWS

Villard New York

Burn Down the Ground is a work of nonfiction. Nonetheless, some of the names and personal characteristics of the individuals involved have been changed in order to disguise their identities. Any resulting resemblance to persons living or dead is entirely coincidental and unintentional.

Copyright © 2012 by Workshop Creations LLC

All rights reserved.

Published in the United States by Villard Books,
an imprint of The Random House Publishing Group,
a division of Random House, Inc., New York.

VILLARD BOOKS and VILLARD & "V" CIRCLED Design are
registered trademarks of Random House, Inc.

Library of Congress Cataloging-in-Publication Data
Crews, Kambri.
Burn down the ground : a memoir / Kambri Crews.
    p.   cm.
ISBN 978-0-345-51602-2 (hardcover) — ISBN 978-0-345-53220-6 (ebook)
    1. Crews, Kambri.   2. Children of deaf parents—Biography.
        3. Texas—Biography.   I. Title.
            HQ759.912.C74 2011
        306.874092—dc23   [B]   2011040828

Printed in the United States of America on acid-free paper

www.villard.com

2 4 6 8 9 7 5 3 1

First Edition

Book design by Diane Hobbing

For my mother

It doesn't matter who my father was;
it matters who I remember he was.

—ANNE SEXTON

CONTENTS

New York City, 2002–2008

PROLOGUE

Dear Kambri,

Thank you so much for the "USA Today" and for more money in Trust Fund. I wish you were rich so you can send more.

I am in solitary for 30 days. What I did was insult the interpreter Mrs. Heath. Called her "Bitch Whore" after we argued. Anyway I don't care if I stay in cell, and I don't have money for the Commissary anyway.

Will you visit me? Don't forget to sneak a pack of Wrigley's

Juicy Fruit from the Free World. Prison rules say don't dress sexy or short skirt. I bet you know how to do it right. Wear big, loose shirt for hiding a Dairy Queen hamburger.

Love, Daddy

Daddy is Theodore R. Crews, Jr., or Inmate #13A46B7 to the Texas Department of Criminal Justice. He lives in Huntsville—a city of thirty-five thousand located sixty-seven miles from Houston on Interstate 45 toward Dallas. It's a nondescript Texas city, known for decent barbecue, Sam Houston State University, and Huntsville Prison—the former home of "Old Sparky," a wooden electric chair handcrafted by inmates that was used to execute 361 men between 1924 and 1964.

The prison is a lot less ominous than I expected. Except for the barbed wire, it reminds me of a school. It is a large, drab institution devoid of any color but with armed guards instead of hall monitors and a warden instead of a principal.

I have never been to a prison before, so as I drive up to the gate my stomach is in knots. An overstuffed officer wearing cowboy boots, a ten-gallon hat, and a white handlebar mustache approaches my car and rattles off orders in a thick Texan drawl.

"Pop the hood, open the trunk, and show me your ID."

I fumble with my wallet and hand him my driver's license. He takes a glance and declares with a mischievous glint, "New York City? Get a rope!"

I let out a nervous laugh but question his judgment. Is it really wise to joke about hangings at a prison famous for executions?

He must figure that a woman in high heels from New York City would not be hiding a jumbo pack of gum in the waistband of her neatly pressed Banana Republic slacks. When his metal-detecting wand shrieks where the pack of gum is hidden, he dismisses it. "Don't you worry, honey, it's just your belt buckle." I am not wearing a belt. Juicy Fruit, however, is wrapped in foil.

I venture into the visiting area, a large open room that resembles a cafeteria with vending machines along the wall. There are two long tables with prisoners lined up on one side and visitors on the other. This is the contact visiting area, available only to immediate family members of inmates. What you see on television, with thick glass separating inmates from their visitors, is a non-contact visit. Those are for convicts on restriction for misbehaving, or non-relatives.

Dad isn't supposed to be allowed to see visitors here—he is serving a punishment of a year in segregation for striking a guard—but the warden is letting us have a contact visit because I traveled so far.

Always one for small talk, I am surprised at how friendly the guards are. I imagined they would be stoic, with close-cropped hair and hands resting on their weapons.

They give me warm smiles and polite nods and say things like "How're you doing today, ma'am?" and "Sure is a beautiful day, isn't it?" If I just look past their uniforms and guns, we could be anywhere.

I wonder if they know Dad. Will they treat me differently when they see whom I'm here to visit? Should I apologize to them in advance?

My father comes out of the caged holding area. I expect to see him wearing a fluorescent orange jumpsuit or bold prison stripes. Instead, he's clad in all white, from the short-sleeved shirt over long johns down to his cotton pants and Chuck Taylors. He looks more like an orderly at a hospital than a hardened criminal.

My delight at seeing Dad quickly turns to shock. The last time I saw him he was perfectly fit, but now he is hunched over, slowly shuffling his feet.

Did he break something? Was he in another fight? Has he just aged? Has it been that long? Yes, it has been that long. Christmas 1997, nine years ago, when he spent the holidays with me and I bought him a VCR for that dilapidated trailer of his.

I glance away and try to pull myself together. I look back and flash the biggest smile I can muster. With extra enthusiasm, I wave "I love you" in sign language. He weakly waves back but doesn't answer, choosing instead to concentrate on his pained walk.

I have let Dad rot in here alone.

My eyes well up with tears just as my father kicks up his heels and dances a jig. He signs, "Ha ha! See what could happen? You should visit me more! I'm an old man!"

I stand stunned for a second, my mouth literally falling open before I rouse myself to sign with big, sweeping gestures and a huge smile, "You J-E-R-K!" Dad gives me a hug—not a long one. A guard is standing close, hand ready at my father's elbow, waiting to lead him to his designated chair across the long wooden table from me.

But the strongest steel bars can't cage charisma. Dad resumes walking with his trademark strut—cockiness dripping from every pore.

There's nothing to cry about. He is totally fine.

I maintain my composure and act like every woman spends Christmas sneaking Juicy Fruit to her father in prison.

BOARS HEAD

1978–1986

Chapter One

KINGPIN

I tugged on the belt loop of Mom's skintight jeans, and waited for her to look down and acknowledge me. I wanted money to play Space Invaders in the bowling alley arcade, but she was concentrating on reading the lips of a balding deaf man who had two hooks for hands. Despite having no fingers, he tried to communicate with American Sign Language (ASL), scraping the curved metal claws against each other as if he were giving a Ginsu knife demonstration. My mother was an expert lip reader and kept her eyes focused on his mouth to make sense of the flurried flashes of metal; she bobbed her head up and down to let him know that she understood.

I stared at the beige plastic attachments that encased each wrist and wondered how they stayed connected to his fleshy stubs. Did he take them off at night? Were they suction cups or drilled into his arms? I shuddered at the thought and watched how he made the hooks open and close.

Was he born that way or did he have an accident? After contemplating both scenarios, I decided it would be better if he were born without hands. That way he wouldn't know the difference. I couldn't imagine that the world would be so cruel as to take the hands of a grown deaf man.

As I stared at his signing, his hooks brushed perilously close to my face, causing me to reel back in fear. I had a brief horrifying image of running for my life being chased by him, with his grunts and wheezing breath hot on my neck. But Mom, who made fast friends with everyone she met, was perfectly at ease.

I yanked harder and smacked her round bottom. *"MAAAA-MMMMAA!!!"*

"What?" Mom signed by waving her hand with the palm side up, exasperated at my persistence. "Can't you see I'm talking?"

"Need quarter," I signed back.

Mom could partially hear when she wore powerful hearing aids—one of which was always on the fritz, in need of a battery or screeching like brakes crying for new pads—but they were useless in the din of crashing bowling pins. For all practical purposes, she was as deaf as every other grown-up gathered in the dingy Tulsa bowling alley smelling of fried food, cigarettes, and beer. They had traveled here from all parts of the country to compete in the 1978 National Deaf Bowling Tournament, where Mom was scheduled to defend her title as women's singles champion.

This event was the type of activity the Deaf community created so that members could mingle. In the days before the Internet and mobile gadgets, the best way for the Deaf to socialize was old-fashioned face-to-face time through clubs, travel groups, cruises, and sporting events like fishing and bowling tournaments. While some fathers may have gravitated toward fishing and hunting, mine liked bowling because he could smoke, drink, and carouse between rounds. Mom liked it because she was damned good, with a 164 average. Usually her winnings were enough to pay for our trips with a little profit to boot.

The National Deaf Bowling Association was founded in 1964, but the women's singles had only been around for four years and Mom was already a force to be reckoned with. She loved to brag about how she was knocking down pins while knocked up with me. She'd bowled three days prior to my birth and was back in the alley three days later.

The wooden lanes and alley lights may as well have been the stage and footlights of Broadway. She was a star and I was proud to say she was my mother.

Mom answered my plea for a quarter by pantomiming empty front pockets and signing, "I'm out. Go ask your daddy."

Without hesitation, I turned on my heels and skipped to the bowling alley lounge, where I found my father leaning against the pool table holding court among a small gathering of onlookers. He held a cold can of Coors Light and a lit Kool in one hand and was signing with his free hand.

"Two deaf people get married. The first week of living together they find it hard to talk in the bedroom after they turn off the lights."

I caught Dad's eye and he gave me a quick wink as he gave the ASL sign for "wait" by wiggling his slim fingers palm side up, revealing the calluses from his years as a construction worker. Unlike my mother, Dad didn't speak at all other than an occasional shout of a name or profanity aimed at a Dallas Cowboys game. When he did, his voice came out in an oddly high pitch with too much air behind it. He couldn't read lips as well as Mom and didn't move his mouth much when he signed.

I let him finish the joke that he didn't bother censoring, even though I was nearby. I had watched him tell it at least a dozen times. As he signed, the ash on his cigarette grew longer.

"After several nights of misunderstandings, the wife comes up with a solution. 'Honey, we need simple signals in the bedroom at night. If you want to have sex, just reach over and squeeze my breast once; and if you don't want to have sex, squeeze it twice.'

"The husband replies, 'Great idea. If you want to have sex, pull my dick once. If you don't want to have sex, pull it a hundred and fifty times.'"

His audience erupted into a variety of loud grunts and squeals of laughter. One waved his hands, while another signed ASL letters, "H-A-H-A-H-A." Dad chuckled at himself with a slight curl of his upper lip, making a dimple appear in his right cheek. He took a drag of his cigarette and the long, crooked ash finally broke off, landing on the worn, booze-stained carpet. A few flakes floated onto his dark blue jeans and he sent them flying with one forceful burst of breath. He inspected his appearance and brushed off the remaining ashes before he asked, "What's wrong?"

I signed back, "Need money."

"Okay, but don't waste," he warned before making a big production out of retrieving his wallet and fishing through its contents. I'd always thought of my father like a deaf Elvis. Tall, muscular, and handsome with dark hair combed back into a modern pompadour, he could charm the skin off a snake. His friends were caught in his magnetic spell and kept their eyes trained on our exchange. Dad seized the opportunity to remain in the spotlight. He grabbed my shoulder and whisked me around to face his fans.

"Do you know my daughter? Her name K-A-M-B-R-I." In ASL, it is customary to introduce someone by first spelling out the name letter by letter followed up with a shorthand sign, a "Name Sign," to refer to that person. A person's Name Sign often uses the first letter of their name in ASL incorporated with the sign that indicates a physical or personal characteristic, such as a big smile or a goatee or, in my case, my temperament as a baby.

Dad signed each letter slowly so they had time to soak in my unusual name. He then drew a tear on each of his cheeks using the middle finger of the ASL letter "K" to show them the sign he and Mom had created for me.

"Why tears with a 'K'? Because when she was a baby she never cried. No. Never. Always laugh, laugh, laugh."

He patted my head and smiled. I looked back at the adult faces staring at me and forced my lips into a smile—not quite the hyena Dad was describing—as I waited for the money. As was always the case when I was introduced to deaf people, the first question was, "Hearing?"

Dad signed, "Yes, hearing."

I sensed a twinge of disappointment in their expressions, a typical reaction when deaf friends learned I wasn't one of them. I understand it now, but as a seven-year-old kid I found myself wishing I had been born deaf, too. Then I would belong to the tight-knit Deaf community instead of being just an honorary member.

"Very smart," Dad bragged. "Good girl. Nickname 'Motor Mouth.'"

You know you talk a lot when your deaf family nicknames you Motor Mouth.

Dad passed me a crisp bill, and my eyes widened when I saw it was a five. Five bucks would get me an icy Dr Pepper, greasy crinkle fries, and plenty of games in the arcade.

"Share with your brother," he signed with a warning raise of his brow.

David could fend for himself. Besides, I reasoned, he was three and a half years older than me and better at most video games. One quarter lasted him a hell of a long time; surely he didn't need any more money. After a quick thank-you to Dad and a half-assed wave to his friends, I left the dark, smoky hideaway and headed straight for the snack bar.

In the game room, I found David dominating Space Invaders, as usual. He swayed and ducked, jerked the joystick, and repeatedly bashed the fire button as a crowd of admiring onlookers grew around him. He must have been within reach of the machine's high score, a feat I'd witnessed him achieve once before.

"Totally rad!" a kid shouted, giving David a slap on the back.

"Yeah, totally!" said another with a high-five. My brother accepted the accolades from his minions, who always flitted behind him, with a smug smirk.

"That was so neat, man!"

A freckle-faced kid challenged, "Yeah, but can you reach the *end?*"

"Video games don't end," another kid stated with certainty.

"Oh yeah? Well then how far does it go?"

We weren't totally sure. Each round became progressively harder so it was difficult imagining a game lasting forever. But if you were winning, why would a game just quit? David seemed in line to be our exploratory leader, a twentieth-century Christopher Columbus.

I smacked down a quarter on the glass screen with a crack, claiming my place as the next player in line, and waited for him to lose.

"Go away," he demanded. "You're gonna fuck me up."

David was skinnier than a dried stick of spaghetti and, at ten years old, already as tall as many adults. Like me, his hair was as white as hotel sheets with skin browned from frolicking every day in the blazing South Texas heat without a drop of sunscreen. David returned to concentrating on his game, so I ignored his command and lingered long enough to see him lose a turn.

"See!" he yelled as he gave a quick jab to my arm. "Look at what you made me do!"

I yelped in pain and poked the lump where he had knuckle-punched me.

"I told you to go away," he hissed. "Stop watching me."

The End was apparently not in sight as long as I was present. David's cronies sneered at me. I was jeopardizing my brother's attempt at immortality, so I retreated to the Pong machine. When I ran out of quarters, I sprinted back to the lanes, where the hook-handed man was stepping up to bowl. He had replaced his right hook with a special contraption that gripped his bowling ball. As he charged down the alley, he used his left hook to whack some lever or button that sent his ball barreling toward the pins. I had no idea how many he knocked down or if his aim was any good. Did it matter? *A deaf man with hooks for hands was bowling.*

When the bowling was finished, my parents' night was just getting warmed up. Every night out to a Deaf event ended the same way. My mom and dad stood gathered in a circle of deaf family and friends for what seemed like an eternity while I did absolutely nothing, waiting impatiently to go home. Drink after drink crossed the bar—more Coors Light for Dad, Seven & Sevens for Mom—as Deaf community gossip was dished with a flurry of hands.

Unlike other kids absorbing adult chatter, my "listening in" required eyes and dedicated attention. I was tired and desperately wanted to go, but getting a deaf person to leave any social engagement was harder than eating spaghetti with a knife.

Hoping my parents would notice, I made a dramatic production of pushing together three plastic chairs to serve as a makeshift bed. I draped Dad's denim blazer over me and waited for them to call it a night. I almost wanted to walk up to the alley manager and tell him to flick the lights on and off, the best way of telling a group of deaf people it was closing time. Although I was too big to be carried around like a baby, when my father roused me, I pretended to be fast asleep. He scooped me up and carried me to the car. I buried my face in his neck and breathed in his trademark scent of Jovan Musk and beer and nicotine. My parents, never extravagant with accommodations, unloaded us at a roadside motel for the night.

The next afternoon, a local news reporter arrived at the bowling alley to cover the final day of the tournament, creating a buzz. A slim strawberry blonde, my mother was easy on the eyes. For the first few years of her life, she could hear without the help of hearing aids. This meant she could speak more clearly than most of her hearing-impaired peers, making her the unofficial ambassador to the hearing world. Naturally, the reporter chose to interview her.

Mom was scheduled to close the annual ceremony by performing several songs in ASL, accompanied by a live band. More thrillingly, however, the concert was going to be shown on television.

There weren't many occasions for Mom to get gussied up, so when the opportunity presented itself she went full glitz. Seeing her leave the motel room dressed in three-inch heels and a shiny, short-sleeved maroon wrap dress that clung to her tan skin and showcased her enormous breasts, you'd have thought she was headed to New York's Studio 54 instead of a run-down bowling alley. At thirty-one, she was in the prime of her life and the center of attention. She loved every minute of it.

The reporter chatted with my mother, who was standing near the band, two guitarists and a drummer, who were setting up their instruments at the far end of the establishment. The cameraman turned on the bright spotlight and with a quick toss of her head and flash of a smile, Mom was "on." Before the reporter could even ask a question, Mom declared, "We are *deaf* not *dumb*."

To this day, the phrase "deaf and dumb" is the most offensive insult to a deaf person. Mom wanted to make it clear that just because a person couldn't hear didn't mean they lacked intelligence.

I stood directly behind the cameraman and admired how proudly she stood, with both shoulders back. Even now, as a woman in her sixties, she carries herself with the same poise and grace at a backyard barbecue as at a wedding. She gestured to a table of merchandise like a TV game show model presenting an item up for bid. The table had items available for purchase, assorted T-shirts and handcrafted buttons proclaiming, "Deaf and ~~dumb~~ SMART." They rested alongside an abundance of crocheted knickknacks, jewelry, and assorted keepsakes decorated with hands in the shape of the ASL sign for "I love you."

The reporter nodded politely. "You are performing a concert tonight. How can deaf people enjoy music?"

"Even though we can't hear, we can feel the vibration." She simultaneously signed as she spoke. "We dance to the beat of our own drummer." She flashed a wide smile that revealed two rows of straight, white teeth, perfect except for a chip in the front from a childhood spill on a tricycle.

"Deaf people enjoy music. They just don't hear the lyrics," Mom explained. That's where she came in.

My mother loved music and incorporated it into every aspect of her life. Deafness ran in her family. She was born to two profoundly deaf parents, and had a younger deaf sister named Carly and a few deaf aunts and uncles. By having some hearing ability, it was as if she were determined to hear enough music for all of them and listened to it with a junkie's fervor. Anything would do. Hard-rocking Led Zeppelin played alongside the kooky, light pop of Captain & Tennille.

Mom collected hundreds of vinyl records. She also subscribed to *Billboard*'s Hot 100 and music magazines that published lyrics so she could understand the words. Every Sunday afternoon, she piled a thick stack of 45s onto the hi-fi console turntable, the most impressive piece of furniture we ever owned, cranked the volume, and cleaned house while singing to her favorite songs. Mom couldn't carry a tune in a bucket. But it didn't matter: Our weekend ritual was so much fun with Mom vacuuming and David and me sharing the dusting duties.

I plopped down cross-legged, front row and center, in the crowd that formed in a semicircle around Mom and the band. I slapped my hand over my puffed-up chest as they began to play the national anthem.

I mouthed along with her signing as the song swelled to its triumphant end, majestically demonstrated by Mom's sweeping movements, ". . . and the home . . . of the . . . BRAVE!" I applauded wildly while the Deaf showed their approval by raising their arms and wiggling their fingers as if they were tickling God's belly. No one could sign a song in ASL like Mom could.

Mom accepted the praise with a curtsy and thank-you before she continued. "This next song is my favorite. It's called 'Dreams' by Fleetwood Mac." The music started and stirred within her. She grooved in place to the opening chords.

Now here you go again,
You say you want your freedom . . .

Mom was flushed from the heat of the spotlight, the thrill of performing, and the few cocktails she'd been drinking. Dad leaned against a wall in the back of the crowd, sipping a fresh

Coors Light. He smiled with a slight smirk as his wife relished the limelight. I shared his thought: She was beautiful.

From where I sat, my mother was the envy of anyone in that stale Tulsa bowling alley. But the truth was, this trip to Oklahoma should have been our last as a family. Dad had cheated on Mom again—this time on New Year's Eve—and pretty much everyone there knew it except for David and me. Fed up with his philandering, Mom was leaving him. She'd hastily packed everything we owned into a rented storage space and in the days before we set off for Tulsa, she had checked us into an apartment in the bad part of Houston that charged by the week.

David and I didn't know the purpose of our trip to Tulsa. We were unaware that Mom was going to break the news to her parents about her plans to divorce Dad. By participating in the bowling tournament, she was also fulfilling her obligations to the Deaf community. She was the reigning women's singles champion, after all.

My father was just along for the ride to see his friends and keep up appearances for Mom, though he had a hard time staying on the straight and narrow. He couldn't help but party hard and flirt, assuring anyone who questioned his antics that he was going to be single soon.

"Christy left me," he told one woman. "She wants a divorce," he told another. He wasn't lying, but his comments resulted in something Dad hadn't anticipated. He had set the rumor mill swirling and several women approached Mom with the same blunt question: "Are you and Ted getting a divorce?" One thing Mom passed down to me was her disdain for the malicious gossip that seemed to infect their circle of friends in the Deaf community, as if there was some sort of perverse satisfaction in circulating the misery of another. Being married to my father made her hypersensitive to the damage that whispers could cause.

"Who told you that?" Mom defiantly responded.

"Ted," they answered.

She confronted Dad with the gossip. "Why did they ask me that?"

"They're jealous of you," he signed. "They don't want to see us together."

"But they said you told them I left you."

"No! They lie. They're trying to break us up and cause problems." My father could spin shit into gold. Once he told a lie, he committed to it, and with each retelling it became his truth. He grabbed Mom by her waist and smothered her neck and cheeks with kisses, smiling as he cooed in his softest voice, "I luh yooo, Chrisseee. I luh yooo." There was his dimple again.

Some kids might have been embarrassed at seeing their parents be affectionate, but I never was. I loved watching them kiss and cuddle. I was too young to understand my father's motives and see that he was playing upon Mom's weakness: her determination to appear strong, in control, and poised like the woman her fans adored. That night, her pride got in the way—she knew he was a cheater, but by staying with him she could prove the nay-saying gossips wrong. So she took him back, on one condition.

Chapter Two

MONTGOMERY HILLBILLIES

Mom pointed to a red star she'd drawn on our tattered Texas road atlas and said, "That's where we're moving." It was nowhere near the spiderweb-like clusters of routes and interstates. Boars Head, the spot where we were set to live, wasn't even on the map.

"We're gonna start a whole new life," she said. "It'll be like a long camping trip." We had just returned home from the bowling tournament when Mom delivered her sales pitch. She made the move from our industrial neighborhood in the outskirts of Houston to the wild woods of Montgomery sound like an adventure from *Little House on the Prairie*. She left out the part about my father cheating on her again. For Dad, moving to the woods was meant to be his penance and keep him far away from smoky nightclubs and fast women.

If we had owned a doghouse, my father would have been in it. We weren't rich, so buying Mom's affection with fancy jewelry was out of the question. Instead, Dad would restore his marriage and his wife's faith by building her the home she dreamed of on this little patch of land in the woods. Hard labor was to be my father's sentence. Not his first and, as it turned out, not his last.

David and I knew the spot. We'd been out there a handful of times to scope out the heavily wooded property that Dad had bought a year earlier on a whim after a long drive in the country with a friend.

My father was raised on a farm in Oklahoma and owning a piece of nature was a lifelong dream of his. The five and a half acres didn't cost much and Mom agreed it was a good investment. During the good times, they both liked to talk about building a two-story dream home where they could enjoy their retirement.

Dad was a construction worker during the height of the population explosion in Texas in the late 1970s, when people flocked to Houston to find work in the booming oil industry. He worked on shopping malls and skyscrapers, impressing everyone with his natural talent. His handiwork decorated the homes of our extended family—dressers, cabinets, you name it. During a visit to one relative, Mom pointed out a wooden sideboard filled with china and said, "Your daddy made that."

Our family's furniture was so beautiful that I couldn't imagine my father crafting it with his own hands. As a young boy, he built a rabbit hutch from scratch and showed it to his father, who replied, "Where did you buy that thing?"

Conveniently, he didn't need to hear to work in construction; when jackhammers and power saws are in action, everyone is deaf. My father was the best of the best, so he was made a foreman on many sites, put in charge of his hearing colleagues. His skills were in constant demand in Houston's expansion, although he didn't earn enough money to allow my mother to stay home and raise her kids.

Mom had been working on an assembly line since graduating from high school and was highly skilled at putting together intricate electronic panels and devices. She had wanted to attend Gallaudet University, the nation's largest college for the Deaf, located in Washington, D.C., but her father convinced her that a higher education wasn't necessary. He thought she was better off getting married and staying close to home. She was the only one in her immediate family with any kind of hearing ability. Therefore, she was their lifeline to the hearing world.

Before we moved to Houston, we had lived across the street from my mother's parents in Tulsa, Oklahoma. Mom had a full-time job at Century Electronics when my brother was born in 1967, so my grandmother became his primary caregiver. She was almost as much of a mother to him as Mom was. She and my brother rarely left the house, and because she wasn't able to communicate orally with him, David learned to speak at a slightly slower pace than the other kids. Although she could say his name and make noise to get his attention, she relied on ASL to interact with him.

When I was born on June 22, 1971, Mom quit work to stay home and raise us. My mother and grandmother talked, sang, and read books to me in both spoken English and ASL.

As a child with deaf parents, commonly referred to in the Deaf community as Children of Deaf Adults (CODA), I am frequently asked, "How did you learn to talk?" The query is often delivered with astonishment, as if having deaf parents should have shriveled my vocal cords. I learned to speak orally the way any hearing child does: by listening to the world around me. I had Mom, television, music, neighbors, and people in stores. Other deaf parents, worried that their hearing children wouldn't learn to speak as well as their peers, would expose them to media to the point of overstimulation. Keith Wann, a popular CODA comedian, tells an anecdote of how his deaf mother required him to listen to the radio, not realizing the only sound being emitted was static.

My first ASL word was "Daddy," signed at five months old. Days later, I spoke the word "Mama." By eighteen months old, I was using ASL and could speak English better than other toddlers my age. I liked to entertain my father by performing my favorite nursery rhymes in both sign language and song. Dad even built a "stage" for me around our mod red freestanding fireplace. I'd sing into my mother's hairbrush as if it were a microphone and put on a show. "Watch me, Daddy, I'm going to sing for you," I would sign. "I'm going to be a movie star when I grow up."

Dad would grin and sign, "Okay, I'm watching," then made a big production of putting away the paper so I knew he was obeying me.

~

Mom didn't return to work until I entered kindergarten. I could never tell if she was unhappy with her decision to forgo college. She seemed to like her factory job and was always getting promotions. When we moved to Boars Head, she quit her job at Welex Jet Services because it would be too far to travel to, but my father planned to keep working and commute the two hours each way to and from Houston five days a week from our land on Boars Head. But moving out there with only an uninhabitable cabin and a ramshackle outhouse seemed to be ill advised, and I wasn't sure how this plan would work. My only experience "camping" was draping sheets over a clothesline in the backyard and having Kool-Aid and popcorn delivered by Mom. However, the idea of living without modern conveniences, like Laura Ingalls, sounded thrilling to a seven-year-old girl like me. This camping trip included kerosene lanterns and my own nylon sleeping bag, which reversed to blue or red depending on which way I zipped it. I practiced rolling and unrolling, zipping and unzipping, and sleeping in it on the floor.

With only the bare necessities piled in the back of our baby blue 1966 Chevrolet pickup, we reinvented ourselves as modern-day pioneers.

David and I rode in the bed of the Chevy, sitting on our own wheel wells as we sped north on Interstate 45 toward Montgomery. Pamie, our one-year-old Chihuahua mix, wasn't as lucky; she had to ride in the cab on Mom's lap.

Situated sixty-five miles northwest of Houston on the edge of the Sam Houston National Forest, Montgomery began as an Indian trading post in 1826, making it the third-oldest settlement in Texas. It is considered the official birthplace of the Lone Star flag because the man credited with its design, Charles B. Stewart, was a resident. The fact is debatable, but the city of Montgomery still holds it as its claim to fame.

The city officially measured one square mile, with a population just shy of 250 people, though outlying communities boosted that tally. The center of town consisted of a single intersection: a four-way stop that led to a post office depot, convenience store, gas station, or cemetery depending on which way you turned.

The longer we drove, the less inhabited things got. Shopping centers dwindled down to roadside markets that soon disappeared altogether. The roads got narrower and bumpier as we rumbled by pastures of grazing cattle and fields of bluebonnets until we were so deep in the middle of nowhere there were no traffic signs, fire hydrants, streetlights . . . *nothing*.

While we'd moved a number of times during my seven years, my life to date had been spent in cities where houses were in subdivisions and convenience stores occupied every corner. I was a typical latchkey kid. Why would parents bother paying for a babysitter when they could tie a key around their kids' necks with a piece of yarn and let them watch cartoons for an hour or two until they got home from work?

As I sat in the back of the Chevy watching civilization vanish, I began to worry. I thought of the 7-Eleven where my friend stole wax candy while I served as a decoy. *Where will I get candy now?* I had a slew of friends in Houston, so many they couldn't all fit into our dining room during my last birthday party. Montgomery was so deserted I couldn't imagine humans lived there, much less kids.

I was jerked out of my troublesome thoughts when a tree limb scraped the roof of the Chevy. David and I held on tight to the truck's metal edges, made hot by the Texas sun, ducking and dodging to avoid getting knocked over the side. Frightened, I waved in the rearview mirror to get my father's attention and signed, "Daddy! Slow down!" I threw myself around to show him how I was being tossed like a rag doll. He broke into a big smile, then pumped the brake and jerked the wheel, causing us to slide like we were riding the Scrambler at a carnival.

Finally, the Chevy rounded a hairpin turn and I saw a hand-painted chunk of wood nailed to a tree that read "Boars Head." Flanked by solid walls of pine trees, we proceeded down the bumpy, single-lane dirt road turned bright pumpkin orange from a coating of iron ore gravel that had been laid by some of the locals for traction. We drove over a bridge made of railroad ties that was so rickety it rippled from the weight of the Chevy. Although it was only ten feet above a half-dry creek bed, I began praying to God that I would live to see my eighth birthday.

The truck came to a quick stop, skidding on the pebbles, and creating a cloud of orange dust. We couldn't drive any farther. A wall of trees blocked our way and we had to walk the remaining six hundred feet into the dense forest to our campsite. As I hopped out, my mother shouted a warning: "Watch where you step! There're snakes hiding everywhere."

I kept my eyes focused on the ground as I followed Dad, trekking over the forest floor layered with pinecones and needles as we passed wild palms and aloe plants. Soon we were so deep in the forest that despite the early afternoon hour, it was as dark as a moonlit night save for an occasional glimmer of sunlight when a stiff breeze blew the treetops. Before each step, I looked for a snake. I wasn't even sure what one looked like, but I knew they were our enemy. Pamie seemed oblivious to the danger as she bounded along, craning her neck to see over the brush, leaping over sticks and bushes.

At last, we reached it: the cabin.

I marveled at the sheer size of it. The logs of the cabin were at least two feet in diameter and stripped of all bark. Oddly, there was an old diesel truck parked smack dab inside it.

"Home, sweet home!" Mom gushed. She looked positively dazzled.

"This is where we're going to live?" I asked. "How can we stay in a house with a broken-down truck in it?"

With or without the scrapped semi, the cabin wasn't habitable or even salvageable. There was no roof, windows, or doors, and the logs, many of which looked half-rotten, weren't chinked.

The plan wasn't to *live* in it. We were going to start from scratch. We would sleep in tents until my father could convert an outbuilding on the property into something sufferable while we cleared and readied the land for a mobile home.

Mom's father was a fisherman and a hunter, so she was accustomed to living with an outdoorsman. Though this was a far cry from a weekend camping trip or a visit to a favorite fishing hole, my mother seemed willing to accept being homeless in order to start fresh with Dad.

My father loved working with his hands. He seemed inspired by the challenge that lay before him, completing this enormous undertaking all on his own while restoring his wife's faith. I dreaded what appeared to be a monumental job, but David was euphoric. I hadn't seen him this excited since he got his knockoff Evel Knievel bicycle for his ninth birthday.

By nightfall we had set up our campsite. But the night was so hot and muggy that the only way to sleep was outside of our tents in sleeping bags under the stars. Who needed a cabin anyway? The woods were so dense that once the sun set I couldn't see my own hand in front of my face.

That first night, I had to visit the outhouse. Nestled in a cluster of trees, the latrine was constructed from leftover tin and rotted wood. It stood fifty feet from where we slept, just far enough away that the stench of stagnant waste wouldn't waft through our campsite. To avoid any embarrassing moments with deaf visitors, Mom had painted a block of wood for the door that read "Occupied" on one side and "Vacant" on the other, since there was no lock and they wouldn't hear a knock at the door.

Wearing a T-shirt and underpants, I shuffled along the dirt path, following the beam of my flashlight. The cacophony of owls, crickets, and croaks of bullfrogs didn't frighten me much. As a child reared around deaf people who had no idea how loud they could be, I was used to turning a ruckus into a white noise symphony.

But as I reached the stall, I remembered Mom warning me, "Be sure to check the hole before you sit. You don't want a snake to bite you in the ass."

I pointed the flashlight into the reeking hole, sending a dozen daddy longlegs scurrying for cover. I shuddered.

Finding it free of snakes, I started my business. But when a tree grazed against the rusted tin roof, I stopped midstream. I imagined the branches to be the metal hooks of the deaf man from the bowling tournament, scraping against the side of the outhouse and coming after me.

I burst through the outhouse door and bounded barefoot down the path, yanking up my underwear along the way, a flash of towheaded lightning. I'd learned long before that there was no use in crying; my parents couldn't hear me.

Nevertheless, sheer terror forced a guttural wail out of my skinny frame. As I ran, my flashlight turned every tree into a looming bogeyman. My body involuntarily convulsed, desperate to shake off whatever I imagined was touching me before I reached the safety of my sleeping bag.

I made sure to never again go to bed without first emptying my bladder while everyone was still awake.

Dad had big plans for our five and a half acres. Our land on Boars Head was raw, wild terrain and the top priority was to clear a driveway so the Chevy could haul tools, food, and water to our campsite. We also needed the driveway to allow the delivery of the three-bedroom mobile home my parents had picked out from a sales lot.

My father wasn't wasting the opportunity to show Mom that he was committed. Five days a week he drove to downtown Houston to work on a construction site. Before leaving each morning, he handed us a list of tasks that Mom, David, and I could accomplish in his absence. Arriving home in the late afternoon, he picked up more tools and toiled on the property as long as the setting sun would allow. Every waking moment on weeknights and all through the weekend, he worked tirelessly to convert our land into something livable.

A neighbor in Houston once said of my father, "I don't like that man who always has a beer can in his hand." But now that we were in the woods, I hadn't seen him drink anything other than jugs of water or Kool-Aid from a Tupperware container. Mom's strategy was paying off. My father was isolated in the woods and sober. Still, they didn't seem as affectionate as they usually had been. I was used to seeing them steal smooches or give each other playful smacks or pinches on the rear, but I chalked up their current lack of intimacy to the fact that lately Dad smelled like a dirty jockstrap.

Our first weeks were spent clearing the layers of pine needles, cones, and plants that housed centipedes, scorpions, and every kind of snake imaginable. It was exhausting, especially in the oppressive heat. At night I was so tired I collapsed into my sleeping bag. Some days I was dragging ass but if I got caught slacking Dad knew exactly how to motivate me.

"Kipree!" he'd call out to get my attention, then sign, "Come on, no sitting. The more you help, the faster we can get the trailer." I desperately wanted our mobile home delivered. The novelty of sleeping on the ground had lost its appeal on night three when I found a centipede crawling in my hair. I would have shoveled shit out of the outhouse if it meant I'd get a real bed and some protection from the elements.

After a few weeks, we could make sense of the site and it was time to cut down trees. Using fluorescent pink construction ribbon my father had lifted from a job site, he and my mother worked together marking which trees would stay and which were destined for a bonfire. Dad and David did most of the chopping, while Mom and I were in charge of hauling the felled trunks, limbs, and branches into piles for torching.

After breakfast one morning, Dad gathered us in a circle to review the next step. He signed, "Now we clear the leaves about a foot around every tree."

Every tree? I bleakly scanned the property. There were hundreds still standing! My parents were lucky we didn't have a phone to call a child protection agency.

"Smooth out the piles to thin layers," Dad continued. "Then we start a fire and let it burn real slow. If you see a fire growing too big, spread it out even more and keep it away from the trees."

We were going to burn our land? "Why're we gonna do that? The fire will kill everything."

"It's already dead, dummy," David said, rolling his eyes. My brother had the ability to make me feel stupid with one quick criticism.

David was in cutoff jeans with tube socks pulled up to his knees and his favorite red, white, and blue mesh shirt, which exposed his midriff. He loved that shirt so much that when he outgrew it, he merely cut off the bottom to make it into a half shirt. So, between the ages of nine and fifteen, he was wearing it in nearly every photo taken of him.

"We have to burn it so the grass can grow from scratch," Mom said. "It can't be pretty without being burnt first."

My father saw the skepticism on my face. "Wait and see. In about two or three weeks it will look beautiful. T-R-U-S-T me," he signed with a smile, then handed Mom a double-edged weed cutter and me a heavy metal rake.

While I doubted the practicality of burning the land, I never questioned my father, and I was eager to please him. Ever since I could walk, I'd been at his side helping him on projects by handing him tools, sweeping up, or fetching him a fresh Coors Light. He "paid" me with rides in a wheelbarrow, by having me sit in his lap to steer the Chevy, or by letting me take the first sip of his beer. Although I'd wished I were his indispensable right-hand man, my brother had always filled that role. Dad had just been humoring me.

But now that we were on Boars Head, there was real work for

me to do and I was ready for whatever task he assigned. Over the weeks, Dad taught me how to till and plant a garden, use a level, and build a bonfire. In time, my blisters turned to calluses and I believed my favorite T-shirt, which read, "Anything boys can do, girls can do better." I *could* do anything with the right tools.

Taking the metal rake, I headed to one of the smaller trees.

"If you find a snake, freeze and yell for David," Mom called after me.

Hearing this, I wished I were back at the 7-Eleven in Houston playing decoy for my sticky-fingered friends. At least that danger had the payoff of Kit Kats, Bubble Yum, and camaraderie. I hadn't even seen another kid and with all this work, didn't have time to go in search of one. What would raking get me other than blisters? I was seven years old, and all I wanted was a friend.

One miserable tree at a time, we created circles of damp dirt around the base of each trunk. I was on my third one when I scraped back a blanket of crunchy pine needles and found my first real live snake.

"David!" I shrieked and pointed to the baby copperhead tightly curled at the base of the trunk. "Snake!"

It didn't matter that the reptile was small and hadn't budged; I was petrified. I wanted to bolt, but I heeded my mother's instructions and stood as still as a statue. David walked over, hatchet in hand, and gave a quick chop-chop. The snake didn't even flinch until the blade severed it. Still petrified, I stared down wide-eyed at the gory chunks.

"Don't worry," David assured me, wiping off the bloody hatchet on his cutoff jeans. "Once the fire gets going they'll leave." He slipped the axe back through a holster hooked to his belt loop and strutted away as if he had slain a dragon.

I ran to Mom and patted her butt to get her attention, "David killed a snake!" She inspected David's deed and said, "Oh, that was just a baby. Be careful, there're bigger ones out here." My mother was unfazed by my near-death experience, so I tried to mimic her by acting brave.

We tended to the fires for two days. The moist, smoky odor clung to me like the lingering smell of burnt popcorn. Smoldering piles spotted the scorched earth. The dead growth was reduced to ash and the snakes were gone. Time for new life had begun.

Just as my father predicted, fresh grass soon burst forth in a green so bright it looked neon against the blackened ground. He walked through the trees inspecting our work, then bent down and plucked a shiny, smooth blade to show me.

"See, I told you." He placed it between his calloused thumbs, clasped his hands together, and blew into his thumbs, making a loud squeak with the grass.

Amazed, my mouth fell open. "Did it make noise?" Dad asked.

I nodded then signed, "How?"

He waved me to follow in search of a perfect fresh piece of grass for me. Once we located one, Dad held it in place for me as I intertwined my fingers. I blew a hard breath, making the grass quiver with sound.

He could see by my beaming smile that it had worked for me, too. I giggled as I rubbed my lips. "T-I-C-K-L-E-S!"

He chuckled then asked, "What does it sound like?"

"Like a duck's honk," I signed. But Dad had never heard a duck before, so I tried to think of a better description. I furrowed my brow and tapped my index finger on my chin as a sign to show him I was still thinking. "Or, better! Like a noisemaker on

New Year's Eve." He'd blown those before and knew what the vibration on his lips felt like.

Dad wrinkled his chin and thought about it for a bit before he patted my head and signed, "Come on, let's go. We've got work to do."

Soon, the burnt ground was sprouting grass, wild palms, bluebonnets, Indian paintbrushes, black-eyed Susans, bluebells, and buttercups on our little plot on Boars Head.

"See, Kambri. We told you," Mom said. "It can't be pretty without being ugly first."

It wasn't long before we stopped sleeping outside and moved into a tin shed that sat a few feet away from the now-dismantled cabin. The rusted-out diesel truck remained. Our new living quarters, the size of a one-car garage, had a concrete slab floor. For fresh air, we pushed out panels Dad had cut into the metal walls and propped them open.

Since we had left all of our furniture in storage, my parents got creative. "One man's trash is another man's treasure," Mom said, beaming as she plopped down on our new couch, a discarded black vinyl restaurant bench Dad had found in a ditch. She propped her feet on the coffee table, an oversized electric cable spool Dad had salvaged from a construction site, took a big gulp from her plastic cup of iced tea, and patted the dusty seat. "Not too shabby!"

Dad made two sets of twin-sized bunk beds out of chicken wire pulled taut over two-by-fours that we pushed together. My parents slept together on the bottom while David and I shared the top. We didn't mind. Back in Houston, David and I had had our own rooms, but growing up we shared beds plenty of times when family came to visit. If I was scared or lonely at night, I'd even beg him to let me sleep with him.

Many afternoons, thundershowers gave us a much-needed break. The first few drops of rain clattered like acorns dropping from a tree. Once the clouds let loose it sounded like millions had been dumped from the sky. I tried concentrating on a book but the ferocity of the noise rattled me. Dad didn't notice and once Mom took out her hearing aids, neither did she. They puttered around the shed working on their own projects, lost in deaf thoughts. Inside, the shed was sticky and blistering hot and smelled of musty, moist dirt.

Mom made frequent trips to the Safeway supermarket in Conroe, the biggest town within a forty-five-minute drive of our land. We had no refrigerator so we resorted to using two coolers filled with ice to preserve our groceries. We had camping gear for cooking but we usually ate easily prepared meals like bologna sandwiches on Wonder Bread. Having no electricity also meant no television or radio. At night, in the peace and quiet, it was as if we were the only humans on earth. Mom hemmed our clothes, Dad worked on our list of tasks, and David flipped through MAD magazines while I read Mom's old Nancy Drew mysteries to the steady whoosh of the burning kerosene lanterns.

With no running water, we resorted to petty thievery. At night my father loaded the back of the Chevy with a few bright blue ten-gallon jugs and drove to help himself to water from Webb's, a mom-and-pop shop a couple of miles down the road where we bought bags of ice for the coolers, the newspaper, and cigarettes for Dad. I never worried about the consequences if someone caught us. We were under the cover of darkness and, besides, it was just water. Surely Mr. Webb wouldn't mind since it wasn't like he paid for it; the water came from a natural spring well.

That hijacked water was treated like liquid gold. We cooked, cleaned, and bathed with it very sparingly. Mom boiled pots of it, storing the distilled water in reused milk jugs.

Most of our water was used trying to keep ourselves and our belongings clean. Aside from snakes, dirt was our most intrusive enemy. Layers of orange tinted dust coated everything. Dad fashioned a closet by stringing a rope between two posts and covered our clothes with sheets for protection. But his handiwork failed to protect my favorite baby blue corduroy jeans, which had dirt embedded in every groove.

Bathing was a nightly chore. Every evening around dusk, Mom dragged a metal trough from outside to use as a bathtub. To further conserve, we all shared the same bathwater. Luckily, I was the youngest and the smallest, so I had the honor of washing first. My father lifted a blue jug and poured a thin layer of water into the trough before Mom added pots of freshly boiled water to warm it up.

I was eight years old, having recently celebrated my birthday with a card and cake bought at Safeway, and was self-conscious about my body. Because it upset me to think anyone would see me nude, especially my brother, Mom haphazardly hid the cold, hard galvanized tub behind a dusty white sheet clipped to the ceiling with clothing pins for privacy. But she stood uncomfortably close nagging, "Don't forget to wash your neck and ears. Hurry up, Kambri, the water's getting cold."

As if being naked in a horse trough with my family inches away weren't embarrassing enough, I had to undergo a nightly tick check. I stood in my underwear as my mother inspected every inch of my body. When one was found, she lit a match, blew it out, and pressed the smoking sulfur against the tick.

The whole ritual was so humiliating that to this day I dread showering as a guest at other people's homes. I'd rather use a wet wipe and a heavy dose of perfume than bathe in a tub other than my own.

Once we were all clean and tick-free, we spent the remainder of our evening studying floor plans of prefabricated homes featured in advertisements and brochures. My mother sketched elaborate landscaping schematics on pieces of lined notebook paper. I loved talking about the day when we would have a trailer. I was sick of reeking of insect repellent and kerosene. The outhouse was so grotesque that I tried to minimize the number of times I needed to use it and my sides always ached from holding my pee too long. I had once known such luxuries as electricity and running water, but after a few months without them, they had become as foreign as chopsticks.

All this work was the perfect antidote to my parents' marriage ills. Not only was Dad staying sober and close to home, but the devotion he was showing in providing a home for his family made Mom warm up to him again. They took off alone together on long hikes through the woods and drives exploring the back roads of the country. They'd return walking hand in hand with new discoveries, like genuine Indian arrowheads, a funky-shaped piece of driftwood, a turtle, or a shortcut to a highway. They looked happy.

Life on Boars Head wasn't always work. On summer weekends, we piled into the Chevy and headed for the beach at Galveston Bay. Along the way, we picked up my parents' friends Linda and

Peter Sloan, another deaf couple who lived in Houston. The Sloans had two deaf children, Lisa and Skip. My parents had known the Sloans since childhood; they had all attended a state school for the Deaf in Oklahoma. The eight of us spoke solely in ASL and Linda and Peter Sloan became like a second set of parents to me. We were so close that the two sets of parents were comfortable disciplining each other's children.

When we lived in Houston we saw them all the time. My parents and the Sloans were heavily into smoking weed, and never hid their marijuana use from us kids. I never thought anything of it. I assumed it was something adults enjoyed that kids didn't, like antiquing. The four spent hours getting stoned, playing cards or dominoes, and talking and laughing into the wee hours of the night. They rolled joints with a mechanical cigarette roller or smoked from a fancy bong that my father handcrafted using a glass tube and pewter. The year 1971 was engraved into the base.

We kids entertained ourselves with games that Lisa and Skip had learned at Deaf school. We'd dream up goofy characters and comedy skits and have fun acting them out. When our parents weren't around, my brother and I practiced making "joints" with rolling papers and loose tobacco collected from my father's cigarette butts and argued over which of us would inherit their bong when they died. My claim was that since it had my birth year carved in it, I was the rightful heir. David's rebuttal was that he had actually used it. I had heard he first smoked pot at eight years old. Whether it was true or not, this retort was enough for me to presume it would be his someday.

Since moving to Montgomery, our visits with the Sloans were sporadic and we relished the beach outings. Mom made deviled eggs, potato salad, and dip from Lipton's onion soup mix and a tub of sour cream. She packed plenty of soda for the children and cans of Coors Light for Dad, who could never be found without one, even as he drove.

The Chevy would barely have come to a stop when we'd make a break for the water. I'd spend the entire day frolicking in the brown waters of the Gulf while our moms chatted and our dads drank beer under a beach umbrella.

I'd swim out as far as I could, where the waves were biggest and the bottom too deep to touch. I'd count the number of somersaults I could do in a row, while hearing faint muffled laughter and chatter above the waterline. I'd wonder, "Is this what being deaf sounds like?"

In fact, any time I found myself submerged in water, in a bathtub, a swimming pool, or the ocean, I would take the opportunity to test out how it might feel to never hear again. But I was never sure if I achieved the desired effect. I could not know what it was like for Mom and Dad.

Sometimes, the currents would pull me down the beach some three hundred yards. It was terrifying to emerge from the surf to realize no one was watching after me. Sure, there was a lifeguard on duty, but what worried me was finding my family. Not an unnatural fear for any child but heightened because of my parents' inability to hear me calling out to them. Besides being deaf, they were usually engaged in adult conversation and having their own fun. I often wondered how long it would be before they even noticed I was missing. After one lengthy, terrifying search for a colorful beach umbrella that had been planted by a neighboring party but had since been packed away, I realized I needed to scope out a more permanent landmark like a buoy or jetty to mark my family's location.

Heading home from one beach outing, David and I and the two Sloan kids hunkered down low in the back of the Chevy. We zipped along the highway, and the wind whipped my long blond locks, stinging my salty burned skin. I was daydreaming and playing with a jagged edge of a rotten wood slat in the truck bed with my foot when one of my Flintstones flip-flops vanished through a hole. Seeing it tumble out of sight shocked me into a burst of tears.

Lisa banged on the glass and signed to my father, "Kambri lost shoe!" Dad took one look at me crying and brought the Chevy to a screeching halt. I was surprised when he shifted into reverse and drove backward until we saw my flip-flop stranded on the asphalt. A car had run over it, sending it spinning into the path of another. What my father did next was so reckless he had to have been drunk. Hopping out of the Chevy, he bounced on the balls of his feet, ready to spring into action. I was in awe.

Seeing a lull in traffic, my father sprinted across four lanes of Houston highway and scooped up the flip-flop. Triumphant, he raced back waving the plastic thong in the air, dodging cars that honked in protest. Everyone erupted into cheers except for Mom. She slapped her forehead and shook her head in relief. I was still slack-jawed when my beaming father handed me the shoe and signed, "Don't cry, baby girl." Using his big calloused thumb, he wiped away my tears and kissed my head and cheeks a dozen times before he hopped back in the driver's seat.

Back home, I could smell the beach salt for days. Tiny grains of sand found their way into my sleeping bag and scratched my burnt skin. As always, I had gotten too much sun and was covered in blisters by bedtime.

Mom patted me down with vinegar to take away the fever and

chills. Then she squeezed cool, oozing juice from a stem of an aloe plant that grew wild behind the shed and spread it across my bubbling skin. I drifted off to sleep while thinking about what my father had done and felt a twinge of guilt. That flip-flop was a cheap old thing. It didn't even really fit me anymore.

I thought I'd be overjoyed when our brand-new cream-colored mobile home with chocolate-brown trim was delivered—complete with its own furniture—but I could hardly stand it for the smell. We had been sharing that one-room tin shed all summer long and were all looking forward to the upgrade, but the stench of the formaldehyde used to make the cabinets and walls was overwhelming. It burned my eyes and throat and made me retch.

"You'll get used to it," Mom told me. I was tempted to stay in the shed, but I wanted to sleep in a real bed in my own room, so I slept with a sheet over my head and breathed through my shirt.

David's and my bedrooms were at the opposite end of the trailer from my parents'. Their room spanned the width of the trailer and had its own en suite bathroom. There was a living room, kitchen, dining area, and den separating their bedroom from ours. Each room was carpeted in thin brown acrylic shag. The walls were constructed with fake wood-grain panels so thin they couldn't hold a nail. We still didn't have electricity or water, but we finally had privacy and liberation from dirt.

The trailer was on stilts, so David and I made an extra effort to walk around on tiptoes because the entire mobile home would vibrate if we didn't and that would annoy our parents. Vibration is one of the best ways to alert a deaf person. In fact, there is a whole product line of alarm clocks and smoke and carbon monoxide detectors that shake the bed of a deaf or hard-of-hearing person.

Besides vibration, another way to get a deaf person's attention is by waving your arms in the air or flicking a light switch on and off. Mom always preferred a flashing light to wake her up, but my father needed a good shake to rouse him from a deep sleep. Even Pamie knew how to get Dad's attention. Instead of clanging her empty food dish for me and my brother to fill, she'd pick up the bowl and place it in my father's lap.

In the evenings, I loved to help Dad with whatever project he was working on. Dad customized the kitchen floor with fancy tiles he brought home from a construction site, and made a larger breakfast nook where all four of us could eat together. David and I helped him build decks for the two doors exiting the trailer.

By the back porch, my father hung a tire swing from a fat old oak tree. David and I took turns pushing each other high enough to kick the other branches of the tree. I loved twirling the rope tight before letting go, making myself spin so fast my hair stood straight out.

We found the smoothest patch of land we could to serve as a basketball court, where Dad installed a backboard and hoop. He made sure to hang it two feet shorter than regulation height since the tree he nailed it to would keep growing taller, just like my brother and me.

By the front deck, we executed Mom's sketched landscaping design with logs from the dismantled cabin and planted elephant ears, yellow daffodils, and wild crape myrtles she dug up from the side of a road. Dad handcrafted a wooden bench swing and hung it from a pole attached to two trees. It was sturdy and could fit all four of us at once. If I ever wondered where Mom was, I would usually find her on it reading a book with Pamie curled on her lap. After she and I painted the swing a rustic red color, I could have sworn it came from a factory.

We had done it all ourselves, and it was beautiful.

Months went by before my father completed the water line that tapped into the natural spring that flowed freely beneath our land. Then he dug a hole for our very own septic tank, rendering that nasty old outhouse practically useless.

One day, Mom beat her palm on the side of the trailer and yelled, "David! Kambri! It's time!" We didn't need to ask, "Time for what?" We dropped everything and ran to the pole where Dad had hooked up the box that would catapult us into the future. He posed as Mom snapped a picture, his white smile gleaming through the grime on his face.

"Ready? Let's count down."

"Five, four, three, two, one!" we shouted while signing the numbers for Dad. On "one," he flipped the switch.

Electricity!

"WOO HOO!" We whooped and hollered and danced and raced back to the trailer to turn on every single light. Not until Hurricane Alicia blew through the Gulf of Mexico a few years later would I have to read by the light of a lantern again.

My father had accomplished everything he'd set out to do. In my eyes, he was Daniel Boone, Frank Lloyd Wright, Ben Franklin, and Elvis Presley all rolled into one.

Chapter Three

YOU'RE THE ONE THAT I WANT
(OOOH, OOOH, OOOH)

S oon after the trailer arrived on Boars Head, Dad brought
home all the belongings we'd placed in storage. While emptying one box, I came across report cards, yearbooks, and glossy
black-and-white pictures affixed to construction paper with adhe-

sive photo corners. I recognized my parents in some of the photos, but they were much younger.

"Mama, what's this stuff?" I asked.

"Those are my things from when I was a girl."

I traced the letters on the cover of one book with my index finger and asked, "What's Will Rogers?"

"That's where I went to school before I had to go to Deaf school. It was named after the famous cowboy."

"You went to hearing school?"

"Yep, and that meant I could live with my parents all year."

Mom's parents, Carlus and Betty Worth, were fluent in ASL and active in the Deaf community, and they lived a traditional suburban life. Her father worked full-time in a factory while her mother tended to their modest two-bedroom brick house.

Back then, manual labor was a good job for deaf people. The assumption was that they were not capable of doing much of anything else. My grandfather was one of eleven deaf people to find work at Century Electronics. The others were either from his extended family or former classmates of his from the Oklahoma School for the Deaf. It was such an unusually large concentration of deaf employees that *The Tulsa Tribune* featured them on its front page with a photo of Dad's eldest deaf sister, Norma, hard at work wiring an electronics panel.

When my mother was born in 1947, services for the Deaf were practically nonexistent. The only way to communicate with the hearing world was by using pen and paper. So as soon as my mother was old enough to talk, she became the family's de facto interpreter. This was not uncommon for CODA.

"We went to the ice cream parlor every week," Mom recounted. "Your grandpa would lift me up and place me on the counter and tell me what kind of ice cream they wanted. I'd say to the cashier, 'My mama wants brown and my daddy wants white.' I was only about three years old, so I didn't know the words for chocolate and vanilla."

The only story I recall Mom ever telling about her deafness having any negative effect was about the time when she was eight years old and had dinner at a hearing friend's home. Midway through the meal, the friend's father banged the table with his fist and shouted at my mother, "Would you quit that damn smacking?!" Mom was so embarrassed and upset at his outburst that she ran home in tears and never saw her friend again. But she never smacked again, either, and she made sure to share with her deaf family her new knowledge that eating food made noise that was apparently very irritating to hearing folks.

Mom spoke clearly. So clearly, in fact, that most of the time you wouldn't even guess she was deaf. But if she said a word filled with extra s's, you'd know. For fun, David and I used to trick her into saying them.

"Hey, Mama," David asked. "Where's Boston?"

"Masssssaaa-sue-ssesss," she answered. David and I burst out laughing and tried to elicit more.

"What state's next to Alabama?"

"Georgia?"

"Noooooo, not that one," I led on as I zeroed in on her teeth and tongue.

Knowing we were waiting for a payoff, she gave wrong answers until finally she said, "Missssssisssssssippi?" sounding like she had been to the dentist and the hiss was waiting for the novocaine to wear off.

David and I erupted into cheers, "Yeah! Mississippi!"

"You know how to spell it?" she asked. On cue, the three of us sang (shouted, really) in unison, "M, I, crooked letter, crooked letter, I, crooked letter, crooked letter, I, humpback, humpback, I!" and dissolved into heaving laughter.

I think sometimes it embarrassed her, but I loved it. I just loved it when Mom said, "Mississippi."

"Look here," she said, pointing to a picture of her in a group with other young girls, dressed in gingham-checked uniforms. "I was even on the pep squad. We had pom-poms and would go to all the games. I even remember our cheer, 'Hey! Hey! What'd ya say? Bobcats get that ball away!'"

I was awestruck. Mom looked like Sandy from *Grease*. We spent the whole afternoon going through her mementos, as she fielded my questions. "Why did you fail gym class?"

"Because I didn't want to swim."

"Your school had a pool?" I thought Will Rogers sounded pretty impressive.

"Out of all the girls at school I wore the prettiest sweater sets with matching wool skirts and spent so much time on my hair. Swim class was first period. I *refused* to get my hair wet, so the teacher gave me an F."

My parents were always so proud when I brought home my report cards. I would have swum across the Gulf of Mexico and back to avoid an F. And I was such a tomboy, the idea of being so concerned about a hairdo seemed really prissy. I didn't even own a brush.

As long as Mom didn't have to board at Deaf school, her parents had a live-in translator who could use the telephone and help with day-to-day tasks. But her hearing got worse and her grades started slipping. "I sat in the front row and tried to keep up but I got tired of it. And my sister and all my friends were at the Deaf school anyway." So she moved to the boarding school for the Deaf to finish her education, and there she met Dad.

If my mother was Sandy Olsson, my father was definitely her bad-boy love interest, Danny Zuko. He was slim, good-looking, and had a bad reputation. His smooth skin was bronzed and his thick hair was slicked back. In every picture, he posed with classic cars of the 1950s, his arm slung around the shoulder of various girls. He wore a tight white T-shirt, dark denim jeans with the cuffs rolled up, and black leather dress shoes.

"Your daddy picked on me from day one. He told everyone I wasn't a natural redhead and dyed my hair. When I wasn't looking, he emptied a full shaker of salt in my milk. I took a few big gulps and swallowed a huge chunk."

"Why'd he do that?" I asked. It sounded like something my brother would do to me.

"He said, 'I just thought you'd take a sip and it would taste funny. I didn't think you'd gulp it.' Well that night, I got so sick. I vomited and started coughing up blood so they had to take me to the infirmary. My very first night! Your daddy came to visit and told me he was sorry. From then on, he pestered me to go out with him but I told him, 'No, I'm already dating Garland.'"

Garland was a senior and Mom's first boyfriend. She pointed him out in the yearbook and her voice got dreamy. "He was an all-pro football and basketball player, six foot four with blond hair and blue eyes. Everybody loved him, teachers, my mom and dad, everybody." I wasn't surprised to hear that Mom was in love with another boy before she met my father. My parents didn't censor much of anything. They were openly affectionate in front of us and weren't uncomfortable teaching David and me about the human body or the birds and the bees at an early age. When I was five, Mom bought us the Peter Mayle books *What's Happening to Me?* and *Where Did I Come From?* and instructed us to read them whenever we wanted. The pages were dog-eared from all the times we consulted them, while the *World Book Encyclopedia* set we bought at the grocery store gathered dust.

"Your daddy wouldn't take no for an answer," my mother sighed. "When I went to get my books, he jumped in front of my locker and asked me again. If I bent down for a sip from the water fountain, he stepped in between to ask me again. This went on for four months!"

Even though I knew how the story ended, I found myself rooting for my father to win Mom's heart. Dad was smart and played basketball and football, too, and he was much better-looking. Garland looked like a dork.

Against the urging of virtually everyone, including three different teachers, Mom eventually relented. One date with my father was all it took, and Garland was kicked to the curb. But judging by my mother's far-off gaze and wrinkled chin, it was a decision she sometimes lamented. Without knowing about all of my father's infidelities, I couldn't see why she was so disappointed. Her brooding silence confused me. I thought she was pretty lucky. She'd been the best-dressed, most popular girl on the pep squad. I was a grubby tomboy who liked to play tackle football rather than cheer from the sidelines, wore discount clothes with patched-up holes, and had stringy hair that could have used some chlorine from a pool.

Our life on Boars Head was as adventuresome as her sales pitch had predicted. And Dad had built our piece of heaven from scratch. What was there not to love?

I searched her face for clues as to what could have been so bad to cause her gloomy daze. Mom caught me staring, snapped herself out of her thoughts, and rationalized, "But if I had stayed with Garland, I wouldn't have you and David. You two would never have been born, and I would have Garland's babies instead."

She made us seem like we were her consolation prize, lovely parting gifts she got for losing out on a life with Garland.

My father hadn't even wanted kids. He hated not being able to hear and feared he'd pass his "damned deafness" to his children. The fact that 90 percent of deaf parents have hearing children and 90 percent of deaf children are born to hearing parents didn't ease his fears.

Dad's childhood had been fraught with hardship and frustration. He had been isolated on a farm with no prior knowledge of deafness or its culture. Mom's family, however, with two generations of deaf people, was an anomaly. She had grown up immersed in ASL and in the care of deaf adults who were confident with their place in the world. In her insular community, the hearing were the minority. If her children had been born deaf, she would have considered that a blessing. She would be contributing to the preservation of ASL and survival of Deaf culture, a common, staunchly regarded feeling among many deaf people.

Mom got pregnant right away and every night my father worried his baby would be born deaf. "I tossed and turned and had terrible dreams until your mama finally gave birth," he told me.

When my father held his son for the first time he got big butterflies in his belly before he screamed "DEHVIH!" David was startled awake and Dad let out a big sigh of relief to know his son could hear.

Mom had pressured him to have another baby but he resisted. "I wanted a little girl, but your daddy said no." My father didn't want to tempt fate, but he finally gave in to Mom's pleas. Again, Dad took his new baby in his arms and screamed in a high-pitched voice, "KIPREE!" I shook and he knew I could hear.

Though my father's technique wasn't foolproof, in our case it was spot-on. David and I could hear perfectly.

For days I pestered my mother for answers about her courtship with Dad and life in a dorm. She finally got fed up. "I only went to Deaf school a few years; your daddy lived there almost his whole life. Why don't you ask him? He's sitting right there." She pointed to my father reading the Sunday sports section of the *Houston Chronicle,* oblivious to our conversation. Mom buried her nose back into Stephen King's *The Stand.*

I tapped Dad's newspaper. He folded down a corner so he could see me. "Tell me about living at Deaf school."

"Why do you want to know?"

I shrugged. "Just wondering," I signed. "Mom told me you met there."

I had never really asked my father anything before except for money or permission to sleep over at a friend's. I didn't know what to expect, but he put down his paper and told me his story.

He was one of ten children born to Theodore and Ruby Crews. Together they lived on a farm in the dust bowl of Bowlegs, Oklahoma. Like his older sister Norma, who was the sixth of my grandparents' ten children, and the youngest sisters Cathy and

Reba, my father was born deaf. But his twin brother, Buddy, was not.

Because there had not been a history of deafness in his family, some might call it a fluke. Dad considered it a big "up yours" from the Man in Charge. He arrived a few minutes earlier than his twin, earning him the right to his father's name. But he would have gladly traded the "junior" status for a pair of ears that worked.

Unlike my mother's family, Dad's parents and siblings didn't know ASL, and so made up homemade signs to get across the basics. When Dad saw them talking to each other with their mouths he joined in by moving his lips and tongue with great exaggeration. No sounds came out of his mouth; it was like a puppet missing his ventriloquist.

Grandpa Crews was a cigar-smoking oil rigger who never made it past the fourth grade due to a protracted childhood illness that kept him home from school. I never knew him to be without his dog-eared King James Bible, but according to my father his God-fearing days had arrived later in life. "My daddy's mean," Dad warned before every visit to their farm. "When I was small, my father lashed me with a razor strap. Sometimes my parents made me cut a switch from a cherry tree and used it to whip me."

I shuddered at the thought. I had only received one spanking by Dad, a quick swat on my butt for an epic bout of pouting. The spanking hurt my ego more than my hide.

When my father's sister Norma, the eldest of the family's deaf children, reached school age, she was sent to live at the Oklahoma School for the Deaf, or "OSD" for short. The residential school was about a two-hour drive from the family farm, much too far for her to come home on weekends. Founded in 1908, OSD was located in Sulphur, just off Interstate 35 between Oklahoma City and Dallas. While some Deaf schools were still segregated, OSD housed deaf children of every age, race, and religion living in the state of Oklahoma.

My father was an infant the year that Norma left home for school, disappearing for months at a time. He never fully understood where she went, even when his family tried to explain to him using the small amount of ASL Norma had taught them.

When my father turned five, he was given a brand-new suitcase packed with uniforms. His mother had hand-stitched his name inside each one. Just as I was obsessed with my sleeping bag as we got ready for our move to Boars Head, Dad opened and closed his suitcase and packed and unpacked his clothes until the first day of school finally came.

I was distressed by how emotional my father became as he recounted his first day at OSD. His father had taken care of checking in his sister Norma before taking him to the boys' dorm. There he saw that all the boys had brightly colored toys, some that ran on batteries. Back on the farm, Dad had one cast-iron toy car.

"My jaw hit the floor," he remembered about the first time he watched television. "I watched with the boys for a few minutes, then they looked at the clock on the wall and turned the channel. This time there were real people inside the TV." In disbelief, he ran to show his father but couldn't find him. He had left without saying goodbye.

Grandpa Crews was tormented. Leaving his little boy at the

school filled him with guilt and sadness and he opted to slip out before Dad could see him crying.

In truth, hearing parents commonly dropped off their deaf children with little or no explanation. This wasn't because of a lack of love, but because they didn't know ASL. They were simply unable to communicate. Many children suffered from the sudden and unexplainable abandonment. They didn't know what was happening. Some didn't even know their own names.

My father gulped some air, wrinkled his chin, and pinched his lips tight as he explained how he thought he was being left at an orphanage. He covered his mouth and massaged his lips to fight back the tears. I had never seen my father even close to crying, but this experience had traumatized him. Seeing him so vulnerable made me upset, too. To this day, he can't get through the story without choking up.

One reason he was certain he was being abandoned was that it had happened before.

"I was maybe three or four years old. I was misbehaving a few times one day and my parents got fed up. My father drove me to the railroad tracks where all the poor black people lived in a shantytown. He made me get out of the truck and drove away. The sun started going down and it got cold, but I stood in that spot all day. I had never seen so many black people before and when they walked by they stared at me. I couldn't hear what they were saying but they were moving their mouths so I knew they were talking to me. Some kids threw sticks and laughed. When it was almost dark, my daddy finally came back. He said if I didn't behave, he would leave me there to live with the 'niggers' forever."

Picturing my father as a deaf toddler dumped off at the shantytown sent a similar jolt of fear through me. I remembered my own terror when I was six and had flown home alone to Houston after visiting Mom's parents in Oklahoma. I disembarked the plane but my parents weren't at the gate waiting for me. Panic set in. A man who saw me wandering offered to have them paged over the intercom. I explained they were deaf and wouldn't hear the announcement. Taken aback and not knowing how to help, the stranger walked away apprehensively.

Just then I heard my father's high-pitched voice. "KIPREE!" His head bobbed up and down as he jumped to see over the crowd. He swept me up in his arms, hugging and kissing me all over.

"Sorry, sorry, sorry, Kipree."

I changed from being scared to livid. I didn't speak the entire ride home or the remainder of the night. I even refused to join them for dinner, so Mom left a plate of food outside my bedroom door.

Remembering that day in the airport made me feel sad and confused. I couldn't believe my grandfather would leave his deaf son alone like that. Believing he was left at an orphanage, my father described how he grew hysterical and bolted for the door. The housemother caught him and held him down on his bed till he stopped thrashing. Dad cried himself to sleep, but later in the evening the housemother woke him up by toggling the lights on and off. He and the other boys walked to the dining hall, where he saw his sister Norma. She smiled and waved like everything was fine.

"My heart felt a little relief to know I wasn't alone, but I couldn't stand staying in the dorms all the time. It was like a prison to me."

~

Being incarcerated has not been kind to my father's looks. He was handsome before, but now he is covered in tattoos—the crude type inmates give each other. "This one I got in jail in Mexico," he explains, pointing to the spider on his left forearm.

"Wait," I stop him. "Mexican prison?"

"Oh, yes, bad story. Your mama doesn't even know about it. I'll tell you later." He continues showing off his new body art. "This one my girlfriend wanted me to get. Ha! Silly! And this one"—he points to a Tasmanian devil with both hands in the air waving the ASL signs for "I love you" and its tongue sticking out—"this one a black boy gave me for my birthday."

Dad explains that the "black boy" is a fellow inmate who works in the Huntsville Prison's textile mill. He had disassembled a machine part to get the needles for his tattooing.

Dad's once lush Elvis pompadour is thinner, receding, and slicked back. His formerly beautiful smile featured white, straight teeth but they have been yellowed from his two-packs-a-day smoking habit. A few back teeth have been pulled out. "Hurt so I yanked it," Dad signs. Many others have been knocked out during fights with other inmates. The missing teeth cause his cheeks to sink in, making him look even skinnier than he already is. Like Keith Richards in prison whites.

But his prison whites aren't really white. Every other prisoner's uniform looks clean and new and bright. Dad's is a dull ecru. His thermal shirt is dingy and the sleeves are too short to cover his long arms. It is haphazardly stitched in some places, but still full of holes.

He's better than this, isn't he? We are better than this.

Dad sees me staring pensively at his tattered sleeves and signs, "Old! Need new ones for winter but too expensive."

He has to buy his own thermals?

I had no idea inmates weren't supplied with everything they needed. Growing up in Texas, I often heard that prisoners had it made, with free healthcare and education and days filled with recreational sports and unlimited cable television. Now I know that jails have a commissary where prisoners can purchase everything from candy to toiletries with money from a "trust fund" subsidized by family and friends, if they're lucky enough to have their support. Dad doesn't receive counseling, take classes, or have a television. And even in the blistering Texas summer, there is no air-conditioning.

His glasses haven't escaped injury, either. The nose pads are missing and the frames are taped together in various spots. Every time he adjusts them, I notice how perfectly the metal frame fits into the fleshy, scarred divot on the bridge of his nose.

Who did this to you? I'm angry Dad hasn't been protected.

I recall a Hallmark greeting card Dad sent me for Christmas. He had just marked his first full year in prison; twelve months spent establishing his pecking order among the other inmates. Inside he wrote, "I had been solitary confinement four times since April for fighting with niggers cause me mad because stealings—all offenders are haters, thief, jealous, etc."

What made them do this to you? You provoked them, didn't you? You accused them or called them names. Just keep to yourself, Daddy.

"You're early. I just woke up, had barely had enough time to brush my teeth and take a shit when they told me I had a visitor," he signs, leaning back in the metal armchair.

"Sorry, but I have to catch a flight home tonight."

"I wanted to smoke a joint before our visit." Dad's favorite pastimes used to be smoking marijuana, sipping a cold beer, betting on football, and conversing with friends. I guess a slightly stoned jailhouse visit with his daughter is as close to freedom as he can get.

Rules don't allow for tobacco, drugs, or alcohol, so my father has quit smoking and drinking. He doesn't usually smoke weed, either, not because of the law, but because of the cost. Complaining that five dollars buys a "tiny joint as thin as spaghetti," he doesn't think it's worth it. Although he hasn't smoked this morning, his access to weed surprises me.

"Joint? Where did you get that?"

"Found it in the pages of a magazine at the library. Somebody must have missed it." He shrugs and smiles. "Their loss is my gain. Did you bring a burger?"

"I wanted to but Dairy Queen wasn't open at nine-thirty."

Dad shakes his head, not concealing his annoyance. "See, you are too early."

I look over my shoulder at the guard to see if it is safe for me to pass my contraband. "I have gum in my waistband."

Dad wiggles his fingers impatiently as I dig the package out from its hiding spot. He rips open the silver foil in a flash of excitement and chomps a piece with his remaining front teeth. It takes only three or four chews for the burst of flavor to overwhelm him. He closes his eyes and leans back with his arms outstretched and palms facing outward like he is praising Jesus.

"Long time," Dad signs. After a few more chews a bewildered look washes over him. He inspects the package and finger-spells the words "Wrigley's Juicy Fruit," as if to ensure that, yes, this is the correct brand of gum. "Tastes different. Long time, I guess."

I watch him. He looks like a little boy seeing fireworks for the first time.

Without warning, my father slips off one of his Chuck Taylors and slides sticks of gum between the cushion and sole of the shoe before replacing it on his foot. He swiftly does the same with the other.

"What are you doing?"

"I can sell them for a dollar a stick," Dad tells me as he reties his laces.

I don't think they are well hidden, but Dad isn't worried. I glance around to see if anyone has noticed and spot a beefy Hispanic guy. His buzz cut reveals a dented skull. He has an eye missing with the lid sewn shut and his skin looks melted. His bottom lip droops, allowing saliva to escape, and he uses a handkerchief to wipe the drool.

ASL has its advantages, including the ability to talk without being overheard by those around us. "What happened to him?" I sign, trying not to stare.

"He killed his wife and kids then tried to kill himself. It didn't work," Dad replies matter-of-factly. "Good man. Quiet."

Quiet, says my deaf dad. And good? It's all relative, I suppose. The disfigured murderer is a good man in my father's eyes.

What does that say about Dad?

Chapter Four

THE MAN OF STEEL

Now that we were civilized and living in a trailer, my brother and I had three rules:

1. Don't leave the refrigerator door hanging wide open. We live paycheck to paycheck and money doesn't grow on trees;

2. Don't drink straight out of the milk jug because it grosses Mom out; and

3. Don't tell anyone Mom and Dad smoke marijuana.

From the minute she enrolled me in third grade at Montgomery Elementary School and David in sixth grade at Montgomery Junior High, my mother sounded like a broken record when it came to Rule #3. "You know not to tell anyone we smoke, right?"

"I know!" I huffed. Her warnings were almost solely directed at me, as if David could be trusted and my history as a motor-mouth would get them busted.

In late July, my mother drove David and me to Weiner's, a discount clothing store in Conroe, to put some school clothes on layaway. Leaving the store without my new jeans and shirts was an enormous disappointment, as torturous as waiting for Christmas morning after the tree had been up for two weeks. In the meantime, she let out the hems of our too-short jeans and ironed denim patches on the knees to cover the holes. Every week, she stopped by Weiner's to make an installment payment.

Mom had found full-time work assembling electronic communications panels at HeliFlight Systems in Cut and Shoot, a town in east Montgomery County that, according to local legend, got its name in 1912 during a community dispute involving the town's only church. During the debate, an eight-year-old boy grew frightened and supposedly cried out, "I'm going to cut around the corner and shoot through the bushes in a minute!" The boy's statement stuck and thus the name was born.

Even with Mom's income, money was tight, so professional haircuts were out of the question. Using salon scissors, she gave me a wedge haircut in our trailer's kitchen. I wanted to look like my idol, Olympic ice skater Dorothy Hamill. I was so enamored with the gold medalist that I spent hours practicing her skating moves in a corner of our living room, sliding around on the carpet in my socks and a leotard. But Mom's chop job was unsuccessful. After nearly an hour sitting still at the kitchen table, I came out looking more like Moe from *The Three Stooges*.

My brother didn't fare much better. He got his trim from my father. Dad must have tipped back one too many Coors Lights that day because a sober man could see that was no straight line that crossed my brother's forehead. The edge more closely resembled the curved and jagged coastline of Texas.

Since the school bus wouldn't come down Boars Head—the bridge built with railroad ties was too unstable—my brother and I had to walk the half mile to the hairpin turn where the wooden "Boars Head" sign hung from the tree. A homely black Lab mix named Taffy accompanied us. She became ours after a neighbor abandoned her when they moved to Dallas. Taffy flopped on her back when anyone came near, revealing swollen breasts, bumpy, pendulous nipples, and a belly full of ticks and fleas. She followed David and me to the bus stop just about every morning then disappeared into the woods, returning to the back porch a day or two later.

We had no choice but to trudge along with our heavy book bags in the oppressive heat and humidity. Unlike Houston, where our schools were within a few blocks of our home, we were now more than an hour's drive away, longer when you added all the stops. Even in late summer, it was early enough to still be dark outside as we waited for the morning school bus with the handful of children who'd emerged from the woods. I recognized just two of the boys, Chris and Billy King. I had glimpsed them downhill from the spot where we'd planted our garden earlier in the summer, but I'd been too busy working to make friends with them.

This would be my first time riding a bus and neither David nor I had seen our new schools—my fifth one in four years. I would soon learn that there was an unwritten hierarchy to the seating on Bus #9. The youngest kids and social rejects sat in front under the protective eye of our bus driver, Mrs. Buttercase, or Mrs. Butterball as the older kids called her behind her back. The rear seats, the most revered, allowed for privacy from her prying eyes and ears. They had the added bonus that when the bus hit one of the dirt road's many bumps, their occupants were flung out of the green vinyl benches, sometimes high enough to hit the ceiling. The boring hour-and-a-half-long trip turned into a thrill ride, with us laughing, cheering, and begging Mrs. Buttercase to drive faster over the next big bump.

The older and more popular you were, the closer to the back you were allowed to sit. At twelve years old, David would become a member of the bus royalty, a position he held for the duration of our time on Boars Head.

The riders on the bus ranged from five to eighteen years old. Out of the fifteen, there were only two other girls: Haley Miller and Tammy Sverck. Haley was a delicate thing who looked younger than her seven years and spoke in a whisper, although she rarely talked. Tammy, David's age, was only interested in talking about boys and baton twirling.

The King brothers were closest to my age. They sat in the seats right behind Mrs. Buttercase. They lived in a junky mobile home a few hundred yards downhill from ours, making them nearest in distance, too. Chris was older than me, but after failing two years he wound up in my class. The front part of his greasy, dirty blond hair stuck up in a cowlick like Alfalfa from *The Little Rascals,* and he had odd facial tics, smelled like urine, and bullied kids half his age.

Billy was a scrawny, blue-eyed boy with naturally curly bright blond hair. He could be observed on Bus #9 sucking his thumb while simultaneously picking his nose with his index finger. On occasion, he'd stop to lick his index finger clean before going back to mine for more boogers.

Who was I to judge? I wasn't known for brushing my teeth or wearing clean underwear. I had loathed washing up ever since the onset of the nightly horse trough bath and tick check ritual and did what I could to avoid bathing altogether. I showered only when commanded, which averaged about once a week. I had nobody else; the King brothers would have to do.

On my second day as a third grader, the principal sent me from class to class to teach students the ASL alphabet. David and I were proud of our Deaf heritage, and we weren't afraid to talk about it. We'd tell people right off the bat, and we'd sign to each other on the bus. I don't know if it was because we were in a small community, but having deaf parents made us special. Montgomery had nothing going on. We were unique.

Teaching the other kids ASL made transitioning to the new school easier. By the end of my first week, every kid knew me and asked me to help with their signing skills. I was even put in charge of teaching a group of girls an ASL version of "Silent Night" for the annual Christmas pageant. Excited to sing in sign language, just like my mother had at the Deaf bowling tournament, I practiced in front of a mirror every chance I could. Because of Mom's experience, I asked her to tutor me on hard phrases like "round yon virgin," knowledge that I passed on to my pupils.

On opening night, the school cafeteria was transformed into a theater with the unfolding of a portable stage. The room was packed, with parents, students, and teachers overflowing into the hall. I took my position at center stage and led the girls in signing the hymn in ASL as a chorus sang behind us. I saw my parents standing in the back glowing. I tried not to let them distract me, seeing them so proud, but I was exhilarated to be in the spotlight. At the end they applauded the longest and loudest.

"Beautiful," Dad signed over the crowd, as I took my bows.

Our ASL interpretation was a showstopper and was so memorable that my classmates never fail to recall the event. Thirty years later, I was in Houston and saw one of my former classmates who, without hesitation, performed the song flawlessly in ASL from start to finish.

After the show, I was excited to introduce my teacher to my parents. I wanted to hear her talk about what a great job I had done. When she discovered that my father was not working because of a knee injury, my teacher asked him to volunteer as a chaperone for our class field trip. He looked amused, but agreed. "Sure, I can do that," he said. I squealed a pitch so high Mom thought her hearing aids were malfunctioning.

I counted down the days until the outing finally arrived. I spent the whole field trip interpreting questions for Dad from my classmates. Like paparazzi chasing a celebrity, they swarmed in a circle around us as he and I walked hand in hand. I beamed with pride.

After the trip, Dad drove my two new friends, Shana and Stacey, home. Like most new people I meet, they quizzed me about life with a deaf parent. "My brother and I can do anything we want and my daddy won't hear a thing," I bragged.

Stacey seemed skeptical. "How do you know he's really deaf? What if he's pretending?"

"Here, watch this." I screamed at the top of my lungs. "SHIT!"

Dad gave me an inquisitive glance. My shrieks inside the metal cab of the Chevy must have given his ears a piercing shock. Shana and Stacey froze and their eyes grew wide with fear. My father just grinned and looked back at the road ahead.

The girls and I burst into heaving laughter. We caught our breath and they joined me in screaming, "BITCH! SHIT! ASS-HOLE!" Dad grinned with eyebrows raised in suspicion. I could bet money that he knew exactly what we were up to, but still he just smiled and kept driving so as not to spoil our fun.

"Your daddy is the best!"

"Yeah, he's so cool!"

They didn't have to tell me. I already knew.

The pride I had for my father was reinforced every school day when Bus #9 rounded the corner to drop off the older kids at Montgomery Junior High. A row of shanty houses was directly across the street from the school. The dwellings were so tiny and dilapidated that I would have thought they were abandoned if not for the fresh laundry hanging from the clotheslines. Most of the shacks had broken windows, some haphazardly boarded up. Porches were collapsed, structures tilted, and roofs were patched like quilts.

Often, I stared at them from the bus window, wondering who lived there and imagining how tough their lives must be. Seeing such extreme poverty, I thanked God I wasn't so unfortunate.

These tumbledown houses helped put everything my father had done on Boars Head into perspective. Dad was smart and skilled. He had managed to provide us with water, plumbing, and electricity and I was certain he'd never allow us to live like these poor folks.

My father's accomplishments on Boars Head over the past year and a half were extraordinary. And when a young man driving a large truck filled with sand caused the bridge on Boars Head to collapse, he became a superhero.

The loss of the bridge stopped all traffic in and out of Boars Head. We were stranded. Dad immediately took charge. Unknown neighbors emerged from the hidden recesses of that forest. Most of them had never seen a deaf person, but they trusted my father as a leader capable of ensuring their survival.

After clearing the wreckage and disassembling the remains of the bridge, Dad designed a new one and constructed it with more modern, solid materials. Members of the neighborhood pooled funds together to pay for the supplies and Mom photographed every step of the process so we'd have evidentiary proof of this catastrophic event and epic recovery. Once the framework and metal rods were in place, a ton of concrete was poured and evenly spread. When it was almost dry, Dad signed one corner with his name and the year, 1980. As long as we lived there, I proudly pointed out the signature to anyone who visited. If they were skeptical, I had the pictures to prove it.

The Army Corps of Engineers inspected Dad's handiwork and deemed it capable of holding up to a thirty-thousand-pound load. The new overpass changed our lives. It opened up the remote area to more comforts that other people took for granted. Dad's bridge connected our private hideaway to the world. Years later, it allowed the passage of oil tankers and drilling equipment.

But back in the spring of 1980, the new bridge meant that Bus #9 could drive down Boars Head. We were spared the long slog to the bus stop at the crack of dawn and the afternoon trudge home in the blistering Texas heat.

By building that bridge, my father became a living legend both on Boars Head and among my friends. But every hero has his weakness. For Dad it was his deafness, and the hearing world held the kryptonite.

One afternoon, Dad and I were on an errand in Conroe and I suggested we stop at the Pizza Inn.

"No! We will NEVER eat there, EVER!" my father signed. His eyes became angry slits as he mouthed the word "EVER" through clenched teeth and lips pinched so tight they turned white.

"You want pizza? We'll go to Pizza Hut instead."

"But Pizza Inn is the same!" I argued as he circled the town in search of a Pizza Hut. "Why can't we just eat there?" I didn't see the point in rejecting one over another when they were practically identical, even down to their red roofs.

"Because," my father signed, "they had me arrested."

"Arrested? Why?"

"Why? For nothing!" Dad pulled into a Pizza Hut parking lot and turned off the ignition. "On my way home from a construction site, I stopped in for dinner and a beer. The next thing I knew I felt a tap on my shoulder. I opened my eyes and saw a policeman standing over me. I was tired from long hours of work and fell asleep in the booth. Why didn't the waiter or manager try to wake me? Why send a cop? They said I was passed out and arrested me. I wasn't drunk; I was *sleeping*."

The story was infuriating. Even though I was a child, I was convinced that if I had been with him that day I would have been able to prevent the whole misunderstanding.

"They didn't even bother trying to talk to me because I am deaf. They discriminate!"

I nodded my head in agreement. I knew that some people treated deaf people differently. While staying with my maternal grandparents during one summer vacation, I befriended a girl named Tina, who lived next door. I asked my grandmother if she could spend the night.

"Sure," Grandma Worth signed. "She can have dinner with us if she wants. We're frying catfish Grandpa caught."

Excitedly, I called Tina and was disappointed when she told me her mother wouldn't permit it.

"How come?" I whined.

" 'Cause your grandparents are deaf."

I was dumbfounded and pressed her for an explanation. Tina said her mother was concerned about what might happen in case of an emergency.

"Well *we* can hear and your house is just right next door," I rebutted.

"It's dangerous to have children in a house without any hearing people," she said, parroting what she had probably heard her mother say. "What if they had a heart attack or the place caught fire?"

My face started to burn. Tina's house was barely fifteen feet from ours. Help was right there. Besides, my brother and I stayed home alone all the time. Having two adults with us, deaf or not, was more supervision than usual.

During dinner, my grandmother asked why Tina wasn't with us.

"She's grounded," I lied. There was no use making her feel bad because Tina's mother was ignorant.

When my father was arrested at Pizza Inn, his older hearing sister Edith was visiting us from Oklahoma. She was staunchly religious and her icy cold stare could scare Satan himself. Accompanying Mom to bail Dad out of jail was as offensive to her as Darwin's theory of evolution. "Does this happen often?" she primly asked Mom.

"Oh no! Never!" Mom replied, sticking to my father's version of the facts. "He wasn't passed out; he was just tired from working overtime." But my mother wasn't telling the whole story. She conveniently left out the fact that Dad, alone, had downed a full pitcher of beer. Not only was he passed out drunk in public, but this *had* happened before, just never at Pizza Inn.

My mother could paint a rosy picture. While my father would tell a lie to dig out of trouble, my mother liked to pretend that everything was in order by slanting the truth. She protected her own image by keeping her husband's problems private.

A week after Edith returned to Oklahoma, cash and checks arrived in the mail from my father's family, though no one said anything about Dad's public drunkenness and arrest. "We don't need money," Mom sniffed. "But we'll take it. Heck, if they're just giving it away."

When Dad's court date arrived, Mom called in sick to work so she could serve as his interpreter. Her poise and eloquent speech seemed to sway the judge and he tossed out the charges. The ruling granted my father smug satisfaction that he was right. Pizza Inn was overrun with discriminating bastards and had him arrested because he was deaf. We never ate at Pizza Inn again, with or without Dad.

Before school recessed for Christmas break in 1980, my fourth-grade teacher gave us an assignment to make a homemade booklet of gifts. Each page was to be dedicated to a member of our family. It was up to us to describe the gift we would present if money were no object. It could be anything, not necessarily something that only came in a box. It could be a hope, a dream, anything.

I was a dedicated, eager-to-please student and I took the assignment very seriously, giving deep thought to what I would give to my parents and brother. Each page started the same: "If I could give you anything in the world it would be . . ." I gave my brother "peace." I gave "happiness" to my mother. And to my father, I gave "the ability to hear."

Initially, the thought of sharing my book with my mother excited me. I thought that happiness was something that she would really appreciate. She was always stressed and worried about money. She often complained about needing help around the house. She worked all day and lamented at how exhausted she was from the workload. Sitting at her desk with piles of bills and her checkbook, she sighed heavily and snapped at David or me if we interrupted her.

My excitement at presenting Mom with her gift began to fade when I considered how my father might react to his. The usual presents he liked were tools, cartons of cigarettes, or a "World's Best Dad" beer koozie. I worried that he would misinterpret my hypothetical gift. I didn't want him to think I didn't like him the way he was.

After Dad read my present for him, his only reaction was a quick "Thank you." He looked back down at the page and his chin wrinkled, a sign he was contemplating my wish. He set the booklet on the counter and went into the living room to watch television.

I was too uncomfortable to ask him how it made him feel, so I asked my mother instead.

"I'm sure he liked it, Kambri," she reassured me. "He would finally be able to hear music."

My father hated being deaf. To this day, he dreams about getting a cochlear implant, an electronic device that can help the profoundly deaf or severely hard of hearing hear. There are two components to the implant. One part is the microphone, sound processor, and transmitter, worn externally on the scalp. The other is the implanted receiver and electrode system, which is surgically inserted under the skin behind one ear.

The Deaf community is divided on the use of cochlear implants. Many deaf people don't perceive their hearing loss to be a handicap, but a cultural identity. That's why the *d* in "Deaf" is capitalized when referencing the community, while a lowercase *d* for "deaf" means the inability to hear. The Deaf have their own language, arts, churches, and universities. Because of this, they are strongly bonded through shared history and life experiences, and view themselves as a distinct society.

Implying that implants are necessary is labeling deafness as a defect that must be corrected. In actuality, a deaf person's ability to live a full life is not compromised by their hearing impairment. It simply requires making a few accommodations.

The contentious debate has some going so far as to say that implants are nothing short of cultural genocide, fearing that the devices will render the Deaf community and ASL extinct. Most deaf children are born to hearing parents who often choose implants without first learning about Deaf society. After being implanted, deaf children are often not taught ASL, which fuels the fear that the community will die.

Others in the Deaf community view implants as a matter of personal choice. Since the devices don't cure deafness, but merely restore some sense of sound, deaf people will continue to exist and ASL will remain a necessary and vital language. Opting for an implant is capitalizing on the advances in technology. Parents who elect to have the surgery for their underage children want to give their children advantages and choices. Even with implants, the device is "optional" and can be turned off at any time. And their opinion is that a child can always be taught ASL at a later age.

Dad viewed implants as no different as wearing glasses to correct his vision. To him, an implant would be like a really powerful hearing aid and he wanted one. But in 1980, cochlear implants were rare and expensive. The cost of one today averages forty thousand dollars and is often not covered by insurance. For my father, this meant an implant wasn't even an option.

Like any deaf person, he was very proud and didn't want to be treated like he was stupid or inadequate. He portrayed himself as too cool to be spoken to, and thus avoided rejection.

My father strode through stores with a swagger. When greeted by a cashier, he'd wink and flash a mischievous grin. With his good looks, he usually made the counter girl clam up and blush. If they needed to ask him a question, though, he had to explain. He'd point to his ear and shake his head, "No."

Since Mom was able to hear, she could share things like music and movies with David and me. Dad was undoubtedly frustrated by this. When we shopped for a second car, he refused to pay for a radio as an added option. Every other kid at school had nice cars with air-conditioning and radios, so I pressed him for an explanation.

"Why should I pay extra for something I can't hear?"

Dad's reason annoyed me. I agreed that it wasn't fair that he couldn't enjoy music, but we lived in a democracy. My mother, David, and I represented the majority, Mom raked in a good portion of our family's income, and we wanted a radio. Why didn't her opinion count? But Dad was such a strong leader and I so desperately wanted to please him that I chose not to protest, and neither did Mom.

Our enjoyment of music wasn't the only thing that separated Dad from his family. On rainy weekends, Mom drove David and me to the six-screen movie theater in Conroe. Horror movies were our favorites, so we planned our trip to see films like *Carrie, Halloween,* and every *Friday the 13th* movie.

In the early 1980s, there was no such thing as closed captioning in movie theaters, and even today the showings are limited in big cities and rarely offered in rural communities. Rather than join us for the movie marathons, Dad stayed behind to work on the Chevy or watch football by himself.

Despite public options being limited, he was still able to enjoy movies with us privately. My parents' deaf friends, the Sloans, liked to borrow films with English subtitles from the public library or their Deaf club in Houston, and they showed them on a wall in the living room using a 16 mm reel-to-reel projector. But the selection was limited, so they often chose titles that were highly inappropriate for us kids, such as *The Exorcist*. I know full-grown adults who shudder at the mere mention of the movie, but I don't. I laugh at the memory of a screening in the Sloans' makeshift theater.

I was just five years old when I curled up on a couch under a scratchy blanket in their living room ready to watch what I thought would be an exciting horror movie. When the film opened with an archaeology scene set in a Middle Eastern desert, I quickly grew bored and fell asleep by the end of the opening credits. Soon I was jolted awake at the frightening sound of Linda Blair talking in the voice of Satan.

Things got worse for Linda. Her head spun; she levitated and found herself covered in crusty sores. To everyone's shock, Linda Blair began stabbing herself in her crotch with a crucifix. Dad and Peter did a double take while Mom and Linda shielded their faces in horror. I ducked under my blanket and plugged my ears. Suddenly, Skip's piercing screams broke the tension. "Fuh meh! Fuh meh! Fuh meh!"

I peeked out from under the blanket and saw Skip writhing on the shag carpeting assaulting his crotch with an imaginary cross.

My brother doubled over with laughter, then joined in shouting between gulps of air, "Fuck me! Fuck me! Fuck me!"

Their antics sent me into a tizzy. They were such a welcome comic relief that I jumped up and down on the sofa, laughing and cheering as the spasmodic boys wiggled around on the floor. The shrieking and laughter got Mom's attention. She scolded, "David, you cut that out!" She waved her arms to alert Dad and smacked her hands together hard as she signed, "Make him stop!"

Pleasantly stoned, Dad, Linda, and Peter were pretty amused by the boys' antics. Mom, however, judging by the look on her face, was not. She was the only adult able to hear David's and Skip's repeated profanities. "They're cussing! I don't like them being dirty! Make them stop!"

"DEHVIH!" Dad screeched with a pitch so high it could have broken glass. "You want me to get my belt to spank you?" The threat was adequate. Skip and David scrambled to their feet and I plopped back down on the sofa.

Like most CODA, David and I had perfected the art of ventriloquism, the ideal way to communicate in front of our parents when we didn't want them to know what we were saying. We became so adept at talking without moving our lips that we were able to have full secret conversations in their presence. With their attention back to *The Exorcist,* David, Skip, and I resumed our snickering. With perfectly still lips we mimicked Regan's self-mutilation, careful to keep our voices low so Mom wouldn't hear and our hand gestures small so Linda, Peter, and Dad wouldn't catch sight.

These private home showings were fun. As I said, public movie theaters were not for Dad. He wasn't as good as Mom at lip reading and hated relying on anyone to interpret for him, especially his wife and kids.

Without a radio in the car, David and I made requests for Mom to sing her favorite songs during our forty-five-minute rides to the cinema. Dad was right. We didn't need a radio. We rotated who sang backup lyrics but most times the three of us sang at the top of our lungs, turning our car into a jukebox on wheels.

I begged Mom to sing "Teen Angel," a classic song from 1960 about a girl who was hit by a train. I liked it because it reminded me of a story my mother often told about her deaf uncle, Bobby, who was my grandmother's twin brother. He and five other deaf passengers were killed when the car they were riding in was struck by a train. The lights and gates at a railroad crossing had failed. "They never heard it coming," Mom lamented.

Once we got to the theater, Mom bought us each a single matinee ticket. We loaded up on soda, popcorn, plain M&M's, and big sour dill pickles wrapped in wax paper and plotted our show schedule.

Plan in hand, the three of us spent the day sneaking from one theater to another in the multiplex, waiting for the coast to be clear before dashing inside where darkness concealed us.

On the long ride home we laughed, rehashed the movies, and, of course, sang our impromptu songs with delight. Movie days were bonding times but my father was left out in the cold.

Dad didn't like our inside jokes or secrets that he didn't understand. Like when we watched the evening news that featured investigative news pieces by Marvin Zindler, a flashy reporter with white hair and blue-tinted eyeglasses. Zindler had gained worldwide notoriety for closing down the Chicken Ranch, a house of prostitution that later became known as "The Best Little Whorehouse in Texas." Mom, David, and I loved to join in as Zindler shouted his signature sign-off, "MAAARVIN ZINNNNDLER EYYYYYYEWITNESS NEWS!"

Seeing us laughing and mouthing in unison piqued my father's curiosity. "What?" he signed. "What'd you say?"

Dad thought we were keeping secrets or plotting behind his back. He was visibly annoyed and frustrated and he didn't want to be played the fool because of his deafness. When we all spoke without using sign language, he was threatened. We knew it was rude, but sometimes it was just faster to dismiss him when we were discussing something that didn't concern him.

I felt a pang of guilt seeing the curiosity and hurt on Dad's face when I brushed him off with a quick sign of "Nothing." How could I describe a funny voice to my father who had never heard a voice to begin with? It was easier to let Mom explain. I shrugged my shoulders and did just that.

I was part of the hearing world. I held the kryptonite, too.

HALF BAKED

Despite being deep in the woods, my parents became the same social butterflies they'd been back in Houston. Their first few years on Boars Head had been filled with lots of hard work. In addition to their full-time jobs, they developed and maintained our acreage, planted and sustained a garden, and kept Mom's landscaping in tip-top shape.

As busy as they were, they still found time to play. There were no clubs or associations for the Deaf within a sixty-mile radius of our trailer, but they made plenty of friends at a nightclub they frequented in Conroe. I was ten when, in October 1981, my parents decided to host a Halloween party and invited their favorite co-workers and barflies.

As we cleaned the trailer Mom gave me forewarning: "Some women that are coming tonight are *lesbians*." On the word *lesbians* she dropped her voice to a dramatic whisper. "Do you know what a *lesbian* is?"

I blushed and nodded. I had known what the word meant ever since I asked Dad for "lesbian" money instead of lunch money one morning before school. American Sign Language is far more complicated and nuanced than hearing people may believe. ASL uses hand signs along with facial expressions and body language to convey a rich variety of words and phrases.

Finger spelling, in which fingers are used for signing one letter at a time, is generally used for communicating proper names and other words for which no hand sign exists. Contrary to what some people may think, ASL allows deaf people to quickly communicate thoughts, emotions, and feelings to others in the Deaf community.

But a slight change to a sign can change its meaning—much like a typo on a keyboard—and prompt the occasional mistake from a ten-year-old.

Dad had burst into laughter upon seeing me sign, "I need lesbian money."

"You mean 'lunch' money?" he asked, and signed "lunch" by forming an *L* with his thumb and index finger and tapped his thumb on his chin. "You said 'lesbian.'" He mimicked my mistake by taking the same L shape and placing the fatty part between his thumb and index finger on his chin. "Lesbian means a gay woman." A simple switch of my wrist and placement of the ASL letter "L" could have avoided the awkward lesson in gal-on-gal copulation.

I mulled over Mom's news that lesbians would be at our Halloween party and said, "To each his own." A phrase I heard her say whenever any scandalous gossip was bandied about during Deaf events.

"That's right." Mom smiled. "To each his own."

To prepare for the party, David and I turned his bedroom into a funhouse. We filled our old metal bathtub with apples for bobbing and put boiled spaghetti, chunks of Jell-O, and grapes into shoe boxes and aquariums. My friends Chris and Billy King stuck their hands in to feel the mushy food while David narrated in a spooky voice with a flashlight under his chin. "You are touching my braaains. That is my heart! Ooooohhhhh! Those are my eyeballlllll!" Dad's addition to the decorations included a homemade wooden coffin.

My parents dressed up like vampires with ghoulish white faces and blood dripping from the corners of their mouths. My mother wore a long red wig that she stowed in her nightstand and a skin-hugging, floor-length black dress. My father slicked his hair and wore a black cape. When they posed for pictures, Dad wore plastic fangs and pretended to suck the blood out of Mom's neck. They looked amazing.

"Kambri, these are the ladies I was telling you about," signed

Mom when the four members of the rock band KISS arrived. I was stunned.

"Hello," I whispered, offering my hand for a shake and staring wide-eyed. They looked so authentic that if Mom hadn't told me they were women, I would have sworn the real KISS had hired a private jet to crash our party on Boars Head.

"Gene Simmons" had a really long tongue like the real lead singer and flicked it when anyone came near. A few beers later and "Gene" and "Paul Stanley" were French-kissing. I didn't know which was wilder: seeing two women being intimate or witnessing the "Demon" and the "Starchild" make out.

When the bonfire we had built died down, the party moved inside. We pushed the furniture out of the living room and everyone sat in a big circle on the floor. I squeezed in between two costumed guests while Mom took her place in the center.

"Hey everybody, listen up! I'm going to teach you a game the Deaf like to play called Elephant." Mom signed in ASL as she talked. Even though my father was the only deaf person at the party and already knew how to play, she didn't want to leave him out.

"All right, I'm gonna start. Everybody have a drink?" A few people hopped up to grab fresh beers as Mom went on with her instructions.

"I stand in the center and turn in circles. When I stop, I'll point to someone. If that person is you, then you have to put both your fists on your nose in the shape of a trunk, see?" She demonstrated stacking her fists on her nose. "If you're sitting on either side of him, then you have to make the elephant ears by putting your hand up to the ear of the person I pointed at. Get it?"

A few people weren't paying attention or were too drunk and grumbled they needed instructions one more time.

"Okay, Kambri, you can help me show them how to play." Mom started spinning in circles. "I turn and turn and turn, then *stop*!" She pointed at me and I quickly put one fist in front of the other on my nose.

"Jerry, you put your hand up to Kambri's ear." The mummy to my left did as he was told.

"Dee Dee, you're supposed to make Kambri's other ear, but you gotta be fast or you're out of the game. Got it?" The Raggedy Ann to my right nodded.

Our Deaf party game was a hit. People screamed and laughed when they messed up and screamed and laughed when they got it right. Dad lit a joint and passed it around the circle of players while the onlookers passed around our bong.

When the joint made it to Dee Dee, she took a hit and then handed it to me. Realizing she was handing it to a kid, she quickly pulled it back. "Oh! Sorry!" She coughed and tried to hold in the smoke, but some blew right in my face.

"It's okay." I pinched the joint between my fingers and passed it to Jerry, who didn't think anything of it. Even though I didn't take a hit, the living room was thick with marijuana smoke. I felt dizzy and my mouth felt like I had eaten a sack of flour. To quench my thirst, I stole sips of beer out of half-empty cans that dotted the trailer. Dad always let me take the first gulp of his Coors Light as a reward for fetching him a fresh one. I definitely preferred my beer cold, but these sips were refreshing, and the rest of the night became a blur.

"I think she's high," Jerry said. "Hey, Kambri, smile!" The flash of his camera hurt my eyes, so I pinched them shut and reeled back. Jerry cracked up and said, "Oh, yeah, she's baked outta her mind."

The next morning my mother's impatient voice jolted me awake. "Come on, lazy bones! Time to get up!" Mom flashed my bedroom light on and off like they did at Deaf school to wake the kids. "Come on, let's go. Come help me find my necklace."

My tongue felt like sandpaper. I rubbed it with my finger, feeling each taste bud. I then peeled off a chunk of dried Juicy Fruit I had stuck to my bedpost and put it in my mouth. Outside, Mom, Dad, and David were digging through ashes. The screens were off our windows and piled in a stack by the porch steps.

"Grab a screen from over there and help us look for my rose pendant. You know what it looks like." I had never seen my mother look so upset. The pendant was part of a set that had matching earrings, and the rose represented June, her birth month.

"How'd you lose it?"

"Your daddy threw it."

"Why'd he do that?"

"Oh, I don't know, Kambri," she answered, irritated. She was in no mood to field questions.

I stepped out onto the front porch, and my father waved me over. My mother was visibly angry, but Dad was unfazed. We didn't have money to spare, and her fourteen-karat-gold rose had cost at least a few hundred bucks. It would not be easy to replace. My father didn't seem at all upset or remorseful at having discarded Mom's treasured possession. In fact, he turned the search into a game.

"Let me show you." He shook a screen and signed, "Like California gold digging."

I picked up a screen and my father dumped a pile of dirt and ashes on it. I wiggled it and dirt fell through as Dad spread the pile around in a thinner layer.

"Neat-o, mosquito," I mouthed, since my hands were busy shaking the screen.

We canvassed the entire front yard without finding the necklace. After several hours, our backs and knees hurt.

"I give up," Mom sighed, arching her spine to stretch out the kinks.

For years whenever someone complimented her beautiful earrings, my mother regretfully commented on how there used to be a matching necklace.

I hadn't known about the explosive confrontation between my parents after the Halloween party that night. In a drunken, stoned rage my father had ripped the chain from my mother's neck and had thrown it in the yard, but I had slept through the entire fight.

My parents' relationship seemed to suffer a cold spell after the necklace incident, just like the weather. One February morning, the ground coated with a layer of frost, I was on the back porch tending to our mutt Taffy and two of her offspring. Unlike Pamie, they weren't allowed in the trailer. They were so badly infested with fleas and ticks that if you parted their fur you couldn't see their skin. I hated seeing them so neglected and spent hours with them huddled around the dryer vent. I used my red and blue sleeping bag to keep them warm and scraped off as many of the insects as I could with a lice comb. I heard my parents coming back from a trip to Webb's with the Sunday paper.

I noticed my mother's puffy, bruised cheek the minute she stepped out of the Chevy. Her right eye was so swollen that she could barely open it. Jumping to my feet, I cried out, "Mama, what happened to your eye?"

My father was at her side. He was watching, anticipating my reaction to her answer. She gave it without using ASL. "I slipped and fell on the ice," she replied.

"Ice? What ice?" I asked, and then looked to Dad. The frost on the ground wasn't enough to hold a footprint. It had only snowed once that I could remember, a phenomenon so rare that we raced to take photos and scraped together a wad of snow the size of a tangerine that we kept in the freezer to preserve for eternity.

With my obsession with Dorothy Hamill, I would have been the first one to try skating on it if there had been ice near our trailer.

My father remained expressionless. So I looked back to Mom and asked again, "What ice?" At that moment our eyes locked and I knew that she wasn't telling the whole truth, nor did she intend to talk about it any further. My father took her by the elbow and led her through the back door, and I knew not to ask any more questions.

My parents had never argued in front of me. Their room was on the opposite side of the trailer from mine. Since they didn't bicker and yell like hearing couples do, I wouldn't have had any way of knowing what was happening behind their bedroom door. When they had a disagreement in my presence, I knew because their signing became more animated and sharp slapping sounds accompanied their ASL. Once I was in my bedroom, I wouldn't have heard the angry smacks of their hands.

Dad may have made a shrill sound or grunt but, even if he

had, I might not have paid attention. As a child of deaf parents, I was used to tuning out the clamor and commotion around me. My mother used to take out her hearing aids when she got home from work, and neither she nor Dad was aware of how much noise they made as they banged around the trailer cleaning house, inadvertently slamming doors and clanging dishes.

Mom's shiner lasted for weeks and she seemed withdrawn and depressed. We stopped singing and dancing around the trailer while we did the housework; she wasn't reading books and had no interest in playing cards with me. Instead she took long naps behind her locked bedroom door, disappeared for solitary drives, or, worse, just sat in silence on the swing. I wanted to ask her about it but for more than twenty years, I never did.

Chapter Six

SHOWCASE SHOWDOWN

M y mother was now the lead person at HeliFlight Systems
in Cut and Shoot. Dad was still in construction in downtown Houston. Like Mom, he left home every day before day-
break and got home well after sunset. Our parents logged so
many hours working and traveling to and from their jobs that

most times my brother and I were left at home in the woods without any adult supervision. Life on Boars Head developed into a southern-fried *Lord of the Flies*.

In our first few years on Boars Head, David had flunked sixth grade, survived a bite from a copperhead, and beat an eight-foot rattlesnake to death with a metal pole. After skinning and mounting the hide of the slain reptile, he carried around the snake's severed rattler like a trophy, recounting to everyone how he saved my life. I backed up his tale (I didn't get bitten, so he *had* saved my life, sort of), thus earning him the alpha-male title on Boars Head. He was David, Lord of Montgomery, fearless and feared. His notoriety suited him and he strutted around shirtless with his best friend, Allen, a short, stocky boy with a bushy head of dirty blond hair and a fuzzy new mustache. Allen lived in a mobile home located just over a mile down the road from ours. His dented trailer was propped up on concrete blocks and streaked with red stains from years of rain rusting the nails. The yard was overgrown with brush and littered with old car parts, paint buckets, and tattered clothing. Some windows were cracked; others were patched up with cardboard and duct tape. Like many trailers around ours, it looked abandoned, but Allen lived there with his father and older brother.

In the past, I was always invited to join David in catching turtles and frogs, playing on the tire swing, or participating in a game of tackle football with the other boys that lived on Boars Head. Some days he'd stay inside with me to work on jigsaw puzzles and play rounds of Monopoly or Skip-Bo. But things seemed to be changing and we hadn't played together in weeks. His invitations stopped and I was left at home alone while he and Allen were off to God knows where. I presumed they were up to no good, especially after they were caught sniffing fumes from cans of spray paint in the King family's barn.

Most of my days in the woods were filled with soul-crushing monotony and isolation. I spent countless hours kicking the dirt.

Three summers on Boars Head and I was bored.

"Go outside," Mom would say without lifting her eyes from the latest Stephen King novel.

To do what?

I pouted on our wooden swing and kept vigil for our mailman. When I saw his ratty Buick stop at the mailbox, I would race to the end of our driveway, hold my breath, and pray there would be something for me. On the best days, my Book-of-the-Month Club package would arrive.

My mother was such an avid reader with so many books that Dad had built her a floor-to-ceiling bookcase spanning the width of our trailer. She passed down her passion to me and signed me up for a monthly book club membership. I cherished each new book as if it were part of Shakespeare's First Folio. Deciding that jettisoning my books to gather dust after a few readings was wasteful, I devised a plan: I would transform my bedroom into a public library and share my collection with the world, starting with everyone on Boars Head.

After taking a detailed inventory of titles, genres, and the retail value of each book, I asked my father to build me a custom case like the one he did for Mom. Using skills I learned at school serving as the librarian's assistant, I explained how I wanted it divided into Nonfiction, Fiction, Periodical, and Reference sections. He took careful notes and measurements and made each shelf a different size and shape, painted it glossy black, and mounted it to my bedroom wall.

I was a budding entrepreneur, and my library was just one of several ventures under the umbrella company of Kambri Crews Products. Others included an internal post office, a papier-mâché puppet theater, and a personalized stationery store. The common denominator was their heavy reliance on our teletypewriter, or TTY.

Before email, text messaging, and videoconferencing rendered it virtually obsolete, the TTY (also known as a telecommunications device for the Deaf, or TDD) was a deaf person's lifeline of communication to the outside world. Our machine was a recycled army-green Department of Defense castoff that stood a full four feet high and weighed almost two hundred pounds. When turned on, it sent out a surge of power that made the entire trailer vibrate as if it were a rocket ship preparing for liftoff.

To call deaf family or friends, we dialed the number on a regular telephone, then placed the receiver into a modem device with two rubber suction cups. We typed in a message and the TTY converted the keystrokes into a series of piercing tones transmitted to the TTY on the other end of the line. Basically it was instant messaging, only instead of a digital screen it had a massive spool of computer paper that documented every word of dialogue.

Only one person could key at a time and typing conversations was time consuming. The telephone company charged by the minute for long-distance calls, so universal shorthand evolved. TTYs used only capital letters. So "GA" signaled to the person on the other end of the line that he should now "go ahead" and begin typing. "SK," short for "Stop Keying," meant you were ready to end the call.

Since letters were typed on paper in real time, there was no backspacing to correct a typo. Instead mistakes were indicated with *XX* and then correctly typed. I spent hours memorizing the placement of keys and pecking with my index fingers, so I would never have to use *XX*. When the phone rang, I raced to answer it. If my greeting was met with screeching computer sounds, it meant someone deaf was on the other end, usually Mom's mother or sister Carly calling from Oklahoma. I placed our receiver on the coupler and typed like a pro, "HELLO THIS IS KAMBRI GA."

Although our TTY served an important purpose for the family, without a phone attached to its modem, it became an oversized, clunky typewriter and the heart of Kambri Crews Products. I typed leaflets notifying everyone I knew about the library's grand opening. David and the kids on Bus #9 became card-carrying members.

While such a nerdy endeavor might elicit taunts from kids in other neighborhoods, the children on Boars Head greeted my enterprise like I was the ice cream man. They were equally bored and isolated, after all. This was no child's play; even my parents were frequent patrons. I kept a detailed log tracking who checked out which books and if they warranted late fees. Dad was a big fan of science and technology and my library records showed he checked out every issue of *3-2-1 Contact*. Unlike Mom, he always returned his selections on time. My mother preferred books like *A Separate Peace*, although she owed dearly when she gave it back eighteen days late!

The summer I turned eleven started out the same as the previous three. Like most brothers and sisters, David and I bickered over the basics. Protective over our things, we labeled them with warnings of "DO NOT TOUCH!!!" If Dad brought home a rare treat like Ding Dongs, we divided them evenly. After counting them out, I unwrapped and licked every square inch of cake as a safeguard, then rewrapped them and carved my name in the tin foil.

But somewhere along the way, David seemed to despise the very sight of me. I had no idea of what had changed between us. I was his enemy and I couldn't figure out why. The easiest explanation was that he was nearly four years older and was outgrowing me. He had woods to explore, animals to slay, girls to conquer. I had always been excited whenever my brother stayed home to keep me company but now dread replaced enthusiasm when he started bullying and knocking me around.

The scene always played out the same way. David woke up in relative peace, the grogginess of sleep coating his fury like frost on a windshield. He'd fix himself a bowl of Lucky Charms, onto which he scooped heaping helpings of sugar from a canister. He'd sit in the living room hunched over his cereal, crunching and slurping away, and we'd watch *The Price Is Right,* shouting out our bids to the host, Bob Barker, and the contestants vying for the prize, a shiny new kitchen appliance, a bedroom set complete with wall-to-wall carpeting, or a brand-new car. "Higher! Higher! Higher! Lower! Lower! Higher! Higher! *Idiot!* I said *higher!*"

By the time the closing credits rolled, David's rage would begin to emerge. Just as Mr. Barker was reminding us to spay and neuter our pets, my brother bared his tiny teeth like fangs and said, "You'd better run for your life."

I'd leap off the couch and run in a different direction each time in a weak attempt to outsmart him. If I made it to Mom and

Dad's room, I had more time because they had installed a heavy-duty metal doorknob that used a real key. A spare was hidden in the living room, in an antique metal pitcher on the top shelf of the bookcase. While David was fishing for it, I could barricade myself in their bathroom, where I would stare at the door waiting for its inevitable betrayal.

David's voice got closer. "I'm comin' to get you, Kambri."

My heart pounded and my ears throbbed. The bathroom door handle was a cheap plastic knob that pushed in to activate the lock. Any slim device, like a bobby pin, could be used to pick it. Though I tried pressing against it with both hands, David always prevailed.

"You think you can outsmart me?" Spit foamed in the corners of his mouth and sprayed as he hissed.

He danced on his tiptoes like Sugar Ray Leonard, and jabbed me with slaps and punches. My arms flailed about in a pathetic attempt to fight him off. The more upset I became, the harder he laughed.

"Leave me alone," I whined.

"You should see your face! 'Leave me alone,'" he mocked, imitating my pained expression. "You're so ugly."

He'd grab the back of my neck or a fistful of my long blond hair and drag me to the floor. The carpet burned my elbows and tailbone as I writhed around and kicked David's back with the heels of my feet. He pinned my arms down with his knees and snorted and hocked snot until he amassed enough to dangle a long, gooey string. He let it slowly drip down till it nearly touched my face, then slurped it back up.

Not wanting his mucus to land in my mouth, I screamed through closed lips. Unsatisfied with my reaction, he began tapping his index and middle fingers on my forehead. Exhausted, I pinched my eyes closed and tried turning the torture into the beat of a song.

Thump, thump, thump, thump . . .

Without warning I lunged to bite his finger. He yanked his hand back in the nick of time as I bit so hard my teeth cracked against each other. A close call, David began striking my sternum instead. Harder and harder he pounded.

After his arm grew tired or he became bored, he jumped off me with one final slap to the face. "You're such a whiner. Are you gonna run and tell your mommy?"

He knew I wouldn't. David was a master manipulator. He could convince me to partake in activities that he then lorded over me as blackmail.

"I'll tell Mom how you skipped school," he threatened. "You don't want Mom to find out you beat up Chris King, do you?"

There was an unspoken rule on Bus #9, that in exchange for David's protection, I had to obey him. Beating up Chris for committing any infraction my brother deemed unacceptable during the bus ride to and from school was a frequent command. Chris's offenses could be as flagrant as stealing money from Haley's five-year-old brother or as insignificant as looking over his shoulder at the other kids.

"Get him, Kambri!" David shouted as soon as the bus disappeared around the corner.

Besides the threat of a thumping from David, I also wanted to please him and be part of his growing group of friends. My brother insisted he'd do the job himself if I hesitated.

"You'll be next!" he warned, shoving me toward Chris, who was being held down by another of David's minions.

I pounced on Chris, who twisted up into a ball as I pounded away at his back.

Chris cried and howled until his mother appeared on their front porch, sending us scattering as she yelled, "Christopher King, don't let that girl beat up on you! Kick her ass!"

Sometimes Chris deserved it, but I still felt bad for hurting him. He was my friend. I would pretend to hit him with my full force to convince my brother that I was doing as he commanded.

I knew Mom would never tolerate me being a bully. She always fiercely defended the underdog, perhaps because she was sensitive to any discrimination against the Deaf. But David's tormenting had become so unbearable that I began calling my mother at her job begging for help. At home, our phones had amplifiers so she was able to hear when the volume was cranked up and her hearing aids were turned to ten. Because her work phones didn't have loudspeakers, I had to scream louder than usual.

"David is beating me up," I panted into the receiver.

"Kambri, don't be a tattletale."

"But he's hitting me!"

"Remember the boy who cried wolf?"

Although I didn't want to be a snitch, I wasn't lying.

"Kambri, you can't keep calling me. I have work to do. You don't want me to lose my job, do you?"

Mom was careful to budget her and Dad's paychecks, but it was always a struggle to make ends meet. If my bugging her at work got her fired, the consequences would have devastated us. I couldn't bear that burden, so I hung up and promised not to call again.

My mother chalked up our continued fighting to sibling rivalry, but my instincts—and bruises—told me otherwise. When

I pointed out an injury to my mother as proof that I wasn't a liar, my brother was able to convince her that I was exaggerating.

My brother loved the wilderness and was always off on treks through the woods, armed with his hatchet, knives, and a canteen. When he was feeling particularly charitable, I would be invited to join him and his neighborhood friends, Allen and the King brothers.

We'd throw on our rattiest T-shirts, cutoff jeans, and spare tennis shoes and head through the woods for the creek, where we dove into the rushing water and swam alongside turtles and water moccasins, trying not to get too close to the snakes. We'd tie a rope to a tree branch and take turns swinging off the edge of the cliff, doing our best Tarzan yells. We had to swim with our shoes on or else the mussels on the creek bed would slice our feet. On those days, David was the best brother a girl could have. I loved and worshipped him almost as much as I did Dad.

But this summer, I woke up every day with a sense of dread. I never knew what I was going to encounter when I took my place next to my brother on the couch each day to watch television. Would it be the cruel, domineering David or the endearing one, who gathered and cleaned dozens of mollusk shells for me during our hikes to Lake Creek because he knew how I liked their shine?

The lack of punishment emboldened David. If my parents did impose a penalty, grounding him or banishing him to his room, they were rarely there to enforce it. When Mom and Dad were home his taunting became no less ruthless.

One day I had reached my acceptable limit, which was averaging about thirty minutes of escalating torment. "Mama! Help!" I shrieked loud enough that my vocal cords burned. Knowing Mom had probably taken out her hearing aids, and Dad couldn't hear my screams, I banged my heels on the carpet to make the floor vibrate.

"Stop shaking the trailer," Mom yelled without investigating. "Your daddy's trying to watch TV!"

"MUDDAH FUH!" my father would yell if David or I came anywhere near the television when a boxing match or a football game was playing. David and I avoided the TV area when he was engrossed; we were terrified of hearing his screeching curses.

I broke free from my brother and ran to the living room. Mom threatened, "If you two bother me one more time, I'm going to get your daddy to whip you."

My father was known to dramatically unhinge his brass belt buckle as a gesture of an impending lashing, but there was never any follow-through. Convinced the threat alone would be enough to stop my brother, I returned to my room. David was undeterred, however, and attacked me again.

"MAMA!"

My father's unmistakable footsteps came toward us. David and I were still tangled together when he burst into my room, his belt already unbuckled.

"STAH!" he screamed as he gave the sign for "Stop!" making a chopping motion with his right hand into his open left palm. The sound of his hands coming together made a loud smack. "Why don't you listen to your mother?"

He swished his leather belt through the loops in one quick jerk. He then sat on the edge of my bed, bent David over his knees, and began whipping him.

This was the first time I'd seen my father use a belt, and I was next! I panicked. A scene from an episode of *The Little Rascals* flashed through my mind where Spanky shoved a plate in his britches while his brother got a beating. My eyes surveyed my room for something—anything—to stick in my pants. The only item I found was my pocket-sized, hardcover Bible. If ever I needed God, it was now. I pushed the Bible into my underwear. My pants bulged, revealing a clear outline of where the Good Book was lodged.

Dad released David, who ran out of the room choking back tears. He had often been paddled by the principal at school for misbehaving, but I had never been paddled or whipped, besides the one time Dad gave me a single swift smack on my bottom.

I swallowed a big gulp of air as my father beckoned me over. "You better listen to your mama." I bent over his lap and he came down with two quick strikes of his belt. I was relieved at how well the Bible took the blows, but then Dad stopped at two. I had counted David's spankings and knew at least eight more licks were coming my way. I held my breath. *Oh no! He can see my Bible.*

Dad abandoned his belt and came down with his bare hand. If by a slim chance he hadn't seen the book, I knew he would feel it. When he stopped again and shooed me off his lap, I expected him to tell me I was in more trouble. Instead he stood up, retrieved his belt, and signed, "Be quiet. Your mama's tired."

As my father left my room, I saw him force back a smile.

Many Friday and Saturday nights, my parents went dancing at Gilley's, a honky-tonk bar that was featured in the movie *Urban*

Cowboy. The bar was in Pasadena, a ninety-minute drive from Boars Head. My parents usually stayed there until 2 A.M., closing time, leaving me home alone with David.

My mom loved to dance and my father had better moves than John Travolta. He was better-looking, too, if you asked me. He grooved to the beat of the vibration and wasn't distracted by all the lyrics. The thrill of a night on the town seemed to reignite the spark in their marriage. They came home sweaty and laughing and were still dancing around the trailer all through the next day.

Evenings that they were going out started the same, with my mother trying to pour herself into skintight jeans.

"Kambri, come here," she'd holler.

I'd go to her bedroom and find her on the king-sized bed, breathless and flat on her back. Her blue jeans were open and she'd be pulling on a wire hanger she had threaded through the hole of the zipper.

"Help me," she'd grunt. "I can't zip up my jeans!"

She'd press down on her belly as I yanked on the zipper with both hands, the way you might zip closed an overstuffed suitcase.

"Finally! Now, help me up." I'd pull her arms, as she'd rock back and forth a few times to gain momentum to get off the bed. "I used to be so skinny, till I had you." She'd jiggle the roll of flab that spilled over the top of her jeans and add, "After I had David, I was back to wearing my same old jeans. Now I'm fat and it's all your fault."

Clearly, the heaping bowls of Blue Bell vanilla ice cream and plates of fried potatoes she was so fond of had nothing to do with it, nor did the bags of M&M's she kept hidden in her middle dresser drawer.

She wasn't fat, if you asked my father. He seemed to like her just the way she was, judging by the look on his face. I got that same expression when I was eyeing the dessert section at Luby's Cafeteria.

Dad was wearing Wranglers equally as tight as Mom's, with a shiny brass belt buckle in the shape of a Texas longhorn. He smelled like a mix of Lava soap, Jovan Musk, and freshly applied hairspray. Dad groped her butt and kissed her all over her neck and cheeks.

Mom batted Dad's hand away and signed, "I'm ready." She tiptoed around in a circle to show him the 360-degree view of what he couldn't have just yet. Dad pinched her butt and Mom squealed. As she grabbed her purse and keys, Mom called over her shoulder, "Don't stay up too late."

I nodded even though I planned to stay awake through the end of *Saturday Night Live.* No matter how hard I tried, I always fell asleep during the musical act.

The headlights of the Chevy flickered out of sight. As I watched *Diff'rent Strokes,* I heard David menacingly call after me, like we were in a country-and-western version of *The Warriors:* "Kaaam-mmbriiii, come out and playyy-aayyy!"

A chill ran down my spine. When I turned my head around I saw David calmly approaching me clutching his 20/20 rifle.

My parents had bought the shotgun for David's thirteenth birthday, a rite of passage for most Texas boys who lived in the woods. The gun was perfect for a young kid since it was powerful enough to kill but didn't have the pesky kickback of a bigger gun. My brother hunted rabbits, squirrels, and birds for no reason other than to skin them and hang their dried hides on his bedroom wall along with his turtle shell and snake skin collection.

He'd dig up the skinless corpses he'd buried, scrape off the remaining flesh with a pocketknife, and clean them with different agents like nail polish remover, rubbing alcohol, and gasoline. Mom bought him a three-tiered plastic corner curio shelf that snapped together so he could display the teeth and skulls like trophies.

He peered down the barrel of the gun and said, "I'm gonna kill you."

I had no idea if he was serious or just playing with me, and I had never been more terrified.

I ducked down below the couch and screamed, "That's not funny, David!"

That's when I heard him cock the gun.

I peeked over the sofa to see David aiming the shotgun at me. I bolted outside without shoes, dove under the front porch, and crawled under the trailer. Judging by David's wheezing laughter, the prank had exceeded his expectations. I was sure my brother could hear my heavy breathing but I tried to make myself smaller, wrapping my knees tightly to my chest.

"I'm not gonna hurt you," David called out. He could barely speak, he was laughing so hard.

He pleaded with me to come back inside, probably feeling guilty about how I overreacted. His stunt had worked, but he hadn't meant for me to spend the night in the woods. I didn't trust him, though, especially after he had recently shot my pet salamander point-blank in the head with a BB gun. I stayed crouched in the darkness under the trailer.

The front door slammed behind him as he retreated, but I could still hear his muffled laughter.

Chapter Seven

OKLAHOMA!

D ays after David aimed his gun at me, Mom was on the telephone with a travel agent, but she was clearly exasperated. She shoved the phone in my direction. "Here, Kambri, you talk to her. I can't understand a thing she's saying!"

Mom saw me balk and waved the receiver at me again. "Kambri! I need your help, now take it."

Mom was in the middle of booking round-trip flights to Oklahoma when I took over. Fed up with my calls to her at work to complain about David and the battles at home, she was sending my brother and me to spend part of our summer vacation with our two sets of grandparents. After thirty minutes of relaying available options, I finally purchased plane tickets.

"See, that wasn't so bad, Kambri."

I slammed down the receiver. The excitement about the trip, especially the flight, had been spoiled by the annoyed sighs from the customer service agent on other end. Humiliation pulsed through me. How was I supposed to know "layover" didn't mean staying overnight like a sleepover? I was ten.

"Kambri, you're gonna have to learn how to handle things like this."

As I stormed off to my room Mom trailed after me. "Why don't you want to help me? David does it all the time and never complains."

I hated that my mother always compared my brother to me. I *did* get frustrated when she used me as a translator. David was more enthusiastic for a reason. He was almost fifteen years old and his signing and ASL vocabulary were better. If he was home, Mom automatically chose him to be her interpreter. He relished the responsibility of being indispensable to her, swelling with exaggerated pride and cockiness. I knew I should assist when Mom asked, but I dreaded interpreting phone calls. My signing wasn't particularly fast, even when I wasn't holding a phone with one hand and signing words I didn't understand. No customer service agent wanted to talk to a kid, either.

However reluctantly, I helped when Mom needed me. I made appointments, called the utility company for late-payment extensions, and in this case, booked two economy class tickets out of Boars Head to the sweeping plains of Bowlegs, Oklahoma.

Since moving to Texas, we only visited Dad's parents about once every year or two, in part because of the distance but also because my father wasn't comfortable there. His parents were salt-of-the-earth types seeming to have stepped out of the Depression era.

His mother was called "Mee-Maw" by her dozens of other grandkids. Mom, David, and I thought the name made us sound unrefined, so we called her a more formal title, Grandma Crews. Her skin was a leathery tan from toiling in her garden. She boiled and canned ripened fruits and vegetables in mason jars and stocked them in a cellar that once doubled as sleeping quarters for her eldest daughters, and as a storm shelter to protect the family from tornadoes that barreled through the fields, long devoid of crops.

Then there was Grandpa Crews, built up by my father to be a man fond of using cherry tree switches and razor straps for corporal punishment.

On the way to the airport, Mom reminded us about the rules on the Crews farm. "Remember they're very strict," she stressed. "No cursing, don't say God's name in vain, and no talking back. And don't forget . . . ," she added with a wag of her finger.

"We know," David and I recited in unison. "Don't tell them you smoke marijuana."

Guilt swept across her face. "Right."

Bowlegs, Oklahoma, located a good hour-and-a-half drive on a two-lane road southeast of Oklahoma City, was a simple place. It was as isolated as Montgomery but had a different landscape. Instead of the moist air, lush forest, and natural springs, the land surrounding the Crews farm was an arid, endless horizon of plains dotted with pumping oil jacks that looked like giant robotic grasshoppers pecking the ground.

Off the main road, we followed dirt paths marked by cattle guards and rusted mailboxes. At the entrance to the farm an aluminum metal gate in the fence was meant to keep out more than to keep in. The only farm animal they owned was an aged horse named Clipper. In the distance, I spotted their two-bedroom home covered in gray slate roofing tiles. Nothing there changed except the height of the trees.

Life on the farm was as dull as Boars Head. Grandma woke us every morning just after dawn. "Brush your teeth, then come get your breakfast."

At home I never brushed my teeth unless my gums were puffy and bleeding. I remembered Mom's instructions: "Do what you're told." So I did, careful to save water.

On the farm, water was as precious as it had been when we were stealing it from Webb's Grocery. We filled their porcelain tub with claw feet with one inch of water, no more. They had a toilet, but we were encouraged to use their outhouse. They used a well with a hand pump that collected rainwater. David and I took turns trying to jack it and judging the water level based on how many thrusts it took before we were rewarded with ice-cold, clear water. Grandma Crews made sure we washed up before every meal. Instead of running our hands under a faucet, they kept a bowl and pitcher of water in a mudroom. With teeth brushed and hands cleaned, I joined David in their cramped kitchen, where a plate of food awaited me. I slid into one of the silver metal chairs with the bright teal vinyl cushions that matched the Formica table. David signed, "Look," and pointed up to the wall.

I glanced up at the hanging knickknacks. "What?" I signed back.

With her back to us scrubbing dishes by hand, Grandma Crews kept talking. "Kambri, I don't know how you like your breakfast, but there's ketchup, salt, pepper, and jelly right there on the table."

"Okay, thanks," I answered, noticing the condiment caddy. I looked back at David, who was waving his hand to get my attention.

"Look," he persisted. "See that leather thing?"

I nodded and signed, "What is it?"

He spelled out, "R-A-Z-O-R S-T-R-A-P."

My body went stiff. A "razor strap" was the instrument of terror from my father's childhood. Some fathers might have a "big fish" story they liked to tell, but my dad's recollections were filled with tales of torture. His beatings with a razor strap now had evidentiary proof, hanging a mere foot from my grandmother's grasp.

Grandma Crews turned around and I darted my eyes from the wall back to my food.

"You must be hungry. You two aren't making a peep!"

After breakfast we played in the dirt sandbox built next to a broken-down Chevy pickup just like ours, only older.

"Why do you think they keep that strap hanging in the kitchen?" I asked David.

"So they can grab it in a hurry, I bet."

Watching Grandpa Crews shuffle around the property with the arthritis paining his joints, I couldn't imagine him hurting anyone or anything. His voice was soft and steady. He sometimes whistled when he said an *S*, making my skin break into goose bumps. I watched as he gently brushed and saddled Clipper, then helped boost me up into the seat. As he led us at a slow pace, he shared stories of tornadoes destroying crops and how the old pieces of farm equipment that were rusting away used to work in the olden days. I took pictures with my first camera, a windup Kodak with a flashbulb, which I had received for my seventh birthday.

My favorite part of the farm was Grandpa Crews's pet cemetery. He had buried each animal with its own handmade tombstone and had a special memory to recount about them all. "This old cat liked to kill mice and leave 'em on our doorstep. A snake got to her. This boy used to bite my tires till he got too close to one and got run over. And you remember him. He was a good ol' dog that died at a ripe ol' age, like I'm going to."

"When Clipper dies, will he be buried here?"

"Nah," he chuckled. "He's too big a boy. I don't know what we'll do with him when his day comes."

When we turned back to the barn to unsaddle Clipper, I was overcome with sadness. Grandpa Crews wasn't the tyrant Dad had made him out to be. He had taken so much time with me and made me feel like his only grandchild even though he had dozens. He was my pen pal and we even had a running joke between us about how I could beat him in a spelling bee though I was only a fifth grader. This convinced me that I was his favorite grandchild, a fact I decided to keep to myself so my cousins wouldn't get jealous.

Religion permeated every aspect of life on the farm. It controlled musical taste and television programming. Attendance at weekly church services was mandatory. Even our language was censored. The word *hate* was strictly forbidden, enforced vigorously by Grandma Crews. Lectures about God's goodness crept into every conversation no matter how banal. As members of the Assembly of God church, Dad's family devoted themselves to the Lord's work and relentlessly recruited new members.

At holiday gatherings, the family swapped stories of miraculous divine healing. The wheelchair-bound walked, blind men saw, broken bones mended, and even cavities disappeared. Inexplicably, no deaf person was ever cured, a fact not lost on Dad.

"They're hypocrites," he signed when the subject came up. "They lie and gossip. They judge. They aren't true Christians."

Dad could hardly tolerate this aspect of his family and never attended church. Being on the farm made him visibly uncomfortable.

At home in Montgomery, I could only remember going to church twice. Mom's relationship with God was born out of fear of the unknown, and although she didn't attend services she sent money instead. Not supporting the church would be like not mailing a chain letter. "Good things always happen when we pay our tithes," she said as she filled out a check for fifty dollars. "Once, after I stopped, your daddy lost his job." She ripped the check out of the book, stuffed it in an envelope, and sealed it shut. "Let's hope they don't cash this till Friday, because that's when we get paid."

Trips to visit Dad's parents always included at least one reminder of how my soul was in peril. For years I dreaded the Second Coming. Sometimes on Boars Head when Mom and Dad took off on impulsive explorations through the woods, I didn't know where they were, and I wondered if the End had come.

"I wasn't always the man I am today," Grandpa told me as the two of us sat in his recliner one afternoon. "I used tobacco and wasn't very nice. But then I found God, and I quit all that. Now I go to church every Sunday, and I'm at peace knowing that when the Lord comes I'm going with Him." His voice was gentle but stern. "I want you to come with us, too. You hear me, Kambri?"

I felt uneasy whenever Grandpa Crews spoke about religion. As he talked, his sad eyes got misty. I tried to stay still in his lap and nodded my head politely to prove I got his message.

"To go to Heaven, you have to be saved, and you have to ask for Christ's forgiveness. Kambri, you must accept Jesus Christ as your Lord and Savior. Do you read your Bible?"

"Yes, sir."

It was only a half lie since I really did like the Jehovah's Witnesses' book of Bible stories I had received as a gift from a childhood friend, but I knew my grandfather wouldn't approve. He would want me to read the King James version like his. By the time I left the farm, I was converted, promising myself that when I got home I would read it start to finish. And though I tried, I was never able to make it past the first page of Genesis.

The Crews farm guaranteed there was peace between my brother and me. The bullying had gotten so bad at home that I wondered if maybe he'd been poisoned by venom when he had been bitten by the copperhead snake. But now he was so kind and well behaved. His decision to be cruel to me at home had to be a conscious choice. My father's warnings about my grandfather's temper and the sight of the razor strap hanging on the wall in the kitchen could have influenced him. The daily reminders of God and church may have helped, too. But more noteworthy, my father's parents were hearing. One whine or cry from me, and I would have been out helping David select a switch from a cherry tree for a beating of his own.

Being on the Crews farm on our best behavior for a whole week was exhausting. Although I enjoyed my time there, my brother and I let out a sigh of relief when we saw Grandma and Grandpa Worth's new van lumbering down the country road to pick us up. We would be spending the remainder of the summer with Mom's parents in Tulsa, where we could be ourselves, and heathens or not, they would love us regardless.

Our grandparents' custom van was more befitting of pothead college kids than sixty-something adults. It had backseats folded out into a bed and diamond-shaped mirrors on the walls and ceiling. Each mirror was outlined with bright royal blue fake fur. As we rumbled toward Tulsa, David and I stuck our hands underneath the curtained windows and flipped off passing cars. They honked in protest but of course my grandparents couldn't hear it. Our good behavior didn't make it past Interstate 44.

Grandpa Worth was tall and slender, with dark hair and a persistent five o'clock shadow peppered with gray stubbles. He was a man of few words, in ASL or otherwise. If he did make noise to get someone's attention or express disapproval, he grunted with a deep bass tone but never formed any actual words. He was the only deaf person in his whole family. To protect him, his mother had kept him close by her side while she toiled in the kitchen. Grandpa Worth was her loyal assistant and picked up her talents. He could cook better than anyone I knew, especially when it came to frying up fresh catfish we caught from a day of fishing in his bass boat. Most days, Grandpa Worth worked at Century Electronics, while his wife stayed at home and tended to their two-bedroom house in a quiet Tulsa subdivision.

Out of four children, Grandma Worth, her twin brother, Bobby, and older sister, Wilma, were born deaf. Grandma dyed her hair jet black and wore bright red lipstick every day, even if she was just puttering around the house in her terry cloth slippers and housecoat. She subscribed to the *National Enquirer,* and kept back issues piled in a stack near her recliner. She never missed a single episode of *The Price Is Right* or *The Young and the Restless.* Like Grandpa, she didn't vocalize much, but when she did, hers was a husky, gravelly voice from years of smoking a pack of Winstons a day. She kept her cigarettes in a leather case and her lighter was emblazoned with an eagle made of turquoise, her birthstone.

Since David and I had spent a chunk of our early childhood living across the street, we felt right at home with Grandma and Grandpa Worth. We also identified with them more than we did with Dad's parents, because in Tulsa we were part of the Deaf community. David spent his days with Grandpa hunting, fishing, working in the garage, and doing other things boys and grandfathers do, while I stayed home with my grandmother.

Grandma told me that having me around was like having a miniature version of my mother. I gave Grandma a voice, making her day-to-day life a bit easier. I accompanied her to doctors' appointments, the pharmacy, the bank, and the shoe store; she would give me instructions on her various needs. I never minded interpreting for her the way I did when Mom asked, maybe because she was fully deaf and I was in complete control of each transaction, whether it be simple, like requesting a pair of shoes in her size from a salesman, to complex, like asking detailed questions about her blood pressure from a physician. I would interpret the doctor's warning about the effects smoking was having on her health. It scared me to hear his stern lecture, and I could tell he wasn't sure how much to tell me. I worried if my grandmother was getting the best care from him, but I didn't say anything. Girls at school could keep their silly role-playing games of doctor or bank teller. I was living the real deal.

My grandparents' house was a hub of activity. Deaf friends were always dropping in for unannounced visits. Linda Sloan's father, Fred, kept a lit cigar permanently lodged in the corner of his mouth to leave his hands free for signing. When he signed, his heavy breathing growled and whistled. The noise drove me crazy, so I cranked up the new MTV channel as loud as I could.

My grandparents' friend Otto was my favorite surprise guest. He had been popping in for visits since my mother was a young girl. He always greeted me with "Hey now, brown cow! Where's the cow?" He made as much sense to me as a Spanish variety show, but I loved him anyway.

My grandparents had known Fred and Otto since their school days at Oklahoma School for the Deaf. They had newer friends at their local Deaf club. In fact, they didn't appear to have a single hearing friend. I figured David and I didn't count.

In Tulsa, just like most every major American city at the time, Deaf clubs were centers that served as the nucleus for their community. Many had general elections to select board members. Clubs issued monthly newsletters listing recent births and deaths and upcoming events, and relayed important local and national news that might affect their civil rights. Even though we lived all the way down in Montgomery, we still subscribed to the Oklahoma Association of the Deaf newsletter to stay connected.

These clubs were a necessary part of life, especially for deaf people of my grandparents' generation. Without them, their lives would have been lonely and disengaged. Born in the 1920s and living before civil liberties for the disabled, my grandparents might have lived isolated, friendless lives. Teletypewriters (TTY) weren't around until the 1970s and closed captioning for television began in the 1980s. The clubs provided a TTY and enabled them to connect with friends and enjoy activities like potluck dinners, bowling, and bass fishing competitions. Depending on the number of patrons and monetary contributions by its members, some Deaf clubs owned centers while others rented halls or small houses. In Tulsa, the Deaf club operated out of a two-story home with a finished basement and small backyard.

Every stay with our grandparents included at least one trip to their club and lots of loud, intense play with the other deaf and hearing children. No one ever told us to "settle down" or "hush up." We ran like a stampede of horses under the bright fluorescent lights, playing games of hide-and-seek and tag.

In the past, because the gadgets needed to communicate

weren't readily available or were too expensive, deaf members used the club's devices. Privacy was difficult because the TTY typed out transcripts and eavesdropping was simply a matter of looking across the room at somebody else's signed conversation.

Today, many Deaf clubs have been closed down in favor of seeing close friends at malls, coffee shops, and bookstores without the need to pay monthly dues. Advances in technology have served the Deaf well. Computers and the Internet are readily available, cellphones and texting are commonplace, and video phones put the callers face-to-face. There are far fewer obstacles preventing the Deaf from communicating with one another and the hearing world.

Mom's parents were city folks who lived such a modern life, I felt like a time traveler visiting the future. Their home was also equipped with a TTY similar to the one we had at the trailer. It was hooked up to a table lamp that flashed on and off when triggered, sending their rat terriers, Honeybee and Sammy, into a barking tizzy. They also possessed the holy grail of household accessories: cable television.

Although there was a television at the Crews farm, it got only three channels, like ours back in Boars Head. It was a tiny black-and-white set and we weren't allowed to watch it apart from the nightly news, no exceptions. But Mom's parents had dozens of channels, including uncensored ones like HBO and Cinemax. Grandma Worth didn't care what we watched. During the day, David and I viewed countless hours of *The Little Rascals, The Price Is Right, Let's Make a Deal,* and anything on MTV and Nickelodeon. We scoured the cable guide for R ratings and warnings of graphic violence and nudity to determine which movies to watch. In a pinch, we always counted on Benny Hill for laughs and gratuitous boob shots.

At night, the adults-only channel, Escapades, was unscrambled. David and I waited for Grandma to go into the kitchen to prepare her nightly bowl of vanilla ice cream. We then grabbed the push-button channel changer and hid the long cord that connected it to the television under rugs and blankets. Cord concealed and box in hand, we squeezed under the couch and switched on Escapades.

Grandma emerged from the kitchen and let out an appalled gasp at seeing pornography. We laughed so hard we couldn't breathe. She puttered around, screaming our names "Dehvih! Kahn-rare-ree!" while looking frantically for the channel changer. Eventually she gave up the search and settled into her recliner with her vanilla ice cream, as we stayed curled under the couch near her feet like kittens. If Dad's parents knew that we even had the idea to pull a prank so wicked, I imagined they would have summoned a preacher to make a house call once the razor strap was hung back on the wall.

Stunts like this relied on Grandma Worth's deafness, and we always found creative ways to exploit it. We took particular pleasure in teasing her because she was such a good sport, laughing so hard at our pranks that she devolved into coughing fits.

Unfortunately, once the novelty of being in Tulsa wore off, David was back to bullying me. Our grandparents' home was not elevated like our trailer on Boars Head, but instead rested on slab concrete, which meant that we could run like wild monkeys through the house and no matter how hard I kicked and screamed my grandmother wouldn't feel or hear a thing. She didn't have to, though. Her eyesight was just fine. Their house was small and she was always home to witness David hitting me, pinning me down, thumping on me, and teasing me with dangling spit like he did back on Boars Head all those days that Mom and Dad were away from the house. She also saw that he wasn't mindful of the disparity in our sizes and strengths, and that when he hit me, I was really being hurt. She saw that things between us were out of control and after watching several days of it, she took it upon herself to tell our mother when Mom called on June 22 to wish me a happy eleventh birthday.

Like many summers, I spent my birthday away from home and friends. To make up for it, Mom called and sent a care package. Grandma Worth never baked me a cake. Instead she and my grandfather took us to lunch at Luby's or Wyatt's cafeteria in downtown Tulsa, and then to Baskin-Robbins for ice cream. It wasn't as fun as being with friends, and I was always eager to hear from home.

That evening, when the light for the phone flashed, I raced to answer it, hoping it would be Mom with birthday wishes. "Hello?"

I was heartened when I was correct, and listened to her off-key rendition of "Happy Birthday." I excitedly told her about the fishing trip I'd taken with Grandpa, our visit to the local Deaf club, and the special place we had gone for my birthday lunch. Then it was Grandma's turn to take the line. I put the phone on the coupling device for the TTY and signed, "Mama wants to talk to you."

Grandma shut the door to the spare bedroom and typed with Mom for a long time before finally emerging to prepare dinner. I waited until she was out of sight before I slipped into the guest room, where I dug the paper transcript of her conversation with Mom out of the trash. I was surprised to see that she was upset over the fighting going on between my brother and me.

Mom insisted that it was nothing more than sibling rivalry, which is what she always told me, but Grandma disagreed. "The fighting is terrible. It makes my heart beat too fast and it scares me."

My heart sank as I read on. Grandma was refusing to stay alone another day with David and me, prompting my mother to change her reservation and come to Tulsa earlier than planned.

When she arrived, she laid into us with a scathing lecture. "You two are so bad even your own grandmother doesn't want you!"

David was ashamed he had distressed Grandma Worth. She was so easygoing and rarely complained about anything. Upsetting her filled him with guilt that he had crossed the line. He softened his mean streak, much to my relief. The change was almost immediate. Of course, he still teased me now and again as brothers do, but the physical harassment stopped.

On our last night in Oklahoma, David and I turned in early in anticipation of our morning flight home to Houston. We shared the hide-a-bed sofa in the living room but I couldn't sleep. I lay wide awake, my stomach in knots, listening to the sound of David's low, heavy breathing signaling me he was asleep. In a few weeks, I would be starting sixth grade, joining my brother at Montgomery Junior High, where he was starting eighth grade. I had a respectable number of friends, but David was reigning king of Bus #9 and the proud owner of a yearbook so packed with signatures from classmates, I was sure he was the most popular kid in his class. Facing this unknown entity called junior high, and hoping he had insight from his years of experience that he could pass down to me, I worked up the nerve to ask him for advice.

"David? You awake?"

"Huh? I am now."

His annoyed voice made me second-guess whether I should have awakened him. "Oh. Sorry. Never mind."

"What's the matter?"

"Nothing."

"Liar. What's wrong?"

It took a while for him to draw it out of me, but finally I managed to tell him.

"Well . . . I'm just scared about starting school."

"What's to be scared about?"

"I don't know. I guess I'm worried about finding my way from class to class."

"The school's not that big. You'll see. It's easy." David rolled over and covered himself with the blanket.

I couldn't let him fall back asleep; I hadn't gotten the answers I was looking for and I wouldn't dare wake him again. I took a deep breath and plunged into the real reason I was worried. "I want to be popular . . . like you."

The words had barely left my lips when he broke into a guttural laugh. He looked over at me and saw I was hurt by his laughter.

"It's not something you can make happen. Anyway, why do you want to be popular?"

"I just want people to like me. I want to have a lot of friends like you."

"I don't know, Kambri. You'll be all right. Just don't try too hard."

Chapter Eight

WORKIN' FOR A LIVIN'

David was right. With about seventy-five students in each grade, Montgomery Junior High wasn't big or hard to figure out. But I hadn't confessed to him my real insecurity: I was uglier than an armadillo. Unlike Mom and Dad with their big, white perfect teeth that looked like Chiclets, my adult teeth were growing in like David's. They were crooked and small and my gums were always swollen from chronic gingivitis. My formerly golden silky hair had turned into stringy, dirty-dishwater blond strands. In an effort to spruce it up, Mom gave me an Ogilvie home perm. But the "Afro" only called attention to my long, skinny face and Joker-like smile, so I let it grow out, which made the top half of my greasy hair stick-straight and the bottom half kinky curls. I couldn't attract a magnet if I were covered in foil. While Mom was blessed with boobs so big her bra straps made deep indentations in her shoulders from the weight, I was still flat as glass and so skinny I could hide behind a stop sign.

Money was tight and our trips to the grocery store were scheduled around my parents' biweekly paychecks. Sometimes we ran out of staples before it was time to stock up again, so I scrounged around for anything to quell my appetite. I balled up slices of bread, sucked on dried sticks of spaghetti, gummed spoonfuls of butter, or ate peeled and salted raw potatoes, tomatoes, and cucumbers plucked from our garden. My brother and I were bottomless pits of hunger and never gained weight. For David, Mom purchased special high-calorie protein shakes to supplement his diet. She took me to a doctor, convinced I had worms. Luckily the doctor told her what I already knew—I wasn't getting enough to eat for my rapidly growing body—but I was humiliated just the same.

Not only was I exceptionally unattractive and skeletal, I was shamefully unfashionable. All the girls at school wore Gloria Vanderbilt or Jordache jeans with Izod and Polo sweaters, the iconic logos branding them rich and popular. I wore cheap clothes from the discount department store, Weiner's. I begged Mom for my own pair of designer jeans, but she refused. Not even for Christmas. "I'm not gonna spend all that money on one pair of jeans. You won't fit in them for very long, anyway."

She was right; I was growing fast. A sweater that fit one day was too tight just a few months later. I felt my bones stretching at night, so Mom gave me aspirin and massaged my legs to ease the excruciating pain. David and I were head and shoulders taller than everyone else in our respective grades. We kept track of our growth rate with marks on the kitchen wall. I climbed on top of a stool and marked the wallpaper with a pen where David's head was, and then he'd do the same for me, until the wall looked like a six-foot ruler with all the measurements we had taken over the years.

The weekends at Galveston beach and blistering sunburns had covered me in freckles, which the boys teased me about.

"Hey, Kambri, did you stand too close to a mud flap?"

At home I took out my frustration on Mom, a natural redhead with plenty of freckles of her own. "I'm ugly because of you! It's all your fault I have freckles!"

Mom's attempts to comfort me with the tale of the Ugly Duckling backfired.

"So, you think I'm ugly, too!"

"I didn't say that, Kambri."

"Well, you told me one day I'll turn into a swan but how can I do that without being ugly *first*? YOU THINK I'M UGLY!" I shrieked.

I flung myself onto my bed crying, kicking and screeching hateful rants about Mom into my pillow.

What I lacked in looks, I made up for in effort. I invested all my energy into school and extracurricular activities. Throughout junior high, I was a straight-A student and teacher's aide, served on the Youth Advisory Council, participated in theater arts festivals, and competed in poetry readings, readers' theater, and pantomiming. I was on the track team and a starting player in both volleyball and basketball. If I could have joined the boys' football team, I would have. Instead, I settled for playing with them on Boars Head.

One evening after school, I was in a basketball game against the Magnolia Bulldogs. I heard a familiar voice coming from the stands and was surprised to see my father sitting alone on the top bleacher. My heart fluttered. No one had ever come to see me play. I stopped and gave him a big wave. He waved back and signed, "Don't look at me. Look at the game!"

Energized to have someone there to watch me, I raced down the court, caught up to the other players, blocked a shot, and grabbed the ball in midair. Before anyone realized, I was headed toward my team's net unguarded. The only thing between the basket and me was fifty feet of court. The crowd leapt to their feet screaming wild cheers, including Dad's signature piercing shriek.

I dribbled to the basket and slid a layup toward the hoop. I missed.

The crowd let out a collective groan and everyone took his seat.

I glanced up at Dad. He snapped his fingers as if to say, "Aw shucks," but I still hung my head in shame. After the game, Dad patted me on the back and signed, "Next time. You just need practice."

If the night hadn't been bad enough, Dad made it even worse by driving our old Chevy to the game.

The once-beloved truck that we had decorated with red, white, and blue balloons and streamers to carry David's baseball and my softball teams in parades back in Houston was now a blemish on the façade I was attempting to create. The bench seat had holes worn through and the metal was riddled with rusty spots. Dad had patched them up before spray-painting the interior a bright royal blue.

I was usually one of the last kids to be picked up after practice so my classmates never saw it. But there was no avoiding it now. Ducking my head, I climbed into the cab convinced that every person in the whole wide world knew I was a freckled, ugly loser who lived in a trailer, rode in a rattletrap truck, and missed the easiest shot in the history of basketball. I wanted to die.

The Chevy had outlasted any other car we owned. Mom's four-door sedan still looked decent, but because of the bumpy dirt roads, it was rattled to the core and eventually fell apart. The miles we logged demanded an upgrade to something that could handle the backwoods of Texas, so we became the proud owners of a brand-new four-wheel-drive Toyota truck. I'd never seen anything so cool.

"The cab comes off so when we go to Galveston we can drive it like a jeep," Dad signed.

"We really can't afford it," Mom said. "But it's built to handle these roads so we'll save money on all the repairs and your daddy won't have to spend all his time working on it." She rattled off the speech like she was still convincing herself that getting in over our heads with the high monthly payment was the right thing to do.

To make ends meet, my mother got a second job working nights and weekends as a hostess at the members-only Walden Yacht Club in Montgomery. I took the opportunity to ask her if I could work there, too.

"Why do you want to work? You're only thirteen."

"Please? I can use the money to buy my own clothes and books."

To pinch pennies, my mother had discontinued my book club membership, and I desperately wanted it back.

"Let me talk to my boss and see what he says." Mom told her manager I was fourteen, but very mature for my age. He agreed to meet me so my mother told me to get dressed in my nicest school clothes before we drove forty minutes to Lake Conroe for the interview. Mom told me the Walden Yacht Club was a really swanky restaurant. I imagined it to be like Red Lobster, since anytime I heard adults talking about where to go for a special anniversary or celebration, Red Lobster was *the* choice. I had never been to one, but knew from the TV commercials that it was really expensive and served you fish that you couldn't catch in a lake.

The yacht club was part of a gated community of new estate homes, single-family houses, condominiums, and townhouses under development on the shores of Lake Conroe. I had never seen anything so luxurious. The homes had sprawling manicured lawns and carefully sculpted evergreens. There was a golf course, swimming pool, multiple tennis courts, a clubhouse, and even a playground. "This is how the other half lives," Mom said as she steered us toward the yacht club. She pointed out a house owned by Farrah Fawcett and said, "Beautiful, isn't it?"

The nicest house I'd ever been in was my grandparents' two-bedroom ranch in Tulsa. How rich must these people be to afford homes like these? I couldn't contain my awe as I stared out my passenger-side window trying to imagine what these houses looked like on the inside. We drove for six miles before we reached the yacht club. I was captivated by its grandiosity. It was modern and sleek, using both brick and glass in an ornate, impressive architecture. Enormous columns marked a grand entryway. Two lofty glass doors were reached by a sweeping stone staircase. The clubhouse, a half-acre big, was directly on the waterfront and befitting of such a posh community. As I climbed the stairs, a young, pretty hostess greeted me. She was tastefully dressed in a slim taupe pencil skirt, peach silk blouse with ruffles and lace, and beige pumps. She flashed a beautiful smile and said, "Hello, ladies, how may I be of service to you this afternoon?"

I had never been treated so professionally by a stranger. I was just a teenager, but she acted as though I were a member of this elite world. I let her know that I was there for an interview about a job. She told me to have a seat and disappeared into the kitchen. My mother wanted me to handle this on my own and left to chat with her co-workers. I chose a nearby table and awkwardly sat down, crossing and uncrossing my legs and wondering if I should place my hands on my lap or on the table. I simply did not know how to act in a place like this.

The dining room was grand with a floor-to-ceiling, circular brick fireplace as its centerpiece. The entire back wall was made of glass windows that showcased breathtaking views of the twenty-one-thousand-acre man-made lake.

The manager was a stout, middle-aged man, and almost bald except for a ring of dark hair at the base of his scalp. I was nervous when he first sat down at the table, but he put me at ease by asking basic questions about school and my favorite subjects. He agreed to give me a shot. "If anyone asks, you say you're fifteen," he said.

Because I was underage, I was only permitted to bus tables. I was paid the minimum wage of $3.35 an hour and was given shifts that coincided with my mother's hostess schedule. When I arrived for my first day, I was paired with a waitress named Shelly, who taught me how to balance a tray of dirty plates with one hand. I soon discovered this was the hardest part of the job.

"When you see someone's water glass halfway empty, you take this pitcher and fill it up for them," Shelly directed. "But you need to hold the pitcher sideways so the customers get ice in their glass. If they haven't touched their plate in a while, go ask 'em if they're done.

"The key is to be discreet. The better we are, the bigger the tip. If you do a good job, I'll share my tips with you."

When the first table was seated, I filled all their glasses with water as Shelly had demonstrated. I had a few minor spills but soon mastered it. Then it was time for the salad course.

Shelly emerged from the kitchen carrying the plates on a tray she balanced on one shoulder. "Here, take this," she said, pulling what looked like a giant wooden chess piece from the pocket of her apron. "After I serve them their salads, ask them if they want any pepper."

I looked around for a pepper shaker on the table but didn't see one. Beads of sweat formed on my upper lip and the bow tie around my neck felt tight as I hurried back to the service station in search of pepper.

"Kambri, what're you doin'?" Shelly yelled after me.

Busted, I confessed, "I'm looking for the pepper."

Shelly laughed. "You're holding it. You ain't never seen a pepper mill before?" I shook my head as I stared down at the wooden object in my right hand.

"Dang, you gotta lot to learn."

I had been working there about two months when my classmate Lance came to brunch with his family. I was at the service station and quickly turned away so he wouldn't see me. I knew that some of my classmates lived in Walden, but it never occurred to me that they might be a part of this community. On the very rare occasion my parents took us out to eat, we went to Pizza Hut or Long John Silver's. A trip to Bonanza Steakhouse in Conroe for an all-you-can-eat buffet dinner was saved for special occasions. I didn't know any families that took their children to dine at fancy places like the Walden Yacht Club that had waiter service, live piano music, real china, and linen tablecloths. The realization left me momentarily thunderstruck, like in fourth grade when I discovered that teachers used the bathroom. It just seemed unnatural.

I turned around cautiously and watched Lance and his family take seats at a big round table by the fireplace. I had always thought he was just like me. He was one of the popular kids at Montgomery Junior High, and liked to make the girls laugh with goofy faces and jokes. I had had a crush on him all through seventh grade but always clammed up when he came around. But now our differences were glaringly apparent. He was a patron of a members-only yacht club, and I was his busboy.

I was mesmerized watching him interact with his family. They all looked so proper and well dressed. Lance was wearing pressed chinos and a buttoned-up pink oxford Polo Ralph Lauren shirt and was behaving like a proper young man, not the class clown I was used to seeing. His father was even wearing a tie to breakfast. Lance caught me staring and smiled. In a uniform of black slacks, a white collared shirt, black vest, and bow tie, I was out of context. He looked momentarily confused, as if he was trying to figure out how he knew me.

I tried to look cool as I carried a tray with a pitcher of water and some glasses on one shoulder. Lance's eyes seemed to be following me around the room. So I took the opportunity to show off: I spun a tray on one finger, balanced piles of dirty dishes, and joked and laughed with another busboy, a cute seventeen-year-old. When I reached to fill Lance's glass with water, he fumbled and dropped his fork.

"Let me get you another one."

I came back with a clean fork and the pepper mill and asked, "Pepper for your salad?"

"Um, yeah," he whispered. At school he was full of charm and confidence, but now he could barely articulate an answer.

Maybe he wasn't such hot stuff after all. Filled with newfound confidence and a pocketful of tips, I sauntered away with my tray of dishes like I owned the place. Suddenly the glassware shifted and slid from the tray and shattered on the floor. Two of the other busboys came to help me clean the embarrassing mess. I stole a glance at Lance, but he quickly looked away, pretending he hadn't just witnessed my catastrophe.

Lance never spoke to me again after that day at the yacht club. Instead, whenever he saw me coming down the school hallway, he darted his eyes to the floor and whispered to his friends. I was certain he disdained me on the grounds he was wealthy and I was not.

Growing up deaf, my parents were sensitive to the plight of the Deaf community and the way they were sometimes disregarded. For the first time, I felt like I really understood what that meant. These were the days before the Americans with Disabilities Act was passed, protecting the rights of the Deaf, who were often subjected to discrimination at work and passed over for jobs or promotions. Many times they were gawked at like they were zoo animals when they used ASL in public or made fun of because of the unusual sounds they made when trying to communicate verbally. The most insulting thing for me was when someone deaf was ignored entirely by a hearing person because that person was afraid or even disgusted by someone they viewed as different.

Mom and Dad taught David and me the Golden Rule: to do unto others as you would have others do unto you. No matter what challenges anyone faces, physically or otherwise, he deserves the same respect as anyone else. Many in our circle of deaf friends were born with physical disabilities, so I was accustomed to being around people with special needs and developed empathy for them. As a schoolgirl I took special interest in the class outcast, who took medicine to control his wild behavior: I made sure he received holiday cards and party invitations. I couldn't stand the idea that somebody would be excluded for something they couldn't change.

The bond in our Deaf community was so strong that a person's race, religious beliefs, or sexual orientation was irrelevant. They were deaf first. In the early 1970s, an openly gay lifestyle was almost unheard of, especially in the rural South. But in our community, Uncle Darold, a handsome man with a handlebar mustache who wore leather vests without shirts underneath, and tight jeans decorated with silver studs, was just Darold. Phrases like "whatever floats your boat" or "to each his own" reflected my mother's basic tenets.

I was raised in this community and Lance's reaction of contempt was foreign to me. Like some people who couldn't get past my family members' hearing impairments and chose to reject them from social circles, Lance wasn't able to look past my busboy uniform. To him I was the hired help. His inability to like or appreciate me for who I was and his willingness to judge me based on my social standing made him wholly unattractive to me.

Now that I was employed, Dad was going to teach me to drive. Or, technically, finish teaching me what Mom had started. She wouldn't let me drive the Toyota—it was the nicest vehicle we had ever owned and, job or not, I was only thirteen. But I wasn't too young to learn to drive. Lots of kids in Texas were driving farm equipment long before that age. By that time, I had driven a go-cart, a three-wheeler, and a dirt bike and often steered the Chevy down the busy Houston freeway on Dad's lap as he worked the pedals. I had even ridden a bull bareback.

Mom chose to take me out in the old VW Bug they bought soon after the Chevy died. Its red paint was faded and dull from years of sun exposure and the engine sounded like a go-cart. It had no radio or, more important in the Texas heat, no working air conditioner. But it was perfect for letting a young kid get behind the wheel and give driving a shot.

It wasn't exactly a smooth ride. The Bug had a stick shift,

which was hard to learn. And worse, David decided to tag along. His presence meant I was under extra scrutiny. Mom was on the passenger side and David sat in the middle of the backseat, right in the line of my rearview mirror, where he had room for his long legs.

I soon learned that driving a car was wholly different than driving anything else. The Bug required the operation of a clutch and gear while steering, and it was bigger and faster than anything else over which I'd had 100 percent control.

It was exhilarating. For about five minutes.

Once I got us moving, there wasn't much to do except steer since Boars Head and the adjacent Honea Egypt Road didn't have stop signs or intersections. Despite this, Mom was a horrible passenger. At every twist and turn of the country road, she pressed against the dashboard with open palms and stiff arms.

Bracing for a collision, she screamed in varying degrees of seriousness, "SLOW DOWN!" "YOU'RE GOING TOO FAST!" "KAMBRI, I SAID SLOW DOWN!" The windows were rolled down so the breeze distorted her hearing aids. She shouted even louder to hear herself.

I alternately screamed back. "I'M GOING TWENTY!" "WOULD YOU CALM DOWN?" "YOU'RE MAKING ME NERVOUS!"

For David, this was pure entertainment. I saw his wry smirk and squinty brown eyes staring back anytime I looked in the rearview mirror.

When we approached Webb's Grocery and the paved two-lane highway, Mom told me to stop and turn around. She showed me where reverse was on the gearshift, but I released the clutch and sent us lurching before the Bug stalled. Mom reminded me how to restart it, which took extra effort now that I was flustered. Again the Bug heaved forward and backward and stalled. After several failed attempts, Mom took over.

"You're gonna burn up the clutch!" she said.

My face was hot from embarrassment and annoyance; my rapid heartbeat pounded my eardrums as I stomped around the car and got in the passenger seat with a big slam of my door, folding my arms tightly across my chest. Mom deftly got us moving again, trying to show me what she was doing with her feet. "See, this is how you do it. It's not so hard." I was too angry to look over and she drove us home in silence.

Dad was surprised to see us return home so quickly. "What's wrong?"

I signed a big, fierce, "Mom!" and launched into an animated account of how scared she was. I screwed my face up, braced against an imaginary dashboard, and signed, "SLOW DOWN! TOO FAST!"

Dad smiled, which ticked me off even more. I tramped away as he tried to stifle his laughs. Mom had been his backseat driver since 1966. He knew exactly what I meant.

A few days later, I heard a knock on my bedroom door. "Come in!" I yelled, but nothing happened. That meant it was Dad knocking. A few seconds later, he slowly opened the door to make sure he wasn't invading my privacy.

"I'm going to Webb's, you want Jack Crackers?" he asked, switching the word order of Cracker Jacks, since ASL has rules differing from English grammar about word order and sentence structure.

"Yes, please." I signed and went back to finishing my puzzle in *Games* magazine.

He flashed my light and said, "Kipree!"

I looked up and he asked with an impish grin, "You want to drive?"

My eyes grew big and I signed, "YES!" as I leapt up, threw on my shoes, and ran out of the trailer with Dad following behind me. I walked toward the Bug and waited for Dad to catch up but he was standing by the Toyota.

He swatted the air with a sour expression and pointed at the Toyota. "Better," he signed.

"Really?" I couldn't believe that he would trust me with our brand-new truck. I wasn't sure it was a good idea. "Come on, let's go."

I slid in the driver's seat, so excited that I don't recall adjusting the seat or mirror. I just cranked it up and drove.

Perfectly.

Dad was navigator and signed directions to me as I went. He trusted me so much that at one point he told me I was going too slowly and at another had me turn around on a bridge. He even had me drive into a ditch so I could practice getting myself out. He was an unlikely teacher, since he had wrecked every car we had ever owned. The irony was lost on me. I was thirteen and driving the Toyota!

At Webb's, I loaded up on "Jack Crackers," he on cigarettes and beer, and I drove us home. At the trailer, I handed back his keys and he signed, "Don't tell Mama. She'll get mad. It's our secret."

At the same time I got the job at the Yacht Club, Mom got us a gig running a roadside fireworks stand that was owned by my parents' friend Donna. They'd met her at Johnny B. Dalton's, the nightclub in Conroe where they went dancing and drinking most weekends. My father said she managed Dalton's and another bar called Cooter's off of Coon Hollow Road.

"She's real classy," Dad signed. "She has really long painted fingernails, wears lots of gold and diamonds, and drives a C-A-D-I-L-L-A-C." My father always equated sophistication in a woman with how she kept her fingernails manicured. Perhaps it was because hands were his tools of communication, but in any case, he seemed to fetishize them.

"Donna said we could keep half of whatever money we make selling fireworks," Mom said. "It's all cash so no taxes have to be taken out."

Our first day at the stand, I met Donna. She was just as flashy as Dad had described. Every one of her fingers had big, shiny rings encrusted with diamonds, emeralds, or rubies. Some even had two. Her shirt was tight over her ample cleavage, enhanced with several gold chains and pendants. She was caked in heavy makeup that emphasized deep wrinkles, and her big, hair-sprayed do was dyed jet black, which I assumed was to cover up gray. I was sure she was at least fifteen years older than my parents.

My mother and Donna made pleasant chitchat as I unpacked boxes of fireworks and stocked shelves. Donna gave us quick instructions on safety—we were surrounded by a half ton of explosives—and how to keep track of inventory.

Donna had an expensive car and nice jewelry and ran so many businesses I assumed she must be loaded. But she was generous, too. After our first day of work, Donna gave me one of each kind of firework to take home. The cost of the fireworks was probably chump change to her but I was still floored by the gift. After Donna sped away in her sedan, Mom and I acted like we had just won the showcase on *The Price Is Right*.

Even though there was more than a week until Independence Day, we invited friends over, built a bonfire, and set off our treasure trove one at a time. Some made scary whirrs and whistles and others screamed high into the air before exploding into a shower of sparkles. We collectively oohed and aahed over the beautiful gold, silver, red, white, and blue displays for what seemed like hours before we ran out.

We sat around the campfire recounting our favorite fireworks when suddenly dozens of loud rapid pops like a machine gun detonated through the darkness. We ducked and cringed instinctually before realizing Dad had snuck a pack of Black Cats, ignited the whole brick, and tossed it in our trash can by the shed. The metal barrel amplified each blast, giving Dad's eardrums an extra hard beating. Dad pretended each explosion was a bullet near his feet and danced around like he was stepping on hot coals. Watching him carry on like he was eight years old sent me laughing until my cheeks ached.

Other than that first day at the stand, I never saw Donna again. But she had a cute son named Cash Price, with sandy blond hair that had golden highlights from driving his convertible Mercedes with the top down. Every day he stopped by the stand to check on things and collect our profits. When I saw him pull up, I would race to open his car door, and he always greeted me with a flash of his smile that made his eyes twinkle.

Even though he was twenty-one, he treated me like I was an

adult. He drove me to the general store for Dr Pepper and Cracker Jacks and we talked about our favorite films, TV shows, and music. One afternoon, I was particularly excited about a new movie, *Gremlins*.

"Oh my God, Cash! You just have to see *Gremlins*. It's this new movie and you just have to go see it. It was so good and Gizmo is sooooo cute."

Cash listened intently to my rants, asked questions, and promised he would go see it soon.

Finally, he cut me off. "I gotta run to the other stands. Wanna come with me?"

I looked back at Mom and asked, "Can I?"

"Sure, but don't be too long. We've got work to do."

"Cool! Hey, Cash, can we put the top down?"

"Yeah, why not?"

We peeled away and the sun beat down on my shoulders and the wind whipped my hair and eyes.

"If you sit on the trunk, it feels like you're water-skiing. Here, you can wear my sunglasses so you can keep your eyes open," he said, handing me his Ray-Bans, like the ones Tom Cruise wore in *Risky Business*. I climbed to the back and sat on the edge of the seat. We were going so fast it was hard to breathe without sucking in a blast of air. I lay back on the trunk as the clouds and trees flew by overhead. The motion of the car and the sun beating down made it feel like I was riding a speedboat.

"Aw, man, I love this song," Cash said, cranking up Phil Collins's "Easy Lover" as loud as the radio would go. We drove from stand to stand and picked up the day's take. Each time he hopped out he said, "I'll be right back. You want anything?" I played cool, wearing his sunglasses and acting uninterested, hoping that the people at the stands, whoever they were, would think I was Cash's girlfriend.

One afternoon as I waited for Cash to arrive, I heard a piercing squeal of brakes. I looked up just as a car hit Pamie with a dull thump. Mom gasped and we both screamed. Pamie flew through the air, hit a tree, and landed at its roots. She was alive but we knew it was not for long. Her back was broken and her body twisted. I raced back to the road to see the taillights of the car speeding away, the smell of burnt rubber filling the air.

"COWARD!"

"Kambri! Get away from the road. You don't want to get hit, too!" Mom cried as she hovered over my dog's body.

"They just hit her and drove off!"

I ran back to Pamie and crouched next to her and Mom. As we petted her softly I begged, "Don't die, Pamie. Please don't die. Please, please, please."

She took her last breath.

When Cash got to the fireworks stand, he knew something was wrong. I didn't run out to greet him, and I kept my head down and pulled my shirt up to cover my face so he wouldn't see me crying. Mom told him what had happened. He said we could go home to bury her; he'd watch the stand for us.

Dad picked a spot under the shade of a giant oak tree next to a wild holly bush and dug a hole for my beloved pet's cold and stiff body. I couldn't bear to watch her get covered in dirt, so I hid in my bedroom closet where no one could find me.

The next day Mom woke me up and said I had to help her at the stand.

"Dad calls off work all the time," I cried.

"July Fourth is just around the corner and we made a commitment to Donna."

I reluctantly complied. I figured Mom was sad, too, and if she was able to work, so could I. When Cash arrived to check on us, he was driving a shiny new red pickup truck and gave a great big wave. I was still self-conscious about crying the day before so I ran to hide in the bathroom in the portable offices next to the stand. Mom knocked on the door. "Kambri, Cash wants to see you," she said in a soft voice.

"Tell him I'm in the bathroom."

"Kambri, be nice. He has something he wants to give you."

I splashed cold water on my face and walked out to find Cash sitting in the driver's seat of his new truck fiddling with the radio dial. When he saw me, he turned down the volume and said, "I'm sorry about Pamie."

"Thanks." I chewed the inside of my lip and traced the dirt with the toe of my shoe, trying to fight back tears.

"Here, I got you this." He handed me a stuffed Gizmo doll from *Gremlins*. "It's from that movie you like so much. Shake it." My heart leapt for a split second.

I shook Gizmo and it squeaked noises that sounded like the fuzzy creature in the movie. I cracked a smile.

"So, do you like my truck?" He offered me a chance to sit in it.

I climbed into the driver's seat as he leaned on the window frame. I was playing with all the buttons when "Easy Lover" came on the radio. I turned it up for Cash.

I knew all the words by heart and I sang along with Cash, who was grooving in place. When he and I locked eyes, we broke into big, shy grins but kept singing in unison. I had a fleeting hope that maybe he thought of me as the girl in the song, but I knew better. He was twenty-one and rich with two fancy cars and I was eight years his junior, rode around in a junky VW Bug with a dented roof and missing back windshield, and wore a training bra.

Besides, who would want to be an "easy lover" anyway?

After July Fourth, the stand was closed. Donna said we raked in more money than any of the other stands she owned, and she wanted us to work for her again at Christmas.

I was thirteen, had two jobs, could drive a stick shift, and had my first crush. Flush with cash and determined to reinvent myself, I asked my mother to drive me to a shopping mall in Houston, where I spent my money on new clothes. I even got a haircut from a real stylist at a salon instead of from Mom in our kitchen. It was my first attempt at making a specific request for a new style since my Dorothy Hamill–turned–Moe Howard chop-job fiasco. This time I asked for a spiky Joan Jett mullet and got much better results.

Back at the trailer, I modeled my new outfits for Dad, who took pictures with our new Kodak disc camera.

"You look so pretty," he signed.

"See, Kambri, you just needed to have a little patience," Mom added. "You'll be a swan in no time."

Chapter Nine

HELLCAT UNDER A HOT TIN ROOF

While I was busy working at the yacht club and the fireworks stand during the summer of 1984, David was hanging out with his friend Allen and a girl my age named Maria, who had just moved to Boars Head. On one of my days off, I found them smoking weed in our living room.

Maria didn't say much, but laughed at anything they said. She was a solid foot shorter than me but thick and stout, like she'd been hauling hay. She had exotic features: almond-shaped brown eyes, dark skin, and coarse onyx hair that made her stand out.

Uninterested in whatever they were snickering about, I ignored them and retreated to my bedroom. This continued every day that week until one afternoon David called from his adjoining bedroom, "Hey, Kambri, come here."

I cracked open his door and was met with a cloud of pot smoke. "Come hang out with us," he said with a smirk.

"Here, you want a hit?" Allen squeaked, holding his breath through clenched teeth as he passed me the joint. "Shut the door; we got a hotbox going on."

I didn't know how to inhale, so David offered to help. I sat on his waterbed, a gift for his sixteenth birthday, and he lifted up the ashtray so the rippling tide wouldn't knock it over.

"I'll take a drag and then blow it in your face. You breathe in like normal and hold it for as long as you can." David scooted closer, took a hit, cupped his hands around his mouth like a funnel, and slowly exhaled.

I inhaled deeply but ended up coughing. It made my stomach clench and throat lurch like I might vomit, but I didn't want to seem childish. David took another hit before passing it on to Maria. Like a pro, she pinched the roach between her thumb and index finger and brought it to her lips. Sucking in, she kept her eyes squinted to keep out the smoke.

"So, what're y'all doing?" I asked with another cough.

"We're just hanging out. What're you doing?"

I'd been working on my library, taking inventory of my books, assessing their current retail value. Important stuff.

"Nothing," I mumbled. "Just reading magazines."

"Yeah? Did you see the thing about Ozzy in *Hit Parader*?"

David leapt up and said, "Oh, man, we gotta play them that tape! Go get it, Kambri." Before the words were fully out of his mouth I was bounding toward my room to grab the cassette.

At a recent Crews family reunion, I'd hunkered down in the back of our Toyota with my cousin Colleen. She was a year younger than me, and like many of the Crews, she lived a sheltered, Christian life. She was, quite frankly, a prude. I thought it my duty—nay, my honor—to educate her in the finer points of high culture, namely the genius known as David Lee Roth.

"Isn't he a fox?" I gushed, salivating over photos of Van Halen's lead singer in my favorite magazines. Colleen had never laid eyes on a creature as fine looking as Diamond Dave. That sultry gaze, those pouty lips, and the leather pants slung low on his impossibly lithe limbs, so low we could almost . . . Well, it was obvious from the look on Colleen's face that this was the greatest single moment of her life.

Two weeks later, the postman delivered the package with the sermon on tape, addressed specifically to me. Colleen's mother included a note warning me of the dangers of rock and roll.

Narrated enthusiastically by the minister Jim Peters, *What the Devil's Wrong with Rock Music* was a sixty-minute diatribe about the threats posed to our immortal souls. He cast a wide net; everyone from Ozzy Osbourne to the Rolling Stones was considered a harbinger of evil. Not even the Eagles, Mom's favorite, were exempt. (The Hotel California? Satan's house!) Every record in our collection apparently contained subliminal messages from the Dark Lord himself, which seemed an inefficient system of delivery. But Minister Peters was convincing. In fact, he was so persuasive that Aunt Cathy, who was born deaf and had never heard a single note of music in her life, believed all I had to do to hear the evil propaganda was to play an album in reverse.

"The drummer's beat," the reverend hissed, "is meant to lure you in so you're free to accept the message of Satan!" His sweat seemed to seep through the speakers. "Let me tell you the name of that song," he pressed. "That song's title is 'Runnin''"—he interrupted the title with a deep breath and a long pause—"'with the DEVIL!'"

We laughed so hard we could barely finish our joint.

Maria had arrived on horseback, and Star, her rust-colored Arabian pony, was tied to a tree in our yard. I was bowled over when Maria asked me to ride with her to Webb's, at least a four-mile trek from our trailer. She was only thirteen yet was permitted to ride a horse wherever and whenever she wanted. I thought that kind of freedom only came with a driver's license and a car. This was revolutionary.

After Maria climbed into the saddle, I stuck my foot in the stirrup and pulled myself up behind her on Star's rump. As we headed down Boars Head at a slow clip, Maria dug out a fresh pack of Marlboro 100's, smacked them on the fatty part of her palm, and unwrapped the cellophane. She extracted a cigarette, lit it, took a drag, and handed it over her shoulder to me.

I stared at it, not believing how brazen she was to smoke in public. "What if somebody catches us?" I asked, searching for cars of people I might know.

Maria remained cool, but to help me loosen up she suggested climbing down into the dry creek bed under the bridge Dad had built on Boars Head. Safely out of view, I took a drag from her cigarette, then blew the smoke out without inhaling.

"You're just wasting it," Maria said. "Here, watch me." She sucked the filter, showed me the smoke that was in her mouth, and breathed in. "Try again."

This time the smoke filled my lungs and I was overwhelmed by a tunnel of darkness. Just as quickly, the world was light again. I grabbed a tree to keep my balance.

"Head rush? Cool. You'll get used to it, though."

We finished the cigarette, climbed the embankment, re-mounted Star, and spent the next hour riding to Webb's. I had been a customer at Webb's since I was seven years old. I often bought Dad's cigarettes while he waited in the car, so Mr. Webb didn't question me when I asked for a pack of Marlboro 100's even though Dad smoked Kools. Star carried us the five miles back to Maria's trailer, where Maria introduced me to her parents, Sarah and Eugene Kingfisher. Although I was only thirteen, I towered over both of them. Maria's short stature was undoubtedly hereditary.

As her parents quizzed me about having deaf parents and the fine points of living on Boars Head, Maria lit up a cigarette. I was visibly thunderstruck that she would smoke in front of them. Her mother shrugged and said she knew Maria would smoke anyway. She preferred an honest smoker to a sneak. Maria blew out a puff of smoke with a smug grin.

Maria was an only child and her parents treated her more like a comrade than a thirteen-year-old daughter. They were home every night, eating dinner and watching TV. They shared long walks and talked together about current events without bickering.

Over the next few weeks I became a permanent fixture in the Kingfisher trailer. I cooked myself Kraft macaroni and cheese, bathed in their tub, and turned in for bed when I felt like it. As I snuggled up in my old sleeping bag on Maria's floor, I'd call out, "G'night, Maria. G'night, Sarah. G'night, Eugene. G'night, John Boy."

My days of being bored were over. Each morning, Maria and I packed saddlebags with water, snacks, and cigarettes, hopped on Star, and headed anywhere we wanted. I'd stop at the trailer to check in with my parents or get supplies, but Mom and Dad never questioned me. They were happy that I finally had a girl friend that lived close to us. I was a studious nerd who preferred working on my library to going out, so I never gave my parents reason to worry.

Some days Maria and I searched for arrowheads and other hidden treasures from Montgomery's days as an Indian trading post. Other times we swam in the creek, explored concealed trails, and gathered wild blackberries until the brambles were picked clean.

Star's back was being challenged by our daily five-mile, hourslong trek between Maria's trailer and Webb's. He was a pony barely thirteen hands high, perfect for accommodating Maria's pint size but not much more. We were literally breaking his back. Maria's father put an end to it and said I should get a horse of my own.

I approached Mom with the idea.

I was trustworthy, made straight A's, worked two jobs, and never had gotten anything special. David had terrible grades, never had a job, got suspended from both school and the bus, yet was still given a shotgun and a waterbed.

After what felt like months of closed-door discussions, my parents finally decided that I could get a horse of my own. That weekend, Mom and Dad got gussied up like they were going dancing at the honky tonk. The Kingfishers and I had been going to the auction held behind Webb's every Saturday evening, so I led my parents to the barn to see the livestock that was up for bidding. Strolling from stall to stall, Dad inspected each horse, checking out its teeth and eyes, making note of its age, sex, and size.

We settled on a bay-colored quarter horse with jet-black mane and tail that stood fifteen hands high. The sign on his stall said he was a gelding just shy of two years old and was available at a minimum bid of two hundred dollars. When my choice finally came trotting into the auctioneer's ring, my pulse quickened. I yanked on Dad's arm. "That's him!" I signed.

Dad put his hand out and moved it up and down like he was dribbling a basketball, signaling me to take it easy. "R-E-L-A-X," he spelled.

"This here two-year-old gelding has an opening bid of two hundred dollars. Do we have two hundred?"

Mom tapped Dad's leg and he raised his paddle. "We have two hundred dollars. Do we have two twenty-five?"

Mom was the interpreter for Dad when the bidding accelerated between Dad and other interested bidders. At last, we heard the final words: "Sold for four hundred fifty dollars to that good-looking couple in the back row."

I squealed and clapped before bestowing Mom and Dad with hugs and kisses.

"Looks like that young lady just got herself a horse," the auctioneer said.

"Does he have a name?" I asked the seller after the auction.

"Charlie Brown."

"That's cute," Mom said. "Let's keep it."

"He's a smart fella but he's still green; you need to break him. He's got spunk."

We didn't have a horse trailer, so we tied Charlie Brown's reins around the hitch of our truck and slowly drove down Honea Egypt Road toward Boars Head. True to the seller's words, Charlie Brown fought and kicked the whole way there.

Though he was technically my horse, Charlie Brown was a family project. Aunt Norma's husband, Jimmie, was a blacksmith and drove down from Oklahoma to show Dad how to trim hooves. Maria's mother gave Mom a lesson in administering vaccinations with a syringe. "Smack his ass three times then jab him. He won't know a thing," Sarah instructed.

Mom was a fast learner and had Charlie Brown vaccinated on her first attempt. Feeling the sting, Charlie Brown shot a glance at his rear, then returned to chewing.

"Hey, that was easy!" Mom grinned like a schoolgirl getting a first-prize ribbon.

Dad was possessive of the shed, where he kept his expensive tools. He hung them on a pegboard and meticulously painted bright yellow outlines around each one in order to know right away if a tool was missing. The door was secured with a heavy chain and padlock, which only my father could open. I was surprised when he gave me my own key and showed me the space he had cleared for my saddle and tack supplies.

Dad and David dug holes for fence posts, and then hooked up three rows of barbed wire around the entire perimeter of our property to secure it for Charlie Brown. At the end of the driveway, we put up an aluminum gate, just like the one at the Crews farm. While it was being installed, we kept Charlie Brown tied to a tree. We saddled him and stood in a circle around him as he thrashed around trying to throw it off. When the horse calmed down, David volunteered to be the first to ride him but he was bucked off twice in quick succession.

Dad signed, "Let me try." He only lasted a second longer than David. Charlie Brown's saddle was like an ejector seat.

"Kambri, he's your horse," Mom said. "You're gonna have to try."

I didn't weigh much more than the saddle and Charlie Brown was nearly tuckered out. I cooed in his ear, "It's okay, boy. I'm not gonna hurt you." I climbed on and Charlie Brown bucked and kicked, but not very hard. He settled down and Mom led us up and down the driveway the way Grandpa Crews used to lead Clipper and me. After a couple of weeks, Charlie Brown gave up fighting altogether and was broken.

Mom bought a cast-iron bell in the shape of a longhorn at a flea market and Dad hung it on a tree outside the shed. Anytime we wanted Charlie Brown, we clanged the bell and called his name. He'd trot to us to get alfalfa or oats, or have his saddle put on. Mom said he didn't know he was a horse; he thought he was one of us.

Once, I heard a racket outside of my bedroom door and was startled to see Charlie Brown standing in the hallway of our trailer. He had climbed onto the porch, opened the back door somehow, and walked inside. He was stuck at the first corner, too big to make the turn.

"Charlie Brown! What are you doing, boy?" I wrapped my arms around his neck and he nuzzled mine; his hot breath shot down the back of my shirt. "It's a wonder your hooves didn't crash through the floor!" I exclaimed.

He snorted and nibbled my ears as I backed him out the way he had come in. "You just want to be with me, don't ya?"

One afternoon when I went to check the mail, Charlie Brown was nowhere in sight. I stood on our front porch calling his name before he came into view, sprinting along the perimeter of our land.

"Charlie Brown?" I called, but uncharacteristically, he didn't pay me any mind. I clapped and called louder, but he still ignored me. He was tossing his head around as if he were trying to shake off flies. His strange behavior had me worried, so I called out to Mom, who was sitting in the living room with David. They both joined me on the front porch.

"What's wrong?" Mom asked.

"I don't know. Watch him." Just then Charlie Brown came into view. "See!"

He ran through the trees in big, graceful laps, almost in slow motion. He shook his head from side to side before circling out of sight in the woods and appearing on the other side.

"Yeah, that *is* strange," Mom said.

Suddenly David tore off running barefoot into the woods behind the shed and let out a bloodcurdling scream. He reemerged, cursing and snarling. "He ate my plants!" he screamed.

"Your what?"

"My pot! He ate it all!"

"My God, Charlie Brown is stoned!" Mom laughed.

David had been growing stalks of marijuana behind the shed and Charlie Brown chewed the top off each and every one. He was "loping under the influence," satisfied to run in circles.

He really did think he was one of us.

In junior high, fashion was a life-or-death matter. I once saw a clipping taped to the wall of the school nurse's office warning us of the dangers of wearing tight jeans. They caused circulation problems that led to blood clots that could be fatal. In spite of looming death, the fashion consensus was the snugger the jeans, the better. To make them shrink to the form of our bodies, we even wore them while soaking in tubs of ice-cold water.

The week before eighth grade began, Maria's mother drove us to the new Wal-Mart in Conroe. I spent my paychecks on school supplies, new clothes, and cartons of Marlboro 100's. The year before, I had tried to fit in with my best preppy look. Now I had a new Joan Jett spiky mullet and wore dangly earrings in my left ear and studs in my right. Maria showed me how to heat up eyeliner with a lighter to get an extra soft tip for applying layers of black rings around my eyes. We tucked the cuffs of our skintight jeans inside floppy suede ankle boots and tied different-colored bandanas around our wrists.

Oblivious to the rules of preppy-to-punk evolution, I signed up for the basketball team. My first practice was particularly hard work for a pack-a-day smoker like me, not factoring in the times I smoked pot. I found myself heaving and gasping for air, blaming Coach Carter for my shortness of breath. Afterward, my parents picked me up from a nearby shop on their way home from work, but that was three hours later. I missed Maria and her family and wondered about the fun they must be having while I sat there bored. I decided to quit sports altogether, using my parents as an excuse. My departure meant the team was left with five players, the bare minimum, but if this was irresponsible, I didn't care.

I stopped other activities, too. I didn't join volleyball or track, I quit the Youth Advisory Council, and I stopped volunteering as a teacher's aide.

My drastic makeover and withdrawal from the extracurricular activities that had made me so happy should have warned adults who cared about me that I was heading on a bad path. Other than Coach Carter being angry with me for leaving the basketball team in the lurch, nobody seemed to notice.

I still had my job at the yacht club, but that was in jeopardy, too. The excessive cost of gas and time outweighed the benefits.

"You'll have to quit," Mom said. "But not until after the company Christmas party." She and Dad weren't missing a free meal and an open bar. I was excited about the party, too, since I had never been to one outside our own trailer. Dad drove us to the yacht club, and the closer we got the more nervous I became. I was wearing my nicest jeans, but fretted about whom I would talk to.

When we arrived, my parents and I went straight to the buffet, piling on mountains of food before going back for seconds. I asked for extra slices of meat, enjoyed bananas set on fire, ordered ice cream with heaps of every topping, then went back for more.

The instant the DJ started the music, Mom and Dad hit the dance floor. When their glasses were empty, they took turns getting refills and juggled extra drinks so the trips to the bar were less frequent.

Miguel was the only other busboy there. We were the youngest two and gravitated to each other, partly in solidarity and partly in resigned surrender. We only talked during work, so our conversations existed in short bursts before we were called away to pepper a salad, refill water glasses, or clear a table. Now, without distractions, we quickly discovered we had common ground. We each had our own horse, smoked Marlboros, and thought Van Halen was the greatest band in all creation.

"Hey, you want me to try to get a bottle of liquor?"

"Sure." I shrugged. He seemed determined to get drunk, sneaking swigs of abandoned beers and chugging the remains of half-empty glasses.

He went to the bar to start smooth-talking the bartender, Joe. I was sure if Joe knew I was going to share the bottle, Miguel would come up empty-handed. Joe glanced over Miguel's shoulder and made eye contact with me.

Shit.

I darted my eyes away and saw Mom nursing a drink while Dad was burning a hole through the dance floor. His big smile showed both rows of straight white teeth and his arms swept back and forth in wide movements, forcing other dancers to spread back.

I glanced back to the bar, but Miguel was gone. I felt a tap on my shoulder, and I turned around to see Miguel grinning from ear to ear. He was holding up a paper bag in triumph, and pulled out a bottle of white wine just far enough for me to see the label.

We went outside and stood behind a big pine tree. Miguel pulled a corkscrew from his pocket. He didn't know how to use it, so I said I'd try.

Like a basic instinct, cracking open a bottle of hooch came naturally to me. I pried out the cork and took the first big swig out of the bottle before passing it back to Miguel.

"Hey, slow down," he laughed. "I got us some glasses." He held up two Waterford crystal flutes usually reserved for yacht club weddings.

Glass or not, I still chugged so my parents wouldn't notice I was missing from the Christmas party. Miguel discarded the empty bottle and we headed back inside.

As I entered the double doorway, I caught Dad's eye from the dance floor and he beckoned me to join him. Thinking we were busted, Miguel took off running back to the parking lot like a hound dog that had just spotted a rabbit.

"Come dance with me," Dad signed.

I stood frozen for a second. I had no idea how to dance.

Dad didn't know this would be my first time and wasn't letting up. "What's wrong? Come on!" He signed wildly and smiled more broadly than I'd ever seen. I weaved my way through tables toward him, gripping the backs of chairs to keep me stabilized. I reached the portable parquet dance floor just as the DJ cued "Footloose," one of my favorites.

I joined Dad and began dancing with wild abandon. The effects of the wine and my enthusiasm for Kenny Loggins gave me newfound confidence. I bit my lower lip, snapped my fingers, and flailed my arms and legs.

"You're a good dancer," Dad signed. He looked pleasantly surprised and backed up in order to take in the full picture.

I grew self-conscious for a moment, but I quickly swelled with pride. Dad, who danced better than John Travolta in *Saturday Night Fever,* was complimenting *me*!

I must be a natural.

Dad and I boogied all night, improvising dance moves, dips, and twirls until the lights came on and the music stopped. I was sweaty and happy, even though my buzz from the wine had worn off.

No wonder Mom liked going out with Dad all the time.

*D*ad unwraps a fresh stick of gum and asks, "Are you still working in Rockefeller Center?"

"No, I run my own business full-time now. I produce live theater and comedy shows and help plays and comedians get publicity." I tell him about the parties, the different people I work with, and how I once met Tina Louise from Gilligan's Island. He always did like red-heads.

"I'm proud of you." Dad claps his hands to applaud me, then adds, "Please remember, don't take any dopes and drink heavily."

"I know, Dad."

If anyone knows the consequences, he does. As if on cue, he starts to regale me with tales from the Free World, before he was Inmate #13A46B7, many of which involve weed, booze, gambling, or a combination of all three. "One night I was out partying, dancing, drinking, you know. I saw a beautiful woman watching me play pool. I wanted to show off so I acted like that movie Color of Money and twirled my pool cue. I didn't hear her walk up as I swung around. The stick hit her head and her hair went flying. She was bald! I screamed and grabbed the wig and put it back on her head and said, 'Sorry, sorry, sorry!' I never saw her again!"

Dad and I laugh so loud everyone around us stops and stares. I hear a nearby inmate tell his visitors, "He's deaf. He's a good guy. Real good guy."

I smile. For a brief moment I think this isn't so bad. In fact, this is the best I could have hoped for.

I am having fun. I am visiting my father in jail, and I am having fun. So is he. Through all the fighting and his roughened exterior, he has held on to his impish charm. The look of his smile and eyes and the way he tells me stories make it all worthwhile. Though I know he has an agenda, too.

In the past, Dad has sent me cards that say, "Send money. Love, Daddy." No "thank you." No "please." No gentilities. Now I'm overcome with satisfaction seeing him. Other prisoners admire him. His humor is intact. From now on when his notes are brief and beg for money, I will send him some. I will buy him new thermals that gleam white and new eyeglasses and smuggle in more gum and a burger. Whatever he wants.

Suddenly a loud, angry shout breaks the hum of conversation in the prison visiting room. Startled, I jerk around but can't tell who screamed. My adrenaline rushes and I am scared. The men surrounding me are dangerous. I am not in a comedy club. In this place, things could happen.

"YOU!" A tall white man in beige slacks and white shirt with a tie screams again. I recognize him from the picture on the wall. The warden.

Surely he isn't looking at us. We're just sitting here.

I raise my eyebrows and point to Dad. "Him?" Dad, finally aware that something is happening, turns his head in the direction of where I'm looking.

The warden knows Dad is deaf, but he still shouts at full volume and overemphasizes each word so Dad can read his lips. "YES, YOU!"

The warden curls his index finger back and forth with each word as he commands Dad, "You! Come! Here! NOW!"

Dad struts over, cool as a cucumber.

"WHAT'S IN YOUR MOUTH?" the warden demands. Dad opens wide and shows a mound of chewed gum resting on his tongue.

The warden gets a crazy-eyed look and nearly pops a vein as he screams, "WHERE DID YOU GET THAT?"

Without hesitation, Dad points straight to me.

My head spins. Not only are we busted, but Dad has ratted me out. I smile at the one-eyed murderer seated nearby, watching the events unfold. Hoping the warden will think I'm deaf, too, I act unfazed by what's happening.

The warden holds out a garbage pail and Dad spits out his wad of gum.

Just like school.

I squirm at seeing Dad being scolded like an unruly child. Dad is no longer the cool Danny Zuko of his youth, but a pathetic institutionalized version of himself. He saunters back to his seat as if nothing has happened.

"What's wrong?" I sign, with the most innocent face I can muster.

"Not supposed to have gum."

"Oh. Sorry," I say with my own overexaggerated mouth movements to make sure the warden sees.

I sip my Dr Pepper, but my hands are trembling and soda dribbles down my chin. Dad laughs. "You're shaking? You're scared? Pussy!"

Chapter Ten

REPO MAN

O ur unforgettable night dancing at the yacht club party was one of the few times I saw Dad that year. Things at home were deteriorating between Mom and Dad. He wasn't home as often, even when he wasn't working. During one particularly prolonged absence, I confronted Mom.

"Where's Daddy?" I asked her, dozens of times over the course of three or four days.

"I don't know, Kambri," Mom sighed.

"What if he had a wreck?"

"He didn't have a wreck."

Why doesn't she care? Why doesn't she call anyone?

I fretfully paced the driveway. I had tried preoccupying myself with my library or puzzles in *Games* magazine, but any creaking sound made by the trailer caused me to race outside to see if Dad was home. I preferred to stay outside and pick fleas and ticks off our dogs, a pair of boxers named Duke and Duchess and an American Eskimo pup named Cookie that Maria had given me. If the dogs were off on their own adventure, I drew patterns in the dirt with my big toe or shot baskets at our hoop, now about regulation height.

Dad's disappearances had become regular occurrences over my thirteenth year, ever since I started working at the Walden Yacht Club and fireworks stand.

What if he's dead? What will we do?

Mom gave me terse answers highlighted with exasperated sighs, which confused and frustrated me. I was no longer a kid. I was a teenager with responsibilities. I had even managed to work two jobs. I was accustomed to handling adult transactions, including interpreting conversations that were oftentimes inappropriate for my age. If my father's frequent absences were troubling her, I didn't know why she wouldn't talk to me about it. Since his deaf friends were all in Houston, I wondered if he was too tired to drive home so late and slept on one of their couches instead. It seemed odd that Mom never panicked like I did.

This day, when I finally saw my father's car advancing down our driveway, I ran to meet him.

"Where have you been? I was worried!" He smiled. To my annoyance, he looked amused that I had raced to greet him. "I'm sorry. I was with friends," he signed.

Dad grabbed the basketball and signed, "Let's play a game of 'Around the World.'" Discussion about his absence was abruptly dismissed.

Mom and I spent hours playing competitive rounds of backgammon or the card game Skip-Bo, but my father and I never challenged each other. Although I didn't play on a team anymore, I was thrilled to be asked to play basketball, especially by Dad. I took an early lead, scoring basket after basket. On his turn, Dad made a few. But after a miss, he elected to take a risk to start from the beginning. He missed again and my lead doubled.

The only other time my father had seen me play was the night I had flubbed the easy layup. Now I was down to my final shot for the win. As I took aim from the three-point line, Dad attempted to distract me by squealing and hollering. Despite his efforts, the ball went in.

"I won!" I signed, overjoyed.

"No, no, no!" Dad signed. "You didn't win yet. Rules say you're supposed to shoot two three-point shots in a row."

"No!" I scoffed, grinning from ear to ear. David and I didn't have such a rule. But Dad insisted and tossed me the ball. Again I sunk the basket. Dad continued to improvise and complicate the conditions of winning but I thrived in the challenge, making shot after shot on my first try. He and I laughed in amazement.

"Okay, to win the game, you must shoot from half court, backward with your eyes closed," my father signed.

I stepped up to the line Dad had drawn in the sand, took the ball, pinched my eyes closed, and tossed it. We stood frozen, watching it hurtle through the air and swish through the basket. Nothing but net.

I jumped up and down, screaming with victory as Dad finally conceded defeat.

As we went inside the trailer, I realized that Mom had never bothered to leave her bedroom to greet Dad. Undoubtedly she knew he had arrived. She would have felt the trailer vibrating when his car pulled into the driveway.

When Dad did stay home, he was nursing a hangover. Mom called his boss to give lame excuses on his behalf, cars not starting, nonexistent dental appointments, and family crises. His body betrayed the lies. Every pore reeked of liquor as he slept off his previous night's antics. The consequence of getting fired didn't bother him. Construction work was abundant and his skills unparalleled, so he figured other jobs were available. But the oil bonanza was slowing. Although the industry crash wouldn't hit until 1986, Houston's boom development had stalled. Dad's reputation for drinking on the job and insubordination were threatening his future opportunities.

To make matters worse, Mom lost her job when HeliFlight Systems went bankrupt, and she found work as an independent contractor for the Texas Rehabilitation Commission, where she helped deaf people and others in need find work. But her invoices were never paid on time, so her income was sporadic and unreliable.

My parents always pinched pennies but now Mom was floating checks to cover groceries. Excesses of the past Christmas, when we were lavished with videogames, telephones, and televisions, exhausted any line of credit. I think my parents knew they were close to filing for bankruptcy and had gone on a spending spree. However, Mom tried to protect us from their money troubles, but I knew. I was the one who fielded the calls from the bill collectors.

"Yes, may I speak to Mrs. Crews, please?"

"She's not home right now."

"What about Mr. Crews?"

"He's deaf."

The creditors resorted to threatening me when no adult was home. "Tell them if they don't pay the outstanding balance, the electricity will be shut off." The stress was devastating Mom. Her once lush red hair was thin and dull. She looked like she might go bald at any time.

One afternoon, I went home to find her vacuuming my bedroom, which she had stripped of all my belongings except my bed frame and my library collection.

Out of breath from her furious efforts to clean, she announced that our trailer was being repossessed.

"Today?" I asked.

"Yes, today," Mom puffed. "Now go through your books and pack up the ones you're keeping."

I began loading a couple of cartons with my most treasured selections. I packed my binder labeled "Library Records," my Choose Your Own Adventure books, and everything by Agatha Christie. The rest went into a pile to be thrown out. I tried to minimize how upset I was at destroying the collection of books I had cherished. I rationalized that I had already read those books anyway and I had outgrown running my own library. I was distraught but knew there was no use in pouting.

When I was done, I found myself in the kitchen running my finger along the markings on the wall indicating David's and my heights over the years. Mom stopped packing the last of her pots and pans, came to my side, and put her arm around my waist.

"Look how little you were. You still have about four more years to grow. Girls don't stop growing till they're about eighteen."

A lump formed in my throat. Didn't the bank know it was more than just a trailer?

"Why can't we keep it?"

"We weren't gonna live in the trailer forever anyway. Now we can finally build that dream home we've been talking about all this time."

We're not building any dream home. We're moving into the shed with Charlie Brown.

I retreated to my empty room. I was flushed with anger and my stomach was clenched. My pens and pencils were gone, moved somewhere with my desk, so I dug through my purse to find one. All I found was a mostly dry bottle of mascara. I scraped the inside of the tube with the wand and scrawled "FUCK Y" in big black letters on my wall.

"Kambri!" Mom shouted. "Stop that!"

I didn't know she was there. I spun around, as tears streaked down my face. "Why do you care? The bank's just gonna take our trailer anyway! I want 'em to know they suck!"

"The more they get for the trailer, the less we owe on our loan. Now come on and help me finish packing."

"FUCK Y" is all I wrote, but I figured the people at the bank would know what I meant.

Dad divided the shed in half lengthwise with plasterboard walls. One side was turned into a kitchen with a small living room, where Mom and Dad could sleep on one of our two ma-roon hide-a-bed sofas. The other side served as a bedroom for David and me. We separated out sections with a pilly blue blanket hung with clothespins from the tin roof. Mom bought a new breaker box and installed wiring, lights, plugs, and a 220-volt circuit to power the avocado-colored refrigerator we took from the trailer and a used electric stove we bought to match.

The shed had an overhang where Duke, Duchess, and Cookie stayed with Charlie Brown to keep warm or safe from the rain. Now, however, our family needed the square footage beneath the overhang. Dad transformed half of it into a bathroom by installing a sink, toilet, and tub that he hooked up to our existing septic system. The other half he turned into a closet for all four of us to share. Charlie Brown would have to make do without.

Since meeting Maria, I was smoking at least a pack of cigarettes a day. We'd drink two bottles of Boone's Farm wine every Saturday night in the stables of the horse auction, which attracted the attention of older boys looking for a good time. They were more than happy to oblige Maria's request for a hit off their joint, and I did what she did, oblivious to consequences. Mom may not have known about the booze and pot, but she had caught me smoking red-handed, and, worse, discovered an unfinished letter I was writing to a pen pal graphically confessing to my sexual exploits with a seventeen-year-old stoner who drove his mother's Buick with the seat pushed back so far his feet barely touched the pedals. I was an "Easy Lover" after all and lost my virginity in the backseat of his mom's car.

Hanging out with Maria was influencing my choices in the worst possible ways. My lack of participation at school, my drug and alcohol use, and my promiscuity coincided with our tightening friendship. As if those weren't serious enough, I had also gotten into trouble with the law on more than one occasion.

January 1985 was the first time I found myself hauled off to the sheriff's office. Maria and I had gotten into a fight. She'd been prank-calling me. I'd been returning the favor, but being the overachiever type, I went overboard. I called her more than one hundred times on Christmas Eve, using several phones in the offices behind the fireworks stand. Mom and I had been working there for the holidays, and the office manager was kind enough to let us use the office bathroom.

A trace put on Maria's parents' phone incriminated me. The police contacted the office manager, who in turn contacted Donna and Cash Price. The Kingfishers didn't press charges because, luckily, Maria confessed to having started the whole thing. Even though I didn't face legal repercussions, Mom and I still lost our jobs at the fireworks stand.

Maria and I patched things up afterward and, by summer, we were back to being best friends. One afternoon, Maria stopped by our modified shed accompanied by our new neighbor Curt and his younger brother Junior. The four of us went into the woods headed toward the creek. Regrettably, we were sidetracked by a more malicious adventure.

"Did you hear 'bout Haley's dad?" Junior asked as we trekked down the path.

"Yeah," I said. "My mom told me."

Haley's father, Phil, had succumbed to cancer after a long

battle. He had been diagnosed about the time we moved to Mont-gomery. The rest of the family had left town, abandoning the house they were building in mid-construction.

"Let's go check it out," Maria said.

We weren't certain if the place was deserted permanently, or if the Millers had gone on an extended vacation. Montgomery was filled with shells of long-forgotten dream homes. Living there wasn't easy. Newcomers usually arrived filled with optimism, like us, but got discouraged when they realized how far away from family, conveniences, and health services they really were. Many times people just abandoned their efforts. Money ran out, isola-tion set in after heavy rain closed the access road, plans changed, or, in Haley's case, someone died.

"My mom told me they're visiting family somewhere in Mas-sachusetts," I said. "They're probably moving there."

When we got to the site, the outside of the home was covered in black tar paper prepped for fresh siding. The blank canvas begged to be defaced and Curt wanted to be the first to mar it. He commanded us to find him something to write with.

Junior broke open the back door and found white bars of soap in the utility room.

Curt took a bar and wrote "FUCK YOU" in big block letters.

I liked Haley and her brothers. I had practically grown up with them, whereas Maria and the boys were new to Montgomery and had only known them a few months. I hated the thought of the Millers coming home to see their home covered in profanities, especially when they were in mourning. But I didn't have the courage to stop Curt, now joined by Junior, from continuing their graffiti. I ran to find Maria, who had slipped inside.

Wandering through the house, I was mesmerized at how big

and beautiful it was. It had two stories with at least four bedrooms and three bathrooms and brand-new appliances in the kitchen. This *was* a dream house. Jealousy, even anger, swept over me. Haley's family called this "home," and my family was living in a shed.

I saw Maria in the utility room and asked for a task. She handed me a box of Tide and a bottle of Clorox and said, "Here, dump these out." I poured out the entire contents of laundry detergent and bleach in the washer and dryer and smeared the bathroom walls with toothpaste before Curt called us to flee.

In a matter of days, the phone rang. A neighbor had seen us running through the woods and investigated. The police were called out, but because we were all juveniles, nothing of real consequence would happen to us. Curt was the oldest, and he was only fifteen. Punishing us wouldn't change the fact that the house was a mess and the Millers were due home any day.

Dad was disgusted with me. "Phil was a good man," he signed. "You should be ashamed."

Truthfully, I had never been more ashamed of myself, but I could find no adequate way to express it.

The neighborhood rallied together and held a kangaroo court. Since the boys were away for the rest of the summer, their mother appeared on their behalf. Maria and I, accompanied by our parents, gathered before the assembly in the living room of Mr. and Mrs. Blankenship's trailer. Mr. Blankenship—or Mr. B., as we kids called him—was serving as judge, jury, and executioner at the proceedings. A leathery-skinned, looming man, Mr. B., dressed in his denim overalls, belied his true grit. I once saw him twist the head off an eight-foot rattlesnake with nothing more than a pair of pliers.

I sat on the Blankenships' couch with my hands folded and squeezed between my thighs, my head hanging low.

"Now one of you girls wanna tell us what happened?" Mr. B. asked.

I had spent the days after the vandalism trying to ease my conscience by justifying my participation. Curt and Junior had inflicted the worst of the damage, and the Millers were planning to move away anyhow. Besides, the Millers seemed rich enough to pay for repairs. But with every adult face in the neighborhood staring at me, including my own infuriated and shamed parents, my excuses seemed ridiculous. I knew I had to accept responsibility. I explained the story from start to finish, quivering and sobbing throughout my narrative. Mom interpreted for Dad, who sat next to me on the couch.

"Who wrote them nasty things on the walls?" Mr. B. growled.

"Curt and Junior!" Snot bubbled out of my nose before streaming down my lips and chin.

"She's just blaming my boys 'cause they're not here to defend themselves," Curt and Junior's mother protested.

"No! That's not true! I didn't write that stuff, I swear," I blubbered. "I just messed up the bathroom. I promise. I'm so sorry."

The attention turned to Maria.

"Maria, what do you have to say?"

I looked at Maria. She hadn't shed a tear. She looked unfazed and even annoyed at being a defendant in the Blankenships' trailer in the first place. She shrugged and mumbled a halfhearted "sorry." I was in disbelief. She glanced over at me with a derisive smirk.

The neighbors agreed that if Maria and I cleaned up the damage we had caused before the Millers returned home, they would not impose further punishment.

"The Millers are hurtin' enough as it is. They don't need to come home and see that filth," Mr. B. assured the mock jury. He promised to deal with Curt and Junior separately, once they returned to Boars Head.

"You're lucky," Dad signed. He was still angry, but he was now able to look me in the face. "You could have gone to jail for that. You'd better clean it like new." His signs were exaggerated and emphatic, relaying his wrath.

Sarah drove Maria and me to the Millers' in their truck full of cleaning agents and painting materials. I averted my eyes from the walls and went straight to the bathroom. I spent the afternoon sweating and scrubbing over my shame before giving the room a fresh new coat of paint.

Satisfied, Maria exclaimed, "It looks better than before!"

"No kidding!" her mother agreed. "I shoulda had y'all come mess up our house."

The crime scene was returned to its pre-vandalism state, and I escaped the worst judgment of all, the shame of a confrontation with the Millers. Haley's family moved to Massachusetts before I ever saw them again. If they were aware of what had happened, I never knew. When memories of my repulsive behavior that day crept into my mind, I quickly pushed them away with reminders of good things I had done on their behalf, like sticking up for Haley's little brother when Chris King picked on him.

Frankly, I was disgusted with myself.

Real classy, Kambri.

My life had turned upside down and I didn't like who I was becoming. I was humiliated, but it was just as devastating to see that I had disgraced Mom and Dad. They may have given me too much freedom but had raised me better than this. Being called to the sheriff's station for prank calling had done little to straighten me out, but shaming my parents and me in front of our neighbors was horrific. I resolved to stay clear of Maria and start the ninth grade as a new and improved Kambri Crews. Other than her full refrigerator and air-conditioning, I couldn't think of a good reason to stay friends with her.

My ninth grade of school had barely begun when Mom delivered more bad news. "We need to sell Charlie Brown. He costs too much money, Kambri."

I hadn't been riding him much since Maria and I had stopped being friends. When I did, he was back to his unruly self, hating the saddle and not wanting to walk without another horse and rider to keep us company. We would barely leave our driveway when he would start bucking or walk under a low-lying branch in an attempt to scrape me off his back. If he succeeded in getting rid of me, he'd run back to the shed, leaving me to walk back on my own.

He carried expenses with oats, alfalfa, and vet bills. Selling him and his tack would help lower our debt. We were living in a shed. Charlie Brown had to go.

We sold my saddles and tack at the next auction. Carrie, a girl on our bus, convinced her father to buy Charlie Brown for a hundred dollars. He was a good horse and worth more than that, but we were not in a position to turn down an offer. Carrie's family had a lot of farm animals and they were familiar with Charlie Brown. I had taken him on overnight trail rides with Carrie and her family, so they had seen how he broke into full gallop on the corner of Boars Head, knowing he was almost home. He turned into our driveway so tightly I could reach down and touch the dirt if it weren't for the death grip I was giving the saddle horn.

Impressed by his ability to turn a corner so fast, they planned to retrain him and enter him in barrel races at the local rodeos.

My heart was broken when I said goodbye to Charlie Brown, but I knew he would be better off in Carrie's care.

Soon every trace of Charlie Brown was gone except for the iron longhorn bell we had used to summon him. "I kept it so you'll always have something to remember him by," Mom said with a consoling smile. Dad hung the bell in the kitchen by the door to the shed. Every now and then one of us would clang it. The piercing caterwaul inside the metal shack made my ears ring, but I didn't care. I liked remembering Charlie Brown.

Today, the bell sits on a shelf against a brick wall in the living room of my Queens apartment with layers of chipped paint where Dad tried covering up rusty spots. The chain is corroded but still attached. Every now and then I get the urge to take it out on my fire escape and give it a good clanging just to hear it ring.

A month after the new school year began, Mom left for Fort Worth. She had gotten a job at HeliDyne assembling wiring panels for helicopters and had been staying with friends while looking for a place for us to live. She'd been away for weeks, and I had barely laid eyes on my father. He still technically lived with us, but he was rarely home. I had no idea where he was but I no longer paced the driveway worrying about him. I had grown accustomed to his long absences the same way Mom had and, besides, I was off on my own adventures with David.

David was a junior and I was a freshman at Montgomery High School and we were now inseparable. He was going steady with my new best friend, a girl in my grade named Amber, who had recently moved to Montgomery to live with her father and step-mother in a three-bedroom A-frame home nestled in the woods. A curvy, green-eyed blonde with alabaster skin and a splash of freckles on the bridge of her nose, Amber was as talkative and adventurous as I was. We met in drama class, where we had an instant connection over our love of poetry, theater, and hard rock music. The three of us had lunch every day with Amber's stepsister Gina, who had lived in Montgomery for several years. Gina had dark brown hair and a slight frame with delicate features; she was much more reserved than Amber and I, who cracked jokes and prattled on so much that Gina could rarely interject a comment.

Moving into your barn because your trailer had been repossessed is what some might consider a low point. For me, it was a fresh start. When school began, I forsook team sports. My smoking habit and transportation difficulties were the same issues from the year before. Instead I joined the debate team, won the election for the position of class secretary, and made the honor roll with straight A's. That was about as opposite from Maria as I could get given the circumstances.

Dad gave my brother an old lemon-yellow Datsun to use. He drove Amber, Gina, and me everywhere and we called ourselves the Four Musketeers. Just like all of our previous cars, there was no radio in the Datsun, so David and I sang songs we used to sing with Mom on our way to the movie theater in Conroe plus new favorites like ZZ Top's "Cheap Sunglasses" and anything by AC/DC. Amber always took lead. She sang more beautifully than anyone we had ever heard.

With Mom in Fort Worth and my father missing in action, there was no food in the refrigerator and no air-conditioning in the shed. David crashed on couches at friends' homes or stayed at the shed while I spent most school nights sleeping over at Amber and Gina's house. If I needed anything from home, I used the school bus to get me there. I slept alone in the shed, and then rode the bus back to school the next morning with my duffel bag packed with necessities.

Sometimes David and I would hang out in the shed together. When I saw that David's friend Allen had a new ear piercing, I decided I wanted one, too.

We implemented the "do-it-yourself" technique, by pressing an ice cube to my earlobe for about a minute while David ran a carpet nail through the open flame of his Bic lighter to sterilize it.

David squeezed my lobe. "Can you feel that?"

I thought I could, but David was convinced it was numb enough. Allen stood on his tiptoes and craned his neck to get a better look.

"Hold this behind your ear," David instructed as he handed over a bar of Dad's Lava soap. He wiped the black soot off the nail with his shirt and lined it up just to the left of where my other earring hole was. I squirmed nervously watching him prepare his tools.

"Dammit, you gotta be still, Kambri. Okay, you ready?" David asked.

I took a deep breath and held it as David reared back with the hammer. I squeezed my eyes shut. I felt a sharp stabbing pain as David grabbed hold of the soap and wiggled the nail out.

"Gimme the earring."

Allen handed over a bowl that contained my stud floating in rubbing alcohol. David fiddled with it until he managed to secure it in the hole. He gave me a handheld mirror for me to admire his handiwork. My lobe was swollen and tomato red, but beautifully adorned with a shiny new gold ball earring.

I was impressed by how quickly the operation went and how little blood was shed. "The ice hurt the worst."

"I told ya," David said. "If you don't like it, just take out the earring and let it grow over."

A few days later, David and I found out AC/DC would be in Texas for their Fly on the Wall tour. We had to go. There was no need to ask permission, and in fact, there was no one to ask permission from. We pooled our money together and David drove us to AstroWorld, an amusement park with an amphitheater in Houston. We wasted time before the concert by riding roller coasters and getting high in the Sky Tram.

AC/DC played to a packed audience at AstroWorld's Southern Star Amphitheater. They were pure electricity. In awe, I stayed glued to my patch of grass, not missing a moment of their theatrics, from the gristly voice of Brian Johnson to the over-the-top stomping and guitar riffing of Angus Young. A giant replica of the Liberty Bell was lowered from the rafters during "Hells Bells." The bell was smashed with great fanfare while a deep *dong* sound seemed to vibrate forever. They even had real cannons that fired blanks during the finale, "For Those About to Rock."

I bought a Fly on the Wall concert T-shirt and changed into it in the bathroom. On the ride home our ears were ringing, so we shouted to hear each other speak.

We were having the time of our lives.

Soon Mom called from Fort Worth with news. She had saved up enough money for us to relocate.

"What about school?" I asked.

"My friends gave me the names of a couple of schools around

here. Your daddy is gonna drive you up here so we can check 'em out."

David and I were closer than ever. He and my best friend, Amber, were in love. I was doing well in school both academically and socially and was living with little parental supervision. Even though I was having fun, the prospect of getting out of the shed and attending a city school with better opportunities was invigorating. I didn't know it then, but wanderlust is a trait that I share with Dad. This was my second drastic move, the first being my move to Boars Head. The thrill of exploring a new town, meeting different people, and beginning fresh adventures had me itching to leave Montgomery behind.

I returned to the shed after school and found my father at home waiting for me. He had already closed and padlocked the "windows" and door of the shed, turned off the breakers, and cleaned out what little was in the refrigerator.

I climbed into the Toyota next to Dad and we set off north to Fort Worth to meet my mother. The next day was spent touring schools. During the admissions interviews, Mom spoke as though I was a commodity greater than gold. "She makes straight A's, she's in all the honors classes, and has never been written up or had any disciplinary issues at school." She wasn't lying; she was omitting. My troubles with Maria and the law were secrets left on Boars Head. "She's really interested in drama," Mom continued, as though we were theatergoers. Never mind I'd only seen a production of *The Nutcracker* during a field trip in elementary school. "Do y'all have a drama program?"

The guidance counselors seemed impressed with Mom's sales pitch and promoted their own curriculum. "Oh, yes, we have a very large fine arts program and a few shows are produced each year. And we have one thousand some–odd students in our sophomore class."

One thousand students? In a single grade? That was almost three times the entire population of Montgomery.

We selected a school and Dad and I drove back to Boars Head. I hadn't seen our dogs for what seemed like weeks. "Duke! Duchess! Cookie!" I called a few times each day but they never came running.

Was anybody feeding them now that Mom was gone?

"Have you seen the dogs?" I asked David when he stopped by one afternoon.

"Nuh uh."

"Where could they be?" They had never stayed gone this long.

The next time I saw Dad I asked the same question, "Where're the dogs?"

Dad shrugged and signed, "I don't know."

Something wasn't right. I recalled my mother's words from years before after our old dog, Taffy, had been abandoned when her owners had moved to the city and we adopted her. I asked how a family could just desert a pet. "She's a country dog, Kambri," Mom had said. "She can't go live in the city with them."

More than once, Mom had taken a litter of puppies produced by Taffy or Duchess to the pound. I panicked that they'd be euthanized if they weren't adopted. Dad told me they were the lucky ones. When he was a kid, he tied up litters of kittens in a potato sack and tossed them into a pond to drown. I knew Dad had tried killing Duke before. The red boxer pup was a financial drain. Duke was accident-prone with his snakebites, broken legs, and a collection of other wounds and had cost us hundreds of dollars in vet bills. Dad wanted to eliminate him.

"I took Duke out into the woods and shot at him, but the gun jammed," my father said matter-of-factly. "Duke heard the click on the gun. His ears perked up, his brow furrowed, and he cocked his head from side to side. He was just too cute for me to shoot."

That was then.

Now I pressed Dad for an answer about the animals. "When's the last time you saw them?" I signed.

He shrugged again and signed, "No idea."

I glared at him but he took no notice.

"Duke! Duchess! Cookie!" I called again and again, but they never came home.

I stayed with Amber and Gina's family while I finished the first semester of ninth grade. After my last day of school before Christmas break, I rode Bus #9 home to the shed for the final time. My father was almost done packing the Toyota with the last of our belongings. We were limited in what we could take with us. Cartons of childhood mementos and furniture were stacked atop an old green crushed-velvet couch we kept in the barn for destruction by fire. With a quick flick of a match, Dad set the pile ablaze. The fire swelled, consuming our discarded possessions. A cardboard box wrinkling in the flames spilled smoldering books from my now-defunct library. Dad raked my tattered, burning Judy Blume paperbacks and collector's edition copy of *20,000 Leagues Under the Sea* back into the flames, then tossed a heap of old clothes on the pile.

The black and white fake fur coat I received for my tenth Christmas rested on top. I thought about how I had worn that coat the first and only time it ever snowed on Boars Head. Mom woke us up early so we could play in it before it melted. It was a thin dusting of dry, light flurries that barely covered the dirt but still delighted my brother and me. That was when we scraped together miniature snowballs and set aside a few to keep in the freezer. Those were gone, too, when the electricity was shut off and the fridge defrosted.

When Dad burned our belongings, I twirled myself on the tire swing to tighten up the rope.

This is the very last time I will ever swing on this swing.

I wanted to feel sadder at leaving behind Boars Head and all our memories there, but I couldn't muster a tear. Fort Worth held promise. There I would be a stranger. I could truly reinvent myself. I was banking on this move to give us a clean slate. Each twist of the tire swing gave me a 360-degree view of the home we were fleeing. The shed's windows were boarded up and the front door was shackled with a heavy padlock and chain. A warning sign that hung on the outside read, KEEP OUT VIOLATORS WILL BE PROSECUTED. Our vegetable garden, tilled by Dad and planted and tended by Mom and me, was shriveled and brown. The VW Bug was rusting by the spot where the old outhouse had collapsed. Weeds sprouted on the rectangular patch of land where the trailer once stood before the bank took it.

We had had our chance, but nature was reclaiming what was rightfully hers.

"Kipree!" Dad shouted from the barn, snapping me out of my reminiscence. I lifted my feet and the tire unwound, sending me into a wild spin. I looked over my shoulder and Dad signed. "Come. Let's go."

As we drove away, the ashes of our burned belongings still smoldered.

GROVE STREET

1986–1987

Chapter Eleven

THE MIRACLE WORKER

M om rented a small house in North Richland Hills, a suburb northeast of Fort Worth in the school district we had
chosen. Our three-bedroom ranch sat at the corner of Grove
Street and Bedford Euless Road on a block of identical houses, all
with simple but well-maintained landscaping. The majority of

our neighbors were retirees who had owned their homes for decades, but a few were renters like us. Within walking distance from our house were chain restaurants, bars, motor inns, and a teenager's paradise: the North East Mall.

What I liked about our new digs was that it blended in with the others on the block. It wasn't an eyesore and, for once, I didn't feel ashamed of it. Mom had rented a three-bedroom because David was still in high school, and he would be living with us. But he was finishing his junior year in Montgomery, so for the first time I was given the bigger bedroom, which had a cool double door and a window that looked out onto the busy roadway.

On one of my first afternoons in North Richland Hills, I was peeking out through the living room curtains. I noticed a girl who looked to be about my age. I raced to the front door and said, "Hi!"

"Hi back atcha," she said.

I stepped barefoot onto the hot blacktop and howled.

"Put some shoes on, girl!"

I had spent my life barefoot on Boars Head. Even after Maria nearly stepped on a rattlesnake, I wasn't convinced of the practicality of shoes. My feet were so tough that after stepping on a nail playing hide-and-seek with the King boys, I just yanked it out and kept on running. I didn't even bleed. Here in Fort Worth, however, all the streets were paved. After baking in the Texas sun, the asphalt was scorching hot.

Michele was a thin girl with flawless, deeply tanned skin and a short bob of tight, kinky curls. Two rows of thick metal braces made her mouth too small to fit her bucked teeth. Despite her awkward looks, she was full of confidence.

Michele didn't want to know the why or how of I came to live on Grove Street. She was my friend without being concerned about my history. She was also boy crazy and wanted to educate me on the eligible bachelors in our neighborhood, which was fine by me. There were plenty and she knew each and every one.

The first day at my new school was approaching and there was no way I was blowing my first impression by wearing the wrong outfit. New clothes were essential, which meant I needed money and a job. I walked up and down Bedford Euless Road and Grapevine Highway looking for work. My fifteenth birthday was a few months away, but I wrote sixteen as my age on each application and Mom's name as my yacht club supervisor. She had worked with me there and at the fireworks stand, so she really was my best reference. I was turned away everywhere, except Showbiz Pizza Place, a restaurant chain also known as Chuck E. Cheese featuring video games and an animatronics band.

I still had my uniform from the Walden Yacht Club, so I was ready to start work the day after I was hired. My white shirts had yellow stains in the pits and my pants were too short, but I let the hems out for an extra inch. Showbiz issued me a polyester red and black apron and a black plastic top hat. Nobody even called Mom.

My first day of work, I was introduced to the other employees, mostly juniors and seniors in high school. The boys had acne and the girls wore hair-sprayed bangs and plenty of makeup. I sounded like Tom Sawyer recounting my adventures in Montgomery, from the run-ins with snakes to swimming in the creek to riding Charlie Brown. I didn't mention that I had just moved out of a shed.

At Showbiz Pizza, I was in charge of children's birthday parties, presetting the tables with party hats and balloons. I served pizzas and soda to the kids and Bartles & Jaymes wine coolers and pitchers of beer to the parents. When the animatronics band, the Rock-afire Explosion, started playing "Birthday" by the Beatles, it was my cue to bring out an ice cream cake covered in lit candles. After everyone had finished, I cleaned off the tables and set another round of decorations for the next party.

Every two hours, Chuck E. Cheese, the human-sized mouse who was the restaurant's mascot, would make an appearance. One of us would have to dress up in the gray, furry costume for the short performance. The girls didn't like wearing the smelly, hot, heavy outfit, with a headpiece that was certain to mess up their hair. But I loved being the center of attention and took the job seriously, making sure each time I stepped out on the floor I was performing. "After all, the *E* in Chuck E. Cheese stands for 'entertainment'!"

The job was harder than the one at the yacht club, but I didn't have to share my tips. I pocketed anything from five to twenty dollars per table. After a particularly raucous party, the birthday kid's father took me aside and slipped money in my hand, saying, "You did a mighty fine job. Thank you, young lady."

He walked away and I unfolded the cash and saw I was holding a one-hundred-dollar bill. I had never seen one before and was sure it wasn't meant for me. I chased after him, "Sir! Sir, I think you made a mistake."

"No, honey, you keep that for yourself. Get yourself sumpthin' nice," he said with a wink. My eyes grew wide and I gushed, "Thank you! Thank you so much!"

I walked across the highway and headed straight to North East

Mall, still wearing my pit-stained shirt and too-short pants and clutching my plastic top hat with my polyester apron stuffed inside it. I soon discovered that stores like Express and Contempo Casuals were a lot more expensive than Weiner's and Wal-Mart. I shopped for new school clothes and bought my first pair of brand-name jeans, Gloria Vanderbilt's. The Gloria Vanderbilt label wasn't that popular anymore and the only ones on the rack I could afford were dressy, baby blue, and pleated in the front, not the dark blue denim with gold thread that I wanted. But there was no hiding the embroidered swan on the right pocket where everyone could see it. Wearing clothes with an authentic, recognizable logo instead of the usual discount duds branded me a freshman fashion icon.

Dad wasn't working, so he was in charge of enrolling me in my new school. After our tour of campuses, we had chosen Birdville Independent School District, home of the Richland Rebels. The Confederate flag waved proudly from the flagpole, was stuck on every bumper in the parking lot, and was pinned on the jackets of all the kids. I was disappointed to learn that "high school" didn't begin until the tenth grade. I was insulted. I had almost completed my freshman year of high school in Montgomery and had served as class secretary. I was bigger than junior high, but I couldn't change the rules.

As the first day of school drew near, I realized that one thousand students was a large class. I decided that Smithfield Junior High, one of the district's middle schools, might be more manageable. For the first time, I was going to a school where David and his bad grades and troublemaking weren't going to precede me. This was my first real chance to debut the new and improved Kambri Crews.

Dad strutted through the hallways of my new school like it was named after him. We entered the principal's office and approached a woman with a desk plate that read "Ms. Butler."

"Hi, my name is Kambri Crews and I'm supposed to start school here," I said, instinctively taking charge.

She looked at my father, who smiled. "Yes, we've been expecting you." She handed me a clipboard with a stack of papers and instructed my father, "I just need you need to fill out these papers."

I interpreted her directions and judging by her stunned expression, Ms. Butler had never seen a deaf person. She stared with her mouth agape, gawking at Dad like he was a sideshow freak. I wanted to scold her for her rude reaction. Instead I snipped, "He's deaf."

"I see that," she nodded, then got back to work.

Dad filled out the emergency contact information and handed me the document pointing to a blank signature line. "Sign your mama's name." The sentence above read that this signature would be kept on file and used as a comparison for correspondence with parents, such as report cards and excuses for absences.

"I can't sign this," I signed back. "You need to sign."

"I know what it's for." Dad raised his brows quickly up and down with a mischievous smile. "You sign for your mama. That way you can write your own letters." I shot a quick look at Ms. Butler. She was none the wiser, answering phones and taking messages.

My eyes grew wide. I was a fast thinker, and immediately calculated that this would give me full authority to cut school without my parents ever knowing. I searched Dad's face trying to figure out his motive for letting me "authorize" my own signature. Maybe he didn't fully understand what it meant.

Seeing my astonished expression, Dad put his index finger to his lips. "Shhhh."

He had such disdain for authority that he didn't even want it for me. At school, I strictly played by the rules, so Dad had to mentor me in how to be a delinquent. I wrote "Christy Crews" in cursive letters, and marveled at my skillful forgery.

Dad glanced at my writing and signed, "Not bad. Looks the same." All of those years playing bank teller with Mom's old checks had paid off. He gave me a conspiratorial wink and I handed the clipboard back to Ms. Butler.

"All right, young lady, let's take you to your homeroom."

Dad waved goodbye and added, "Good luck."

Ms. Butler gave me a quick tour of the school, assigned me a locker, and escorted me to my first class. Students whispered and pointed as I walked past. For my debut at school, I had chosen to wear my new Gloria Vanderbilt jeans and a long-sleeved light pink tunic top with black polka dots cinched at the waist with a wide, black belt. As Ms. Butler introduced me to the class, I grew self-conscious and worried that my outfit might be too flashy. Rather than show my insecurities, I held my head high with my shoulders back, the way Mom always stood. When lunch break came, I was petrified that I might have to sit by myself and considered skipping the cafeteria altogether.

I heard a familiar voice call my name. "Hey, Kambri!" I turned to see Michele walking toward me, flanked by two girls. "She's the girl I was tellin' you about." She introduced me to her friends and showed me how the lunch line worked. "Go get your tray and then come sit with us." I breathed a heavy sigh of relief and relaxed for the first time since I had entered the building.

Across the cafeteria, I noticed a few cute boys huddled together staring at me. One of them smiled and coolly cocked his chin.

"That's Terry," Michele told me as I climbed over the bench. "He told me he thinks you're cute."

Had I heard her right? Terry thought, I, Kambri Crews was *cute*? Nobody every thought this about me except my relatives. Everyone in Montgomery, who had known me since I was seven years old, knew I wasn't cute. I was Kambri, the girl who stood too close to a mud flap, could cut glass with her shoulder blades, and threw a football like Roger Staubach. Now in Fort Worth, I was worthy of the attention of boys my age. Gloria Vanderbilt was already working her magic.

My chest swelled and I looked back at Terry with a devilish grin. Smiling, he slid on a pair of black Ray-Bans.

"All the boys keep askin' me who you are, and, boy, Casey doesn't like you at all."

My face flushed. "Who?"

"Casey. She's one of the cheerleaders. She's a snob."

"Why doesn't she like me? I don't even know who she is."

" 'Cause." Michele grinned with wicked glee. "She likes Terry, but Terry likes you."

By the end of my first week, I realized my education in Montgomery had been better than I thought. I was more than six weeks ahead of the curriculum in every single class. I breezed through homework and aced quizzes with a minimum of attention. This was a blessing because it allowed me to focus on navigating the social scene of junior high.

Unlike Montgomery, where all the kids were integrated, Smithfield was divided into cliques. There were the Jocks, or athletes and cheerleaders like Casey; the Freaks, the kids who wore concert tees, smoked, and sported long hair; and the Ropers, country-and-western lovers named for the type of cowboy boot they paired with Wranglers. Since I wasn't used to such a rigid caste system, I drifted from group to group, able to get along with everyone, with the exception of Casey, who always snickered to her posse as I walked by.

One afternoon in geometry class, my teacher returned our graded quizzes and said, "My teacher's aide marked these so if y'all see a mistake, let me know."

I bristled. I knew Casey was his aide and I didn't like the idea of her grading my work. Fishing through the pile, I found my test and saw the grade of 100 written in the right-hand corner. My name had been crossed out and replaced with "BAMBI" in big red marker. I was mortified and quickly stuffed the paper into my binder. Casey had done this to belittle me. I was bewildered by her contempt. We had never exchanged a single word.

My confusion faded and turned into enormous satisfaction when I deduced the reason for her scorn. She was jealous. Casey didn't know about our repossessed trailer or my trouble with the law. She saw the nice clothes I was wearing, and knew I made perfect grades and that all the other kids liked me. Her vindictive "BAMBI" scrawled on the top of my test was evidence that my makeover had been a success.

~

I was in a good mood returning home from school one Friday afternoon, but when I opened the front door a strange sensation swept over me. "David?" I called, tiptoeing through the house. I passed through the kitchen and noticed glass broken out of a window pane in the back door. I bolted to my room and grabbed my piggy bank from its perch above my bed, tore off the rubber stopper on its bottom, and discovered what I already knew in my gut: It was empty. I had just cashed a Showbiz Pizza paycheck and every penny of it was gone.

I was gonna buy Ozzy tickets with that money!

"Damn it!" I screamed. I called the police to report the break-in. Mom and David came home to see a police car in the driveway and officers wandering through the house asking questions.

"What's goin' on?"

"Somebody broke into the house! You better go check your stuff to see if they took anything."

The officer filling out the report asked, "All right, what's missing?"

David emerged from his room and said, "They took some of my cassette tapes!"

Cassettes? But not the TV or the microwave?

In that instant, I knew who did it. The house was neat and tidy, and, other than my cash, nothing of value was taken. My piggy bank wasn't even broken. It had been carefully replaced in its original position behind a few dusty dolls. No robber would have cared about some silly ceramic pig, but David knew I had made that bank by hand at a pottery store Mom had taken me to near Webb's. I had used special paints, then had it glazed and fired in a kiln. It had taken me weeks to make that pig and was

one of the few things I salvaged from the shed before Dad set fire
to the stuff we didn't haul to Fort Worth. It was special, and David
knew it. I glowered at him, hoping he would realize that I knew
he did it and he should feel guilty.

But I didn't want David arrested. Besides, I couldn't prove anything. Like our dogs Duke, Duchess, and Cookie, who remained
forever at Boars Head, David was too wild to make the transition
from country to city. In Fort Worth, he found trouble, or trouble
found him. Either way, he didn't have a job, didn't have money,
and apparently had helped himself to mine.

David only attended Richland High a few weeks before he decided it wasn't for him. He was eighteen years old, practically
living with his new, older girlfriend and didn't have to abide by
any rules. The addition of the pool table turned our house on
Grove Street into his regular hangout spot.

We bought the table for a hundred dollars at our neighbor's
garage sale. Our neighbor had been diagnosed with cancer and
was selling off nonessentials to raise money for her medical
bills. We carried the table across the driveway and put it in the
garage. Dad was already an expert billiards player, entering tournaments and sniffing out bars where he could run a hustle. With
our own table, he could spend hours honing his skills. David and
his slew of new friends, who all had long hair and wore concert
tees and ripped jeans, loved the new pastime. They played game
after game of pool, getting high and chain-smoking while Metallica's *Kill 'Em All* blared in the background.

One Sunday afternoon, I begged Dad for a chance to play. "David's always hogging it," I complained. "I want to be able to play
against his friends."

Dad agreed and spent the next few hours teaching me the

tricks of his trade. The secret, he told me, was simple: Apply the laws of physics and geometry. I was a whiz at math and took advanced level classes all through junior high. In ninth grade at Montgomery High, I was in the same geometry class as David, who was in eleventh. I even helped him cheat by signing answers in ASL, before we got busted and were made to sit apart.

Dad started with the basics of trajectory and impact, and how the angle at which the cue ball hits the rail is equal to the angle at which it will leave. With my solid conceptual mathematical skills and my father's dedicated coaching, I quickly moved to combination shots using more than one ball to sink another and applying English, a billiards technique that puts a spin on a ball. Dad even shared his strategy when it came to hustling at a new pool hall. "Don't let them know you can play. Bet just a little to start with and lose a few games. They'll think they can beat you. That's when you raise your bet and clean them out."

Using his tips and tricks, I spent hours on my own practicing so that when David's friends came over I could play. I pretended not to pay attention to the game and flirted and laughed like a ditzy blonde, flipping my hair and giggling at everything. I missed easy shots and lost my first game. As his buddies got stoned and drank Busch beers, I raised the stakes from a measly two-dollar wager to five dollars a game, and ran the table. Dad had taught me well.

I was also working as often as possible at Showbiz, taking on extra shifts before school to prep the salad bar. I was an enthusiastic and industrious employee, much to everyone else's annoyance since I made them look like slackers. All my co-workers made me feel like one of the guys, just like on Boars Head. One day as I chopped mushrooms, Kerry, another employee, entered the kitchen practically glowing.

"What's up with you?" I asked. "You look like you're in love."

"I got a new car!"

The boys in the kitchen nearly knocked one another down racing out the back door to scope out Kerry's new wheels.

"Oh man that's rad, dude!"

"It's an IROC-Z," he offered even though the name was spelled out in a decal at the bottom of each door.

It was shiny black and the coolest car owned by anyone I had ever known, including Cash Price. Even the font of the lettering was sleek. The other guys fawned over it, pushing buttons, opening and shutting every contraption before the manager leaned out the door and yelled at us to get back to work. The IROC-Z was the most important topic of conversation at Showbiz until the day Dwayne smacked a kid in the head with the plastic tail of the Chuck E. Cheese costume and got fired.

That week, Kerry took turns giving everyone rides. On my turn, he drove me the two blocks to our home on Grove Street. Mom asked, "Who was that?" when she saw him pulling away.

"Kerry. His parents gave him that car for graduation. Nice, huh?"

Mom, not wanting to be outdone by a high school kid said, "Well, we're getting a new car, too."

Even though Dad had found work as a cabinetmaker, his salary and Mom's paycheck were not enough to keep the Toyota from draining our bank account.

"We just can't afford it anymore so we're trading it in for a new Thunderbird."

I didn't know what a Thunderbird was; I just know Mom mimicked the sound of thunder as she rumbled her voice for the word "Thunderbird" like it was ten times cooler than any old IROC-Z. I pictured a hot rod with a shiny new coat of paint and chrome grille.

Now that I knew that teenage boys were impressed by cars, I went to work ready to share my good news. "We're getting a new car, too."

"Oh yeah? What kind?"

"A Thunderbird." I vibrated the word the way Mom did.

Kerry seemed interested so I kept on bragging. "Yeah, my mom said it's silver with a maroon interior. They're picking it up from the lot on Friday."

"Drive it over when you get it so we can check it out."

When I came home and found a strange gray car sitting in the driveway, I was confused. This wasn't the car mom described.

"Whose car is in the driveway?" I asked.

"That's the Thunderbird," Mom said. "Pretty nice, isn't it?"

Mom had made the Thunderbird sound so enviable. As it turned out, it was the unsexiest vehicle around. It was a boxy, ugly hunk of metal, something a grandparent might drive. To top it off, ours was used and the silver paint was more of a dull gray, almost like a primer coat.

"It doesn't look new."

"It's a few years old." Mom smiled. "But it's new to us."

Mom's willful optimism annoyed me, because it placed me in an awkward predicament. Every day at Showbiz, Kerry asked me when I was bringing by the Thunderbird to show him. I would have rather run a marathon in the Chuck E. Cheese suit than have anyone at Showbiz see that gray heap of metal. It screamed hardship, which was not befitting the new "Kambri Crews" image. I came up with a different excuse each time. By the end of the week, it wasn't an issue. Dad had been in an accident.

"Where's that new car you were talking about?"

"My dad wrecked it!"

"Already?"

"Yeah, my mom said he hit a deer."

"A deer? Where's he gonna hit a deer around here?"

I shrugged. My father's explanation to Mom seemed plausible to me. Dad had wrecked nearly every car we owned except for the Toyota. Once he totaled a Caprice Classic driving it home from the sales lot. I thought he was just cursed to be accident prone.

The Thunderbird collision had left the driver's side looking like a peeled-open sardine can. Mom and Dad weren't bothering to get it fixed. The headlight still worked, so I guessed it wasn't worth the money to worry about the aesthetics.

One evening, as my father drove me to run an errand, we were waiting at a red light when a police car pulled up behind us. Dad kept his eye on him in the rearview mirror. When the light turned green, I waved to get his attention. "Green light."

Dad signed the ASL word "officer," then mimicked using a CB. "The officer is on his radio." He shook his head angrily and continued: "He's watching me."

We weren't speeding and hadn't done anything else illegal, so I shrugged.

"I hate cops," Dad signed, baring his teeth.

I knew he did. He made sure to remind me of that anytime a police officer was anywhere near. "Once I got pulled over for speeding. I pointed to my ears and shook my head no to show the officer I was deaf. I acted out writing on paper and pointed to the glove box. When I reached for it, *whack!* He hit me on my hand with his baton and then shook his finger at me. Again, I pointed to my ear and shook my head and signed writing on paper. I reached to open and *whack!* He hit me again. D-I-S-C-R-I-M-I-N-A-T-E," Dad spelled.

As we drove through the intersection, the lights on the police car started flashing and the siren began to wail.

"Told you," Dad signed, and shook his head, lips pursed and nostrils flaring.

"You interpret what I tell you." Dad had a cautious look on his face and repeated, "Don't ask questions, you just say what I tell you, okay?"

"Okay," I signed, annoyed that he didn't trust my interpreting.

When the cop approached he took a slow walk around the Thunderbird, inspecting every inch of it.

"What's he doing?" I asked.

Dad shrugged as he fished out his driver's license from his wallet. The officer approached my father's window, and Dad handed him his license. He then pointed to his ear, shook his head no, and pointed at me.

"He's deaf so I have to interpret."

The officer looked over Dad's license and said, "All right, tell him I pulled you over because you're missing a front license plate."

That didn't make sense to me. The cop had pulled up behind us. How had he seen the front of the car? But he was an officer of the law, so I didn't want to question him or make things worse for my father.

I interpreted to Dad, who nodded his head in understanding.

"Tell him I got into a wreck," he signed, and pointed to the peeled-back fender. "I have it. I just never put it back on."

I thought that the explanation made Dad seem lazy and disrespectful of the law. I decided to tweak his story. "He said he got into an accident and it fell off."

"Well, in that case, you're better off getting new license plates," the officer continued as I signed to Dad. "Because if someone found the plate they could use it to commit a crime." He handed the driver's license back to Dad, who looked confused.

"No, I have it at home."

"It's okay, Dad." I signed back before telling the officer, "Okay, we'll be sure to do that, sir."

"Show him the hat." Dad reached into the back and grabbed a NYPD baseball cap from the dashboard that Mom got after helping build helicopters for the New York City Police Department.

"No, let's just go."

Ignoring me, Dad pointed at the NYPD logo. "Tell him your mama works with the New York City Police."

"He doesn't care, Dad," I protested.

My father put on the hat and gave the officer big thumbs-up and A-okay signs. I felt embarrassed for him being unable to express himself the way he wanted to. Finally, the officer let Dad go with a verbal warning and walked back to the patrol car.

As we drove away Dad signed, "Whew," by wiping imaginary sweat from his brow. "Lucky."

By this time, I had my first real boyfriend, named Brad. I had met him my first day in town when Michele came over to be my friend. She had pointed him out when she was describing the eligible boys in the neighborhood.

"And there's Brad," she had said. "I don't like him, but I just know he'll like you." Michele looked over my shoulder. "Speak of the devil, here he comes. Hey!" Michele called. "Come meet Kambri."

"This is Brad."

"What's your name?" Brad asked.

"Kambri."

"Like the car?"

"No, Kambri. K-A-M-B-R-I."

"Well, I'd still take you for a spin," he said with a cocky, lop-sided smile.

Tall and handsome, Brad was a junior at Richland and played on the football team. His dark hair was trimmed in a fresh buzz cut, a drastic difference from all the shaggy mullets in Montgomery. He drove his own 1969 Chevy Impala, a tank of a car that he paid for with money he earned as a grocery bagger at Safeway. He made sure to be home every night to care for his disabled mother. I couldn't have designed a better boyfriend in a lab.

Brad and I went out every weekend. Though I had a midnight curfew, I usually missed it by an hour or so. It never mattered. Mom was an "early to bed, early to rise" kind of woman and couldn't hear a thing once she took out her hearing aids for the night.

Living on Grove Street meant easy access to bars. The forty-five-minute drives to drinking halls were now unnecessary. As a result, Dad could find his way home most nights instead of going missing for days. He frequented the Dallas Association of the

Deaf, which didn't close until two in the morning and was about twenty minutes away. I had it down to a science.

One particularly close call came after a night out watching a Richland High basketball game and drinking beer at a bonfire party. Brad drove me home, where we were surprised to see the Thunderbird parked in the driveway. The glow of our television beamed through the gauzy curtains of our living room window. Dad had beaten me home for the first time ever. My heart stopped.

"Shit! Turn off your headlights."

I scampered out of Brad's Impala and he slowly drove away with the headlights still off. I creaked open the front door and braced myself for Dad to jump up off the couch. As I slipped inside, my father didn't move a muscle. He was passed out cold and snoring, with his head tilted back and mouth agape. I broke into a sprint to my bedroom, running on my tiptoes even though we now lived in a house on a concrete slab. My room was spinning, but I changed into pajamas, tousled my hair, and smeared my eye makeup. I inspected my look in the mirror, then ventured into the living room to pretend I was emerging from a deep sleep.

I touched Dad's arm, but he didn't stir. I pushed a little harder. He smacked his mouth and licked his lips but never opened his eyes. I grabbed his shoulder and jerked it back and forth with big shoves. He lifted his head and opened his eyes with a squint to shield them from the bright light of the television. He looked around the room as if he was trying to recognize where he was. His eyes crossed, so I waved my hands in his face so he could focus. He was smashed.

"Dad, go to bed," I signed.

"Where were you? It's late."

"The TV is too loud and you woke me up."

He was stinking drunk but still remembered that I hadn't been there earlier.

"Why weren't you home?"

"I was in bed," I signed. "I've been asleep, see?" I pointed at my pajamas.

Dad teetered backward to get a better look at me.

"Come on," I continued. "Go to bed."

Dad didn't argue—he was too busy trying to stand. He slung his arm around my shoulder and leaned on me as I directed him to the hallway leading to our bedrooms. As we passed my bathroom, he made a pit stop and slammed the door shut behind him.

I stumbled to my bedroom and crawled into bed, marveling at my good fortune, only to hear a loud crashing noise from another room. I dashed to the hallway and yanked open the bathroom door.

Dad was flat on his back in the tub, pissing everywhere. After losing his balance, he had grabbed the shower curtain to stop his fall. The rod had given way and the shower curtain had fallen on him like a blanket. As he struggled to free himself, urine was spraying the shower, floor, toilet, walls, and by a narrow miss, me. I ran to Mom, who was fast asleep.

I shook her awake and signed, "Mom, hurry! Help!"

"What's wrong?"

"Dad!" She leapt out of bed and followed me to my bathroom. When Mom saw him passed out in the tub and covered in urine, she ordered me to bed.

Seeing my father splayed out and exposed should have made for an awkward moment in the sober light of day. But the next morning was like any other. As drunk as he had been, I wasn't sure if Dad had any recollection of the night before. He sat on the couch watching football and reading the paper. Out of embarrassment, I avoided eye contact with him. I was certain Mom would have something to say, but Mom acted like it had never happened. I followed her lead.

Mom and Dad were in financial trouble again. "They always say the only things guaranteed in life are death and taxes," Mom sighed, as she read through another notice from the IRS. During the weeks before the trailer was repossessed, they took the advice of a shady businessman back in Boars Head. He had convinced them that taxes were illegal and had given them a book, *The Great Income Tax Hoax: Why You Can Immediately Stop Paying This Illegally Enforced Tax.* As desperate as they were, they had accepted it as truth. They were always seeking their "fortune" in one scheme or another, and they always ended up on the losing side. That shyster back on Boars Head had led Mom and Dad into a whole heap of trouble. The IRS had tracked them down and began garnishing Dad's wages at the cabinet company. Dad's way of fighting back was to quit working altogether, giving him plenty of time for hanging out at the Deaf club in Dallas.

After a night out, Dad was usually found in the kitchen dancing in place to imaginary music while stirring a pan of potatoes or a pot of boiling pasta. If I bristled at the idea of eating his unusual creations, he got annoyed.

"What's that?" I wrinkled my nose at the sight of scrambled

eggs, sausage, and onions sprinkled with Tabasco sauce and wrapped up in a tortilla.

"B-U-R-R-I-T-O," Dad finger-spelled. "The Mexicans at work taught me."

"A burrito with eggs?" I scoffed.

"Don't make a face like that. Taste it first before you decide."

With trepidation, I took a bite and, as usual, was astonished at how good it was. Dad was pretty handy at whipping up meals around the house, especially greasy concoctions. He had even picked up a few shifts at Bennigan's across the street from our rental house. But one day when he was supposed to be working, I was surprised to see him sitting on the couch reading *Popular Mechanics*.

"Why are you home?" I signed.

"They fired me."

"What? Why?"

Dad screwed up his face and shook his head back and forth. I sat down to watch him tell his story.

"I was chopping up onions and tomatoes and popped a few pieces in my mouth. The manager got angry. He shook his head and finger no and mouthed, 'You can't do that.' I shrugged and mouthed back, 'Okay, sorry.'"

"Why couldn't you do that?"

"I don't know. Who cares if I eat a few pieces? But, okay, fine. Whatever. I went back to chopping and cooking, but when I cook I'm used to smoking. We're not supposed to smoke in the kitchen, but I got a real bad craving. You know me. I need my cigarettes. I opened the back door to have a few puffs. The manager ran over yelling and pointing to my cigarette and shook his finger no. Then he pointed to the parking lot and mouthed, 'Go! Leave!' "

Dad shrugged as if to say, "Whatcha gonna do?"

We stared at each other for a moment as I thought about it.

They seem pretty uptight. I did that all the time at Showbiz.

As that thought entered my mind, I realized that it was as if I heard my own voice speaking to me. Then it struck me: What about my father? Since he had never been able to hear, what happened when he thought to himself? I had never even considered this before.

"Dad, how do you think to yourself?" I signed.

He was taken aback. "What do you mean?"

"When you're just sitting around, lost in thought, what happens? For me, I hear my own voice."

Dad's chin wrinkled and he shook his head slowly. "I don't know," he signed, baffled. He picked up his magazine and resumed reading while I stared at him, contemplating for the first time how different our day-to-day lives were.

I had broken plenty of kitchen rules at Showbiz. I had stolen bites of mushroom caps, sips of Bartles & Jaymes wine coolers, and nibbles of birthday cakes.

If he had been able to hear his manager coming, he could have tossed out his cigarette and shut the door. He can't just go out and get any job.

Dad lowered his magazine and signed, "I see my hands."

"What?" My thoughts fell away and my father's face came into focus.

"I see my hands," he repeated. "You asked what happens when I think to myself. I see my hands signing like they're in front of me."

"Really?"

He stared off into space for a second before nodding. "Yes, I see my hands."

"Cool."

We both broke into big grins at our discovery. A scene from the film *The Miracle Worker*, based on the life of Helen Keller, flashed in my head and I asked my father, "Can you say 'water'?"

"Whaa-er," he replied.

I shook my head no and signed, "Watch my mouth and tongue. Water." Using techniques I saw in the movie, I held Dad's hand up to my mouth and repeated the word again. "Now you." We went back and forth until he perfected it. We only worked on it for about twenty minutes. I was surprised at how easily he mastered it.

Too bad we never spend any time together. I bet I could teach him more.

~

$\mathcal{D}$ad asks a guard for the time—11:30 A.M. Our visit is halfway over. His attitude becomes more serious when he pulls a slip of paper out of a shirt pocket. It is a long list of items he wants to review with me before our time runs out. No more fun and games; it's time to get down to business.

"Send me information about Dennis Rodman. A guy here and I argued about him. He says that Dennis never played in college, just in high school and then the NBA. But I bet him a pint of ice cream that Rodman played in college in a small Oklahoma town. I really want to make him shut up and shit his pants."

Dad is still up to his stubborn, argumentative ways, but unlike his early days behind bars, when he spent a lot of time fighting, he now relies on my Internet access to resolve disputes. Dad has always been a gambling man and since he has a head for trivia, ranging from sports and celebrities to history and current events, he does what any man in his situation would do: He turns it into a moneymaking opportunity. In jail, money's equivalents are stamps, writing supplies, and food. For Dad, a pint of ice cream is as good as gold, ranking third behind the ability to hear music, and the Dallas Cowboys. "You know what my favorite ice cream is?"

"Strawberry," I sign without hesitation.

"How do you know that?"

"Because when Mom would bring home a gallon of Neapolitan, David got vanilla, I got chocolate, and you always ate the strawberry."

Dad smiles, checks Rodman off the list, and adds, "I guess you're tired of hearing about ice cream. Ha."

Dad picks up where he left off on his list of things to discuss before our visitation is over. "Buy me new eyeglasses. These are broken from fighting, fighting, fighting," he signs by striking his fists against each other over and over again. He is, of course, referring to the fights during his early jail days.

Dad says he can sketch out the style and his prescription so I can buy them. The next time I visit, I can wear them as though they're mine at the security check-in. Then, during our contact visit, we can swap out his old, broken glasses with the new pair I have smuggled in. "Don't worry. You won't get caught. Everyone does it."

I'm confused as to why I have to smuggle in something so basic. "Can't you get them from the prison?"

"Yes, but they look like Buddy Holly glasses. I don't like that kind. They're ugly."

I am puzzled by Dad's interest in fashionable eyewear. Who is he trying to impress?

Dad moves on to the next item. "Buy me the Sunday New York Times. Only Sunday—I want to see what the big deal is. Also I want a subscription to Discovery Magazine. I love reading about new technology, computers . . . oh, and what is a B-L-O-G? I can't find that word blog in the dictionary and I asked other inmates but they don't know what it means, either."

I love that he is interested in learning but am disappointed he can't seem to get the information he wants.

Dad checks his list and signs, "I want you to sneak in a hundred-dollar bill." With the money he will be able to buy eight packages of loose tobacco and make over five hundred dollars in profit without doing any of the selling. The jailhouse version of one of his standard get-rich-quick schemes.

"What if we get caught?"

"You can't visit me for six months and I get solitary. Only fourteen days. That's nothing!" With all the time Dad has spent alone for fighting, fourteen days is a minor annoyance.

"Okay, next thing, I need you to deliver a message to Larry." Larry, a fellow inmate and new friend of Dad's, has been transferred to another prison after suffering severe beatings at the hands of guards after they found drawings of nude children in his cell.

"Larry told me he's not a child molester, just a flasher!" Dad declares. "That's nothing. And they beat him? Why? Larry said they weren't drawings of kids. No! They're midgets! Not dwarves, that's different—M-I-D-G-E-T-S."

Larry had spun a line of bullshit that Dad had swallowed. Not that Dad is so gullible but because Dad is compelled to believe in others' conspiracy theories so they will believe in his. If Dad doesn't believe Larry then why would Larry believe Dad? Why would I, or anyone else?

"Any news from my mother or brother and sisters?"

I lie. I shrug my shoulders and shake my head no.

I don't tell him how days after his arrest one of his sisters sent me an email condemning Dad. She blamed his non-Christian lifestyle for everything he had done. She informed me that after removing Dad's belongings from his apartment, she had gone through his photos. Based on what she saw—pictures of him partying or posing with women he dated over the years, in various stages of undress—she decided Dad was evil and she was going to burn everything he owned.

I begged her to reconsider and mail me his photos. She agreed but only if I first sent a check for fourteen dollars to cover the postage.

She gave Dad's cherished cowboy hat to her grandsons to play cowboys and Indians. I am not telling Dad about that, either. He really loves that hat.

"How can they call themselves Christians and still disown me?" My father's biggest fear in life is being abandoned, just like he was as a child at Deaf school. Dad persists. "That is not how to be a Christian. Christians are supposed to forgive."

"I know, Dad, I know." I nod without dispute.

He has gotten so many second chances, but that doesn't stop him from thinking he deserves another. I can't blame his relatives for not wanting him in their lives. He doesn't make it easy for them to help or forgive him.

WEYLAND DRIVE

1987–1989

Chapter Twelve

SIXTEEN CANDLES

Within a year of relocating to Fort Worth, Mom and Dad were behind on our rent. My mom walked into my room one day and told me to start packing. We were moving again, this time into a two-bedroom apartment. Having dropped out three weeks into his senior year, David had already moved into an apartment with his new friend Derek.

I noticed that the lease was in Mom's name, but I didn't think much of it. They had so many problems with the IRS that it was probably best to leave Dad's name off. What I didn't know was that she had intended on moving without him and planned on doing it while my father was out of state on a gambling trip. But he had come home early and found her in the midst of packing boxes.

She wouldn't tell him where we were moving, but he was persistent. He rifled through her purse and discovered the new apartment's address on her checkbook. He convinced her to give him another chance—again. She knew better, but since he had already found out where we would be living, she felt she had no choice.

Our new apartment was on Weyland Drive, about a mile from our old house. It was one of thousands in an ocean of brick two-story complexes with tan roofs. It served mostly as housing for the students attending the junior college across the street. The building had tennis courts, laundry facilities, and a swimming pool. Our small two-bedroom on the ground floor with an outdoor patio was much bigger than our shed on Boars Head. But it was cramped, overstuffed with furniture and Mom's knick-knacks. Mom preferred the convenience of living on the first floor and since she and Dad were deaf, they were never concerned with noise from upstairs neighbors.

In the midst of my sophomore year, I quit working at Showbiz Pizza and got a better job at Malibu Grand Prix, a hip spot for young people to hang out. Unlike Showbiz, Malibu was open late, so there were plenty of shifts I could work. This meant a nice paycheck, definitely an upgrade from Showbiz. The mini–amusement park had an enormous arcade with pool tables, air hockey, the latest video games, and classics like Galaga and Pac-Man. The racetrack itself was equipped with regular go-carts for kids but also had bigger, high-speed models for adults with driver's licenses only. The track was a magnet for teenagers and a dream job for me.

I decorated my new bedroom with a modern racetrack motif using discarded checkered racing flags from Malibu and a coordinating black and white checkered comforter from Wal-Mart.

"Oh, Kambri, look at this," Mom gushed, pointing out a three-piece black lacquer bedroom set in a Fingerhut catalog. Mom was trying to rebuild her credit and Fingerhut was the only company that would lend to her. She needed to use the company's layaway program despite its exorbitant interest rates.

"Yeah, that's beautiful," I answered.

"You want it?" Mom smiled. "It'll look great in your room."

Yes, I wanted it. The shiny furniture would look so much better than the flimsy dresser Mom had picked up at a garage sale. Even though I had painted it black and white, it looked cheap and the splintered drawers always stuck.

"We can't afford that."

"It's my money."

"I don't need it."

"I know you don't," Mom huffed. "I'm *trying* to do something nice for your birthday. You deserve it after all your hard work and good grades."

"Mom, please don't. If you want to buy something, then buy something for yourself."

"But it's your sweet sixteen," she persisted. "How about a new radio?" She pointed in the catalog to a stereo system with three-foot floor speakers, lots of wood paneling, buttons, and lights that served no real purpose but to look fancy. The payment was only a few bucks a month, far less indulgent than the bedroom set.

"Okay," I agreed. "A new stereo . . . but not the furniture! If you buy it, I'll send it back, I swear!"

Mom gave me an offended look, but I was not letting her waste money on an extravagant and unnecessary expense. I had loaned Dad and her lunch money regularly and, worse, our phone had gotten shut off for nonpayment more than once. As a teenage girl, this was a tragedy that ranked second only to getting our trailer hauled off by the bank. I couldn't accept her offer no matter how much I wanted a cool bedroom set. Just like when my library was destroyed, I rationalized that all that shiny black lacquer would be too hard to keep clean.

More than an expensive gift, I really wanted to have a party or a fancy dinner, something to celebrate my official coming of age. The day I turned sixteen, Mom was in the hospital recovering from a planned operation. She had chosen this day, my sixteenth birthday, to schedule a surgery she had needed for a long time. I was disappointed but at least she had made the effort to buy me the stereo as a special gift. Besides, I still had my father and brother, who might help me celebrate. Even though David didn't live with us, he'd usually stop in at least once a day to raid our fridge. But I hadn't seen Dad or him in days, which I suspected meant they were out partying together. Still I had a sliver of hope that they would remember June 22, 1987, my sixteenth birthday, as an important date.

Since it was summer, the majority of my school friends were out of town on family vacations. Most of them didn't know that it was my birthday anyway. Brad and I were no longer together. We had been getting on each other's nerves and our nearly ten-month relationship ended with a loud fight in the hallway of our high school. After the breakup, I promptly went back to smoking a pack of cigarettes a day. I worked more often than usual so I wouldn't have time for much of anything else.

I was used to simple birthday celebrations, a homemade cake, a card containing a five-dollar bill from both sets of grandparents, and, if I was lucky, one or two friends over at the house for a sleepover. But this was my *sixteenth*. No one seemed to remember. No one seemed to care.

Bored and agitated, I dusted the apartment, washed the dishes, and scrubbed the floors, hoping the lack of interest in the date signaled a surprise party was awaiting me. Other girls at Richland High got new cars for these occasions. All I expected was some acknowledgment of this important milestone. Instead I was all alone. Even the phone sat silent till past suppertime. When it finally rang, I raced to answer it.

"Hello?"

"I jushh called to shaay I looooove you," Mom sang, slurring the words to the Stevie Wonder song. Even though she was calling from her hospital bed, I was fuming mad and cut her off with a slam of the phone.

Moments later, it rang again. She didn't wait for my answer; she just picked up where she left off, "I jushh called to shaay I caaaaaaare."

I hung up again. By the third call, she had changed her tune to "Happy Birthday." I made it clear I was livid.

"Yeah, happy fucking birthday," I yelled.

"Kambri! Watssch your mouth! Whash the matter?"

"It's my sixteenth birthday and I didn't even get a card or a cake or anything!"

"Where's your daddy?"

"I don't know. He and David are off somewhere. You sound drunk."

"I'm on morphine. Woooooo," Mom giggled.

"It's not funny."

"Well, how do you think I feel? I'm in the hospital and nobody's come to visit me."

I was silent.

"When your daddy gets home, you tell him ish your birthday."

"I'm not gonna tell him. He should remember his own daughter's birthday. And what about David?"

"Kambri, I can't talk about thish. I'm woozy from drugs and you're making my shtomach upshet."

"Fine!" I slammed the phone down again.

At one o'clock in the morning, I heard the key in the lock and smelled a burst of fresh-cut grass, summer air, and alcohol. It was David and Dad coming home, and they had been drinking.

My father looked surprised to see me standing in the hallway. "Awake?" he signed.

I scowled and stormed into the kitchen with Dad trailing behind me. Casually pulling some food from the fridge, he began to fix something for him and David to eat.

"I did the dishes," I signed, and glowered expectantly.

"Thank you," Dad gestured. He then gave me a quick pat on the head before pulling open the cabinets in search of a skillet.

My parents always had to remind me not to leave the pots and pans unwashed. I hated scrubbing them, and today I had left them dirty and piled on the stovetop. It was my birthday, after all.

When Dad noticed they weren't clean he cried, "Kipree!" Then he signed, "Why didn't you wash the pots and pans?"

"I cleaned the whole apartment!" I signed with wild arm movements. "So, I didn't wash the pots. Who cares?"

My father was taken aback by my outburst. "Whoa," he mouthed and signed, "What's wrong?"

"It's my birthday!"

"Not anymore," my brother snorted. "It's after midnight."

"Fuck you, David!" I snapped.

"Oh, man, I'm sorry, Kambri," he continued, stifling his amusement. "I'm serious. I'm sorry. Happy birthday," he reached out to hug me, but I pushed him off. "Awww, come on, Kambri. We forgot. We still love you."

Dad signed, "I'm sorry. Happy birthday. Thank you for cleaning." I charged to my bedroom and slammed the door.

The next morning, my father invited me to the mall. I thought he was motivated by guilt, but maybe he just needed to buy himself new Wranglers. He kept his sunglasses on as he strode confidently through Foley's department store. Passing a row of mannequins modeling new swimsuits, Dad covertly yanked down their bathing suit tops.

He laughed at my shocked expression as he signed, "H-A-H-A-H-A." When I was younger, he used to try to embarrass me by making vomit and fart noises in public. He may not have known what throwing up or flatulence sounded like, but he knew they elicited disgusted expressions from the other shoppers and embarrassed me. Now that I was older, he'd graduated to this public prank, befitting my maturity.

As we made our way from store to store, my father continued to molest the plastic women, pulling off their clothes and on occasion tweaking a breast or tickling the pubic area with his index finger. The other customers gave us a wide berth and cast disapproving looks over their shoulders. I couldn't help but laugh at the horrified reactions of big-haired ladies, gasping and whispering to their shopping partners, "Did you see what that man just did?" I stood back, just far enough to avoid implication.

It didn't take long for the mall police to catch up with us and I had to interpret.

"Who cares? They're plastic," Dad shrugged.

"It's not right," the guards awkwardly retorted.

Dad would not relent. "They're not real. They don't even have nipples," he signed, with a sly grin.

I relayed Dad's excuse. "But they don't have nipples, he said."

Reluctant to have this conversation with a teenage girl and her father, the uniformed guards resorted to pleading. "Please, just tell him to stop and go home."

I started giggling and repeated in ASL, "Please stop and go."

"Okay, fine," Dad signed. We fled the store to the Thunderbird, laughing the whole way. Dad stuck the keys in the ignition so his hands were free to sign, then animatedly reenacted the scene, mimicking the exasperated faces of the security guards. "H-A-H-A," Dad signed. "People are so U-P-T-I-G-H-T."

I was laughing so hard I could hardly watch him. The mall outing had been a welcome distraction. It was a fun way to spend an afternoon with my father, even if he didn't buy me anything. I still felt deeply disappointed at the hurtful oversight and knew that there would be no follow-up surprise or celebration. The memory of a morphine-laced apology from Mom, a drunken, attempted hug from David, and a trip to the mall with Dad molesting mannequins would be the end of it.

I carried a heavy workload in my junior year of high school. In addition to my honors classes, I chose theater as my requisite fine arts course and quickly became a fixture in the drama room, loading equipment, watching rehearsals, and running errands.

Mom said I came out of the womb with a microphone in my hand. "You weren't even two years old, but you were already talking and using sign language and told everyone you were going to be a movie star when you grew up." But aside from the puppet shows I wrote, directed, and "performed" for the King boys, only one acting opportunity had presented itself during our time in the backwoods of Boars Head. I was only eight years old and Mom informed me I was headed to an audition. I had no idea what play I was reading for or what getting the part might entail. I was ready for the exciting challenge, though, as Mom drove us in the Chevy to a community theater in Conroe. I had already had the lead in my second-grade school pageant in Houston and performed in and directed a group of fellow third-grade girls in a brilliant rendition of "Silent Night" in Montgomery. Mom had never been cast in anything her whole life, but I still listened to her advice: "Remember to speak loud and clear!"

That would be a cinch. I had to do that around deaf people all the time! And as a CODA I could express myself in ways other kids couldn't. A hearing person expresses feelings by changing the tone and intensity of his voice. Just as slight variations in the pitch and volume of one's voice convey information in a spoken language, fluent speakers of ASL can pick up small differences in a sign's duration, range of motion, and the signer's body language. It was normal for me to use body language and facial expressions to convey meaning and feelings in my signing with my two deaf parents and other deaf friends and family. The problem was that I hadn't learned how to drop those communications traits when socializing and going to school with people who could hear. My animated speaking had become my unique accent.

Once inside the theater, I took my place at the center of a wide circle of auditioning actors. When it was my turn to read the script, I read, or I should say shouted, the lines with exaggerated facial expressions and wild arm gestures.

"I HAVE MADE UP MY MIND NOW TO LEAD A *DIFFERENT* LIFE FROM OTHER GIRLS AND, LATER ON, DIFFERENT FROM ORDINARY HOUSEWIVES. MY START HAS BEEN *SO VERY FULL* OF INTEREST, AND *THAT* IS THE *SOLE* REASON WHY I HAVE TO LAUGH AT THE HUMOROUS SIDE OF THE MOST *DANGEROUS* MOMENTS."

With frantic motions, the director waved for me to stop. "Okay, thank you!" she yelled. "Well . . . Kambri . . ." She cleared her throat and bit her upper lip to suppress bubbling laughter. "You enunciate very well, and you certainly can *project!*"

Glancing around the room, I noticed that the other actors were exchanging astonished glances, covering their mouths and snickering. I wasn't sure what was so funny. I spoke loudly and clearly, just like Mom had instructed, and the director had agreed. I had nailed it . . . *right?*

If I had been reading for *Annie,* I may have booked the gig. Unfortunately, I had been auditioning for the role of Anne Frank.

What on earth had my mother been thinking? I could have acted better than Jodie Foster, but it wouldn't have mattered. My

Aryan looks, golden hair, and Texas twang were more like the Hitler Youth instead of a Jewish girl trying to survive the Holocaust.

My mother was undaunted by the rejection and gave me a pep talk during the ride home. "It's just one audition, Kambri. Some actors have to go on hundreds before they ever get a part. Let this be a lesson: You can't hit if you don't swing!"

Texas was a competitive place. Everything from football and basketball to shorthand and using a handheld calculator was an aggressive face-off organized by the University Interscholastic League, commonly known as UIL.

After skipping numerous tryouts for the musicals that my friends were cast in, I confronted my fear of auditions and showed up at the casting call for Richland High's production of *Tom Jones*. The play, a farce, was perfect for my over-the-top facial expressions. To my delight, I landed the supporting role of Miss Western.

The cast and crew of *Tom Jones* had magical chemistry. That spring, we entered and won zone, district, area, and regional acting competitions. For the first and only time in our school's history, our troupe qualified for the state finals, held at the University of Texas in Austin. It was such a big deal that all the actors' parents—even Mom and Dad—made the trip south to see us compete.

Ours was the first play to be presented that day, and we turned in a respectable performance. After we gathered onstage to take our bows, we took our places in the audience. As we awaited the judges' decision, the university theater students presented a parody of the competing plays. An outlandish and, at times, borderline indecent lampoon had us heaving with laughter.

Later, the judges filed into the auditorium and took their seats for the awards ceremony. I sat chatting nervously with friends when I heard the familiar guttural noises and high-pitched nonsensical sounds of my father, but they were reverberating over the theater's sound system. To my horror, Dad had climbed up onto the stage and was now doing his best gyrating Elvis impersonation into a microphone.

"Nyowwww wooo yooo laaahh haaaaa," Dad sang.

Gasps and giggles rippled through the audience.

Seated next to me, my friend Scott asked, "Hey, Kambri, isn't that your *dad*?"

"Shhhh!" I hissed and shrank down into my seat.

"It is!" Scott guffawed. "Oh my God! What is he doing?"

All the attention was again on the stage, but for all the wrong reasons. I felt nauseated as I watched the spectacle unfold. The emcee rushed from the wings and tried to wrest the microphone from my father's hands. The struggle went on for at least five excrutiatingly long seconds before Dad finally let go. But rather than make a quick exit, he continued performing.

"Mooooooo laaa laaaa laaaa wooo yooo!" he "sang," shaking his hips and swinging his arm in wild, giant moves to strum his imaginary guitar.

Breathless and confounded, the emcee wheezed into the mic, "If he belongs to you, would you get this monkey off the stage?"

Mom was standing in the back of the theater and hadn't realized what was happening. Now she sprinted toward the front of the auditorium and scrambled up the steps as my father took his bows to stunned laughter and scattered applause. As she escorted him down the aisle, Dad waved and pumped his fists in the air like he was champion of the entire competition.

Order restored, I was relieved to have the awards ceremony

get under way and focus attention away from my father and onto the event at hand. To my disappointment, Richland High's production did not place. My friends filed out of the auditorium to join their families in the lobby. I chose to hang back and wait until the place emptied before going out to meet my parents. I didn't want anyone to see me talking to the dancing "monkey."

Happy to see me, my father clapped when I stepped into the lobby. "B-R-A-V-O," he signed and patted my back.

Jerking my shoulder away, I scowled and signed aggressively, "Why did you do that?"

"What?" Dad looked affronted.

"Why did you go up onstage? This is the State One Act Play competition!"

"The other kids got up there and acted crazy," he replied, animatedly reenacting some of the more bawdy spoofs of the university students.

"They were allowed to be up there! It was part of the program."

"Who cares? It was funny. People were laughing and clapping for me," Dad signed, looking flabbergasted that I wasn't amused by his antics. He genuinely had no idea what he had done wrong. He had seen a bunch of kids being silly onstage and figured he would have a turn. I had grown up accustomed to witnessing my father's impulsive behavior, but this was the first time it truly mortified me. Representing my school in this prestigious competition was my proudest accomplishment and Dad was treating it like we were at an open mic at a bar.

"It wasn't funny to me," I said, scowling.

Putting the event behind me turned out to be impossible. My father's theatrical stage debut—and the story of deaf Elvis— quickly became legend.

Dad's impromptu performance wouldn't be the last time he would humiliate me in front of friends. In the spring of 1988, I was embarking on my first date with Nick, a tall, deeply tanned eighteen-year-old I met at Malibu Grand Prix. My father sat on the sofa fixated on an episode of *GLOW: Gorgeous Ladies of Wrestling*, a TV series that featured scantily clad women in choreographed matches. I waited at the dining room table for my date to arrive.

Opening the front door, I was happy to find a grinning Nick decked out in tight acid-washed jeans and a turquoise wife beater that showcased his smooth, bronze shoulders. He had a sparsely populated mustache and carefully crafted mullet, his bangs perfectly turned under by a curling iron.

Dad was usually not home when dates came to pick me up. But in that moment, my father tore his eyes away from the bedazzled wrestlers, took one look at my date, and sprang into action.

"Don't fuck," he signed, as we stood in the foyer of our apartment.

I jumped between my father and Nick, hoping to shield my date from witnessing this horrifying display. Dad's warning was accompanied by an intense glare.

"Listen to me. Don't fuck," he persisted. "I don't want you pregnant. I want you to graduate and go to college." His hands smacked loudly as he delivered his passionate fatherly advice.

"I know, I know!" I furiously signed back.

From the way Nick was backing himself out our front door, it was clear he sensed trouble. Although he didn't know sign language, he didn't need to. In ASL certain signs are easily discernible and some are blatantly explicit.

The AIDS epidemic was spreading through the insular Deaf community. It would eventually claim the lives of Peter Sloan, Uncle Darold, and a dear friend of my mom's parents. Some didn't rely on mainstream media, either because they didn't have closed captioning or because, on average, they read at the fourth-grade level. For many Deaf, ASL is their sole language, and reading English is foreign yet familiar all at once. ASL isn't meant to be written and is based on a different syntax than English. To some, my father's letters may make him seem barely literate. In fact, he is very well read, possessing a large vocabulary. He simply writes how he would sign in ASL, his native language. The Deaf who weren't well versed in written English often couldn't comprehend AIDS prevention literature with such technical medical terminology. As a result, some hadn't changed their sexual or drug practices to protect themselves. A local AIDS task force was formed that distributed a special mailing to educate the local Deaf community about the dangers of the deadly disease. When I saw photos in a brochure of the ASL signs used to educate the Deaf so they could better communicate and facilitate safe sex, I blushed. Mom left the pamphlet on the dining table and I pored over the contents, reading about how HIV could and could not be contracted, dispelling some of the myths that were running rampant about how you might catch it from a toilet seat or from drinking out of someone else's glass.

I giggled at the graphic signs for "ejaculation," "vagina," and "condom," and wondered if college frat boys had made them up. Sure, "fuck" and "pregnant" aren't the easiest signs to figure out, but most people—especially a horny teenage boy confronted by a wild-eyed angry father—could decipher them.

Nick seemed a bit shaken up as we walked out to his truck. "What was he saying?"

"Ah, nothing, really. He said it was nice to meet you and don't be late. The usual stuff."

Nick and I had fun on our date playing video games and miniature golf, so we agreed to go out again the next week. Waiting for Nick to pick me up for our second date, I watched television in the living room. Flipping channels, I landed on a rerun of the 1970s sitcom *Sanford and Son* just as my father wandered into the room.

"No!" he shrieked, jolting me out of my television trance. "Don't watch that!" he signed, slapping his right hand, which was in the shape of a "Y" in ASL, against his open left palm, the sign for "that."

The yell and loud smack startled me. "Watch what?" I was confused. Surely he didn't mean *Sanford and Son*. I had watched it nearly every day for years.

"That nigger R-E-D-D F-O-X-X. Don't watch him. He's a filthy nigger."

I bristled when I saw him sign "nigger," a word Mom strictly forbade us from using. It bothered me to see him sign the derogatory term. Dad had black friends, too. How could he be so two-faced? So what if my father thought Redd Foxx was filthy? He was playing a character in a sitcom. My father loved telling crude jokes that were considered offensive to plenty of people. That never stopped him from sharing them, even in front of me.

"It's not dirty," I scoffed, wrinkling my face.

"I don't care. I don't want you watching him or C-A-G-N-E-Y and L-A-C-E-Y," he signed.

Now I was thunderstruck. I never watched *Cagney & Lacey*. In fact, I couldn't imagine a worse fate than sitting through an hour-long drama starring two women. "Why not?" I asked, wanting to know the connection in this bizarre synapse leap.

"Because that actress is married to a nigger."

I didn't know which actress he was talking about, but his repeated use of such an offensive word angered me. Hearing a horn honk outside, I hurried from the apartment to meet Nick at the curb, and slammed the front door behind me.

In our small apartment, Dad seemed omnipresent, crouched and waiting to pounce. The next time I saw him, he demanded, "Don't you leave on a date without me meeting him. I want to see him first."

"Okay, fine." I shrugged. He had already met Nick anyway.

"Don't go with a nigger, you understand?"

My father's sudden intense racism seemed to coincide with my beginning to date. His inappropriate behavior at the mall and his stage antics at the theater competition were one thing. These stunts had always been part of his charm, even if they were embarrassing. But his intimidation tactics and racist rants were behaviors I had never witnessed before. They were in direct contrast to the freedom and culture of tolerance I had been taught my entire life.

Why would my father turn on me like this and in such a vile way? If I had taken stock of his life over the last two years, the answer would have been clear. The trailer had been repossessed, the IRS was after us, and we couldn't afford to keep the Toyota. His wife and daughter were working, yet he was unable to find or hold a job, even one as menial as his stint at Bennigan's. Mom, who had recently tried to leave him, was the breadwinner and was creating a rich personal life for herself without Dad. In sum: He didn't feel like a man. His racism was a direct reflection of his insecurities. He needed to feel superior, exert some control, and demand respect from his splintering family.

My father's pattern of irrational behavior toward my male friends of any race was getting unbearable. The final straw came when I befriended our upstairs neighbors, Tony and Sammy. The two were students at the junior college across the street from our house, and often invited me over to smoke weed, drink beer, and join them for a dip in our apartment complex's pool. Though Dad had never met them, he'd warned me to stay away. And Tony and Sammy seemed reluctant to invite me over unless they knew my father was out for the night.

Like most rebellious teenagers, I wanted to be in charge of my own life. I went to their apartment to hang out anyway, assuring them my father would be gone for hours. But one night he came home early, broke the cheap sliding lock on my bedroom door after his knocking had gone unanswered, and found my room empty and my window open.

Tony, Sammy, and I were smoking a joint and playing video games when we heard angry footsteps on the stairs to their apartment. "KIPREE!"

It was my father, screeching my name and banging on their apartment door. It sounded like an axe murderer was trying to break in.

Tony and Sammy were terrified.

The look on Dad's face and the sound of his piercing screams as he dragged me by my arm back downstairs were enough for them to never talk to me again. Hell, they wouldn't even *look* at me. I was frightened by my father's reaction. For the first time, I was genuinely terrified of him.

I wasn't used to rules restricting my comings and goings. David had never had them and I was more trustworthy and responsible than he was. Wrong or not, enough was enough. I complained to Mom about how my father was behaving. While my mother never verbalized it, I could tell she too was annoyed and frustrated by him. When they were in the same room, she was icy toward him. If he tried to get close to her, she would stiffen and rebuff his advances with a twist of her shoulders. Dad responded by rebuffing her right back. While these scenes played out in plain sight, Mom still wouldn't discuss her feelings with me, and she was dismissive when I attempted to broach the subject.

Maybe each of them entering midlife had been the catalyst for change, Dad for the worse and Mom for the better. She was blossoming socially in a way that she hadn't been able to on Boars Head. In Montgomery, there were no other deaf people or clubs. Now that we were in the city, there were plenty of people that Mom could befriend at the very active Dallas Association of the Deaf. Everyone there loved her.

Her friends were constantly calling our house, never failing to wake me up after my double shifts at Malibu Grand Prix. Whenever the phone rang, I groggily answered only to hear the caterwaul of digital transmissions of a TTY. Our TTY was in the living room, too far a walk in my tired state. Desperate to sleep, I sometimes waited for the phone to stop ringing and then took the receiver off the hook.

Despite Mom's heavy work schedule, she formed a song-and-dance troupe with three other deaf women. She taught them lyrics to songs they could never hear and choreographed dance steps that reminded me of the California Raisins commercial. Each member of Mom's quartet wore a different-color shiny spandex leotard over black opaque tights. The women rehearsed for days on end before debuting their new routines at the Deaf club.

Mom was also becoming more fiscally responsible. She had always been the main breadwinner in our family. But despite her best efforts, the trailer was still repossessed. Now she was working double overtime shifts.

In contrast, my father hadn't worked steadily since our time on Boars Head, and he burned through what little pocket change he might have had. He'd even bummed money and cigarettes off me.

I knew I was the only bond left between them, and even the strength of this relationship was weakening with each new day. I was self-sufficient, I argued, and Dad's behavior was outrageous. Mom said she was waiting until I graduated from high school to split up with Dad. I wanted her to act sooner. My father was a negative distraction to me. I was going to be a senior and had enough to worry about with college applications, scholarship forms, a full-time job, and acting, since I had recently been cast as the lead in a locally produced independent film. I needed to stay focused and the turmoil just made it that much harder. In my mind, my parents needed to move on with their lives.

On July 5, 1988, my wish finally came true. After almost twenty-two years of marriage, my mother asked for a divorce.

Chapter Thirteen

A PETTY OFFICER AND
A GENTLEMAN

Within a week of Mom's asking for a divorce, Dad moved to a studio apartment in a suburb about twenty minutes away, which he paid for with disability payments he received from the government. Mom was surprised at how easily he took the news. Eager to keep the friendly tone, she helped him move his half of the furniture they had divided. She even decorated for him, hanging up photos and putting his pewter car and antique knife collections on display.

My mother was relieved, and I was liberated. The last few months had been stressful and scary for me. I was able to concentrate on more productive things now that my father was at arm's length. I hadn't expected him to leave so agreeably. He had always been so smitten with Mom, but since moving to the city, their marriage hadn't been the same. He finally accepted it was time to move on.

David still dropped by regularly, even after Dad moved. He and Derek came and went freely, raiding the fridge, bumming cigarettes, and asking for money from my mother and me. Each time I saw David, he looked skinnier than the last. His height had topped out at six feet, six inches, but he weighed about as much as I did, which was hardly more than a sack of flour. His shoulder-length hair was dirty and uncombed and his eyes looked wild. In the middle of our conversations, he would go off on tangents about imaginary people, places, and things. I thought he was on drugs, but I didn't know for sure. Sometimes he seemed sober but out of his mind.

One afternoon during summer vacation, I tried to enlist Derek's and his help in catching what I suspected was a man lurking outside my bedroom window.

"You're fucking paranoid," David scoffed, then went back to switching channels on the remote.

I thought that Derek would take me seriously. But my hopes were dashed when he grabbed a saber sword off our wall. "Come on, David, back me up. I'm Zorro, the Gay Blade!" he declared, swinging the blade and slicing a broad, swooping Z through the living room air.

David and Derek—sword in hand—left the apartment. I began my act of undressing, hoping to bait the perpetrator. If somebody was out there David and Derek could apprehend him and tell me who he was. As I pretended to unbutton my shirt, I heard the bush outside my window scrape the glass, followed by cursing and shouting. My instincts had been right! There had been someone spying on me, and David and Derek had caught him in the act.

I looked through the blinds but the three of them had run out of sight. My adrenaline raced as I wondered how long the voyeur had been watching me, and what he had seen. Soon the front door flew open. David came raging toward me, baring his teeth like a rabid wolf.

"Did you catch him?" I asked, my heart racing. "Where's Derek?"

"You fucking set me up!" David screamed. "You knew I was barefoot."

Raving mad, David pointed his finger an inch from my face and continued yelling. "You didn't want me to catch him. You timed it so I couldn't chase him because I'm barefoot."

With each word, I took another step backward. I was confused. David was making no sense and I was scared.

"What are you talking about?" I asked. "Did you get him?"

"You know him don't you? Are you spying for the police?"

"Are you crazy? What's wrong with you?"

David was acting insane. I reached my bedroom, slammed the door, and locked it.

I wasn't sure who was worse: the Peeping Tom or David.

~

I thought I knew why David looked so skeletal and wild-eyed. I suspected he was high on crank, a form of methamphetamine. In Montgomery, we had all smoked our share of marijuana, but David's proclivity for getting high had graduated to stronger drugs ever since we moved to North Richland Hills. To date, high school and the drama club had helped keep me busy and away from questionable behavior, but David seemed to be going further and further astray.

In the past, I'd felt safe under his watchful eye even when I was smoking pot with him. If I had gotten caught, my assumption was that David would be in bigger trouble because he was supposed to be my protector. As long as he was in charge, I thought I could do whatever I wanted.

Most parties were limited to beer and pot, although during the summer we were still on Grove Street we had dropped acid a couple of times and ordered pills from a magazine. They were supposed to be like speed, but they were fakes. But now crank was the drug of choice. My turn to try it came in the wee hours one morning, when I heard my brother and Derek banging on the front door to be let into our apartment. I had just gotten changed for bed, so was very annoyed to see them.

"Y'all, it's late," I complained. "I gotta be at Malibu in a couple of hours and I'm working a double."

Derek suggested that I do a line of crank because then I wouldn't need to sleep at all. I had never heard of it, but it seemed like the perfect solution to get me through my early morning shift. Too afraid to snort the white powder for fear of it burning my nose, I wrapped my line in a little square of tissue paper and swallowed it.

Soon I was jolted with enough energy to run a marathon.

"Oh my God, you weren't kidding!" I paced wildly through the house, singing and talking faster than my mouth could keep up. Nothing could stop me.

"What's got into you?" my manager asked when he found me reorganizing and cleaning every nook and cranny of Malibu's snack counter.

The drug zipped through my veins, energizing me to work. As the day wore on, the high subsided and my head began to pound. Exhaustion was deep and sleep was inevitable. I hadn't eaten a thing. I was coming down hard. A bed was not necessary; the freshly cleaned counter would do. Or maybe the floor; I could sleep right under the cash register.

"We need to get you home," my manager decided. "You look like hell."

I may not have looked great, but the counters and cabinets and popcorn maker never shone as bright as they did that day.

The crash after the high was debilitating. I had planned on going shopping before my next shift at Malibu, but could barely lift my head from my pillow to see what time it was. It was almost three in the afternoon and I was to report to duty in two hours. *If I could take a little bit more crank, just enough to wake me up, then maybe I could still get to work on time.* That fleeting thought frightened me. I knew that was how addictions started. I never did crank again.

Being around David was like living at the base of an active volcano. I couldn't guarantee drugs were the source of his paranoia, but David's unpredictable and ferocious behavior kept me vigilant. I stashed my cash and cigarettes in different hiding places and slept with my bedroom door locked and keys under my pillow. When he stopped by, I quickly left to avoid any confrontations, careful to avoid eye contact. With my mother's work schedule, her dance troupe, and other activities at the Deaf club, she wasn't home to witness most of my brother's rages. When she was, however, David's bombastic rants reached epic proportions. He demanded cash and, if she refused, cursed and called her names, feverishly raving around the apartment shouting like a madman, spittle flying, teeth bared, arms flailing. I could tell she was afraid of him but nothing she said or did could calm him down.

I couldn't tell my mom my suspicions about David using crank. How would I explain knowing such a thing? She would question me. Surely she could deduce that his moods were drug-related. Hadn't the "Just Say No" campaign taught her anything?

"Tough love," I insisted. "Tell him he can't come over here anymore. He can go to Dad's if he has to."

She sighed. She was already overwhelmed with the IRS, bill collectors, her exhaustive work schedule, and my father. Although Dad was settled into his own studio apartment just a few miles from ours, he was still our frequent guest after a late night of drinking. He'd bang on the front door until Mom or I would let him in. Usually too hammered to stand upright, he crawled to our living room couch to sleep off the drunken stupor.

A few weeks after my seventeenth birthday, I began dating Rob, a twenty-two-year-old petty officer in the U.S. Navy. It was summer break, and with no more classes to attend, I was working full-time at Malibu Grand Prix and in training to become a manager. On my nights off, I liked to go dancing with Alexis, my friend from Richland High's drama club. The legal age to get into Panama's, our favorite dance club, was eighteen, but I used a fake ID. Alexis was nineteen, a high school graduate, and was an aspiring art student taking courses at the junior college across the street from our apartment. She had deeply tanned olive skin, a mouth full of braces, and an edgy New Wave haircut. The gobs of Liz Claiborne perfume she wore lingered for hours after she left a room. She never wore a bra, in part to snub society's oppressive rules but mostly because she was so flat-chested she didn't need one.

I was out with Alexis at Panama's the night I met Rob. Our attraction was immediate. He was shy and tanned with a slim muscular build and drove a white Pontiac Trans Am with a bird insignia and fake vent on its hood. My mother thought he looked just like JFK, Jr., but other than their thick heads of brown hair, this comparison was only vaguely accurate.

Rob was stationed at the Dallas Naval Air Station, where he worked on F-14 Tomcats—the same plane flown by Tom Cruise in the movie *Top Gun*. When I saw him in dungarees covered in grease from repairing a fighter jet, I wanted to devour him like a hungry Venus flytrap.

That summer, Alexis snagged a sailor of her own. His name was Jeff and, like her, he had a slight frame and funky haircut. The four of us quickly became inseparable. Since navy rules wouldn't allow for women to stay over in the barracks, we needed an alternate plan. Alexis lived with her elderly grandmother, who wouldn't allow us to bring a Ouija board into her house, let alone two strange men. That left the apartment I shared with Mom as our only logical choice for crashing after a night of dancing. As long as Alexis was there, it wasn't a big deal to Mom to have a coed slumber party. Rob and I slept curled up in my twin-sized bed while Alexis and Jeff slept together on the floor.

That arrangement came to a halt when my father showed up at the apartment one time in the middle of the night and flipped on my bedroom light to find Jeff and Alexis sleeping in my room with me. Rob was working the overnight shift at the naval base and thankfully was not there. When Jeff and Alexis awoke to find my father standing over them, they were terrified. Neither of them knew sign language, so Alexis shook me until I opened my eyes.

"What's wrong?" I asked.

"Who is this man?" Dad signed. Alexis and Jeff cowered on the floor, pulling the blankets up to their chins and squinting at the bright light.

"J-E-F-F," I spelled.

"Who is he? Why is he here?"

"He's Alexis's boyfriend."

"I don't like strange men staying here," Dad fumed, even though it was no longer his house.

Jeff, who was known to start a scrap or two at Panama's, froze. Who could blame him? Dad looked like a lunatic looming over them, flailing his hands wildly at me. To my surprise, instead of interrogating me further or starting a fight with Mom, he turned on his heels and left in a huff. Having Jeff there was a good thing.

"Let's get a hotel room," Jeff suggested on our next night out as a foursome.

"I don't wanna sleep on the floor anyway," Alexis said.

For $19.95 a night, Motel 6 was perfect. We loaded up on cigarettes and cases of Busch beer, filling the tub with bags of ice to keep the cans cold over the weekend. The guys took turns paying for the room, a simple accommodation set up with two double beds.

My relationship with Rob wasn't just about sex. We had a real connection. We drank, chain-smoked, and talked while quietly huddled under the blankets of our bed, as Jeff and Alexis twisted and writhed in theirs. As Rob and I bonded over our parents' divorces and sharing our dreams for the future—college for me, working as an airline mechanic for him—we ignored the awkward sounds of sex going on three feet away.

Not exactly a fairy-tale courtship, but then again I was no princess.

As a member of the military, Rob had to leave town on deployment on occasion. In August 1988, he set out for a two-week stint at Miramar Naval Air Station in San Diego, California. I was devastated.

We had been dating for barely a month. His time away would equal half of our entire relationship. We were young and wildly in love. What would happen to us without constant contact? Our insecurities crept in, both Rob's and mine.

"I'll call you when I can, but they keep us busy in training and work."

"Okay," I cried, as though he were headed to Vietnam. "I promise I'll be here when you get back."

To prove to him how devoted and faithful I was, I decided to keep a journal of my daily activities during his absence. The afternoon of Saturday, August 13, marked the second day of Rob's being gone. Mom had been away from the apartment visiting my father's sister Cathy, who'd recently moved to a nearby town.

Mom looked haggard when she arrived home that afternoon carrying several bags of groceries. As we unloaded the food, a wicked smile crossed her face. "Hey, Kambri, do you want to smoke a joint?"

I froze. *Mom wants to get stoned?*

"Ummm . . . yeah!"

She whipped out a joint from her purse and took a drag. When she handed it to me, I wasn't sure how to act. I was worried she'd be able to tell that this wasn't my first time. Then I realized that of all the things I had tried to keep from Mom, getting high was the least to worry about. She smoked, after all. I took the joint and inhaled like a pro. I saw my mother studying me, so I glanced away to avoid eye contact. Soon we were both too stoned to care about proper social mores.

To satisfy our munchies, I cooked us La Choy Chow Mein from a can while we chatted about Rob's family in Ohio and how he had told me that Cedar Point in Sandusky, Ohio, has the most roller-coaster rides of any amusement park. Mom got another mischievous look on her face. "Let's go to Six Flags!"

We pooled together our singles and counted up loose change, which totaled a little over twenty dollars. Mom stopped by the corner gas station to buy a Pepsi with a "buy one, get one free" park admission offer on the can before we drove the ten miles to Arlington, where the park was located. As we walked toward the Six Flags ticket booth, empty Pepsi can and plastic bags filled with coins in hand, a man approached us. "Excuse me, ladies. I bought these passes for the week but we're leaving town tonight and can't use 'em. I'll sell 'em to you for ten bucks. You want 'em?"

A single ticket to the theme park cost more than double that.

Still, I had once been duped into handing over twenty dollars to a cute boy selling magazine subscriptions in front of North East Mall. Adding insult to injury, he took my phone number and gave me a long, deep kiss while I waited for Mom to pick me up. A phone call never came and the magazines never arrived. I had been conned. Faced with another too-good-to-be-true scenario, I shot Mom a cynical look.

"Really?" Mom asked, slack-jawed.

"Yeah, why not? I ain't got no use for 'em."

She and I stared at each other in disbelief. Nothing lucky ever happened to us.

The guy grew impatient. "You want 'em or not?"

"Sure!" Mom said. She paid him the ten dollars and gave our Pepsi can to a family approaching a ticket booth, figuring we should share our good fortune. I expected rejection when we handed our tickets to a pimply teenager working the turnstile. What if they weren't real? But the ticket taker waved us in and said, "Y'all have fun now!"

Mom and I were overjoyed. "Wow! Can you believe it?"

"We sure are lucky!"

"Yes, we sure are! Now let's hurry before the park closes."

"You know what this means? We've got money for food!"

We stayed until closing time eating cotton candy, fried dough, and turkey legs, racing from ride to ride, and squealing, screaming, and laughing like kids who had been let loose from an attic.

I was two weeks shy of starting my senior year of high school. Mom was free of Dad and I was in love with a man in the U.S. Navy. We were in control of our lives and having fun together again. Everything was as it should be.

It was one of the best days of my life.

Chapter Fourteen

EXCESSIVE NOISE DISTURBANCE

Since my parents never noticed the everyday noises around us—pots and pans banging, dishes being unloaded, the telephone ringing—I became successful at tuning things out. I made myself effectively deaf to sounds that did not matter.

I was such a sound sleeper that I was forced to use the three-foot speaker from my Fingerhut stereo as an alarm clock. Each night I put one of the two speakers in my bed next to my ear with the volume cranked to 10 and set the timer. On occasion, this still failed to wake me. When Rob, Alexis, and Jeff slept over, they thought it was strange that I'd climb into bed with a giant wooden speaker. In the morning, when they had to shake me out of my coma so I could shut off the earsplitting wails of Ozzy Osborne, they thought I must be deaf, too.

But in the early morning hours of August 15, 1988, something else woke me.

It was 3:30 A.M. and bumps in the night were never the bogeyman. They were always Dad, drunk and disorderly. Just the night before, hours after Mom and I had returned from our Six Flags adventure, I wrote to Rob in my diary:

About 3:00 this morning my father came over and was SO DRUNK!! It was PITIFUL! I opened the door and he hugged me and said he loved me, went into the living room, turned off the light and went to bed. Idiot. *You better not end up that way.*

Wearing only my underwear and my AC/DC Fly on the Wall concert T-shirt, I slowly opened my bedroom door. Mom's door was open and the soft glow from her table lamp spilled out into the hallway. I edged down the hall and peered into her room. She was lying on the floor, with Dad straddling her, gripping the back of her head with his left hand. His right arm was cocked back, his fist in a ball. Mom heard me and shot me a terrified look. Dad threw a punch and missed. Dad's fist had already been in motion, but that split second of distraction was long enough for Mom to wriggle out of the way. The loud crack of his knuckles on the thin carpeting confirmed I was not dreaming and they were not playing around.

Mom ran toward me, dressed in her favorite floor-length polyester nightgown and her hair curled in black brush rollers. Dad was wearing jeans and reeked of Jovan Musk and alcohol. Clearly he had been at a bar and was out-of-control drunk.

He followed us into the dining area, where I saw that the plasterboard walls were riddled with fist-sized holes. I had slept through his angry punches.

Dad corralled us into the dining room. I shouted to Mom without moving my lips. David and I used to do that as kids to keep Mom and Dad from knowing what we were saying. Then this secret communication never failed to annoy her. But now my ventriloquism might help save our lives.

"SHOULD I CALL 911?" I shouted, hoping she would understand me.

I had never seen Dad raise a hand to her before. He had only spanked me twice in my whole life. I wanted Mom to tell me what to do, to tell me it was okay if Dad got in trouble, to admit that this couldn't be fixed.

Instead she screamed, "I DON'T KNOW!" making her own poor attempt at talking without moving her mouth. She was so bad at it that I worried that Dad would catch on.

My father paced the room shrieking "MUDDAH FUH!" while flailing his arms and pounding his fists on the tables and walls. At one point he grabbed my mother by the arm and pushed her toward one of the four dining chairs. She resisted, but he shoved her into a seated position. Dad's six-foot-two frame of pure muscle, deeply toned from years of construction work, was too much for the two of us combined. We had to call the police. But how?

Dad was screeching in Mom's face. I couldn't get to the kitchen phone with them in my way, and there was no way I was going to leave my mother to fend for herself. I screamed through my clenched teeth to anyone who could hear me, "SOMEBODY HELP! CALL THE POLICE!"

I was certain our neighbors Tony and Sammy would hear me and call for help, even though they weren't talking to me anymore. The cops would be at our door any minute, I told myself. I would still be able to get in a few hours' sleep before my 10 A.M. shift at Malibu Grand Prix. Minutes ticked by like hours and Dad's temper reached a boiling point. He yanked Mom's hair, then twisted her arm behind her back and began squeezing her face with his free hand. Mom was crying hysterically. She screamed at me to call the police. I ran to my room and dialed 911.

"This is the 911 operator, do you have an emergency?"

"Yes, help!" I screamed. "My dad is hurting my mom!"

"Are you at 1608 Weyland Drive?"

"Yes! Number 1004! Send police fast, please hurry!" I recalled Dad's complaints of discrimination by police and frequent stories of deaf people being injured or shot dead by officers due to miscommunication. Worried that the officers might hurt Dad if he didn't immediately obey their commands, I added, "He's deaf so he might not hear what they say."

When I returned to the dining room, I saw that Dad had let go of Mom's hair and now pounded around the room swinging punches, screeching and signing that he would kill her, and then himself.

I tried to defuse the situation, telling him and Mom that the police were on their way. He began to calm down while Mom sat solemnly at the dining room table. I was sitting in a sea of terror worrying that I had a head full of pink sponge rollers and was only wearing underwear. We already looked like an episode from *Cops*. There was no way I would be caught dead looking this way in front of officers. I turned toward my bedroom to find clothes, but Dad commanded me to stay where he could see me.

When the rap at the door came, Dad didn't try to stop me from answering. Two policemen stood in the entryway, their hands resting on their holstered guns. I noticed the front porch light was shattered. Dad must have also done that while I was sleeping. I repeated to the police what I had told the 911 operator, that my father was deaf and might not obey them.

Dad looked unfazed at seeing the officers and threw in a bit of feigned innocence. His face said, "What's the problem, officers?" That might have worked, if there hadn't been a dozen fist holes in the walls behind him.

I told the officers the basics but they only wanted to know about the status of Mom and Dad's relationship.

"Are they married?" one of them asked.

Domestic violence was treated differently back then. Laws would eventually change, but on this night, what happened behind a family's closed doors was mostly off-limits to the infamous strong arm of Texas justice.

"Yeah, they're still married but he doesn't live here anymore."

Somehow it came up that Dad still had some personal belongings in our apartment, namely some clothes of his in a closet. They hung next to Mom's clothes, all of which now had slashes after Dad had angrily taken a knife to them during a rampage two nights earlier.

"His clothes are in the closet, he has a right to be here," the officer said.

"But his name isn't on the lease," I argued.

"It doesn't matter. All we can do is ask him to leave."

Ask *him*? *How about* tell *him*.

The officers negotiated with Dad by interpreting through Mom. She relayed their messages of "Come on, just go home and sleep it off," and "You don't want to have your daughter see her parents fight like this, do you?" Lines like those must have worked when delivered by men in uniform carrying guns, but they didn't have quite the same effect when signed by Mom, the very woman Dad was threatening to kill just moments earlier.

This went on for twenty minutes before the officers were able to lead Dad through the front door. They pledged to follow him home to make sure he stayed out of harm's way. *Our* way. It all seemed so informal. Nothing signed, no photos taken, no report completed. Just a "he said, she said" and a quick dusting off of the hands. They even helped Dad get in his car, even though he was clearly in no condition to drive. His eyes were glassy and he reeked of alcohol.

Mom and I retired to our bedrooms without as much as a hug. We were in shock, and I had to be at work in a few hours. If I went back to sleep, I figured, maybe I would wake up to find that it had all been a bad dream.

I was just drifting off to sleep when I heard a tremendous crash. I leapt out of bed and grabbed the rotary phone that was on the floor by my stereo. Dad came charging down the hallway and into my bedroom. I was in the middle of dialing 911. The 9 hadn't even finished spinning back into its starting position when my father yanked the receiver out of my hand. As if cracking a bullwhip, he ripped the cord out of the wall.

In the age of rotary phones, 9 was a stupid number to have to dial in an emergency.

Throwing down the phone, Dad whipped out a folding knife from his back pocket and charged after Mom, who was standing in the hallway. I trailed behind and saw that our front door was knocked off its hinges and the wood splintered where the bolt should have been.

Dad grabbed Mom by the arm and forced her back to the dining room and into a chair. I stood paralyzed with fear as he planted himself at the head of the table. He pointed me to the empty chair across from Mom. "SIT!" His high pitch and ferocity was startling. I took a seat as ordered.

For hours, he interrogated my mother about her dating and sex life as I sat with my head down on the table. Occasionally he punctuated his sentence with a slam of his fist on the table or a quick jab to the wall. His balled-up hand crashed through the drywall with ease.

Each time I tried to get up, he bared his teeth and screamed, "SIT!" I tried to shrug him off with my best teenage hostility act, signing, "Going to bed." He quickly jumped up, standing tall and puffing out his chest like a king cobra as he shrieked, "SIT! NOW!" I sat at the dining room table with my parents, something we had not done since Thanksgiving when I was nine.

Mom sat in silence as though she was in a trance. Frustrated by her lack of emotion, Dad turned his attention to me. He pointed at a photo of my mother with her co-workers proudly lined up in front of a helicopter they had just built. He grabbed it off the wall—the same wall that sported fresh holes the size of

Dad's fist—and ferociously signed, "Did you know your mother fucked him and him and him and HIM?!" He pointed so hard that his index finger cracked the glass. It didn't cut him through his thick calluses, but it gave him an excuse to get even angrier. He broke the frame in two and hurled the shards and splintered mess against what was left of the wall.

Our eyes locked. He signed to me with forced emphasis on each sign, "Your mother S-L-U-T!"

I searched his livid face. *Are you in there, Daddy?*

"Did you know your mother gives good head?"

He searched my dazed face, as if he were asking if I was on his side.

I wasn't.

He had just told me that my mother was a slut, that my mother gave blow jobs. *Told me, the daughter he was trying to protect from the evils of men.*

He snapped.

In one swift move Dad lifted Mom by her neck and slammed her back against the foyer wall. I looked down and saw that her feet were writhing desperately as she tried to dig her heels into the wall. Her polyester nightgown was bunched up around her waist as she held on to his wrists and strained to make her neck muscles tight. Her eyes bulged and the vein in her forehead grew fat.

I pried at one of Dad's hands but it was firmly in place. So I concentrated on one finger; if I could bend one backward he'd have to let go from the pain.

Please, just one digit, Kambri. You can do it. Just get his index finger. Just one finger.

He was too strong.

I switched tactics. "Daddy, Daddy! Look at me, Daddy!" I signed in his face, breaking his focus. He turned his eyes my way but never lost his grip. "Daddy," I continued. "Please, don't do this. Why are you doing this? Why? Why? Why?"

He was cracking; I could see it. "Daddy, look at me. It's me, Kambri, your baby girl, remember?"

His glassy eyes welled up with tears. I repeated it over and over again. "It's me, Kambri. Daddy, it's me. Remember? Your baby girl, Kambri." Finally he let go. Mom choked and gasped for air. I raced to the kitchen phone, still connected to the outlet, and dialed 911. Dad caught me and yanked the receiver out of my hand just as I heard the operator answer, "911, what's your emergency?" He slammed the phone back into its cradle, disconnecting the call.

I was now the enemy, too.

He whipped out a hunting knife from his pocket and held it to Mom's throat. His top lip was tight and pinched and his bottom lip jutted out, exposing his bottom teeth; he looked like a salivating, growling bear on a rampage. He pulled Mom's head back by her hair and made her throat long and tight, just begging to be slit open. She held on to his wrist with both hands as they stared into each other's eyes.

The phone rang.

I had a choice: I could try the baby daughter route again, or make a break for the phone and hope that he was too caught up in his hypnotic rage to notice me. I ran to the kitchen phone.

I screamed to the 911 operator, "HE'S BACK! He's trying to kill my mom! He's got a knife to her throat! Please help!"

Dad saw me talking into the phone; he knew the police would soon return and he brought himself back under control. As the seconds ticked by, he tried to make things appear a bit more normal. He folded his knife and put it back in his pocket and made us resume our places around the table as we waited for the police.

This time the officers immediately handcuffed Dad, looking to me to interpret his Miranda rights to him. They didn't see me as a victim, too. "You have the right to remain silent," one of them began.

After a few sentences the other officer decided that the teenager might not be the best person to deliver Miranda rights. Legal matters could be taken care of at the police station and they all tromped out through our broken door.

While I was busy translating with one officer for Dad, the other cop dealt with Mom. Other than some bruising, she didn't seem in need of medical attention, and she refused to go to the hospital for an examination. Mom wasn't crying anymore; she seemed to be in a daze and anxious to put the whole event behind us.

Mom and I headed back to our respective bedrooms, again with no hug, no discussion, no comforting, even though this was by far the most traumatic incident I had ever experienced in my life. I had survived being uprooted to live in the wild on Boars Head, defending myself from my brother's bullying; having our trailer repossessed; selling Charlie Brown; watching my beloved library burn to ash; moving to Fort Worth not knowing the fate of our dogs; seeing David's scary descent into the world of drugs; and experiencing Dad's long absences and alcohol-fueled exploits. But witnessing my father's violent attack against my mother was catastrophic. I knew my life would never be the same.

Mom and I were both exhausted, and I just wanted to retreat to my bedroom and shut out the world. It was impossible to feel safe there. The front door was propped up against the frame, and my telephone was ripped out of the wall.

It was almost eight o'clock in the morning and I finally gave up the idea of going to work my morning shift at Malibu. I picked up where I had left off in my journal to Rob:

I wish I could get away from here, but I can't leave my mom and I still have school to think about. I need you so much right now but you're not here. So, if I die right away . . . I love you with all my heart. Kambri Crews.

Chapter Fifteen

COME SAIL AWAY

Dad was charged with aggravated assault with a deadly weapon and placed in Tarrant County Jail with a bond of $5,000. For just $1,000 he could be free. But even at that price, Dad didn't have that kind of money. No one he knew was willing to pay for him, either, so he sat in jail for several days, one of which happened to coincide with my parent's twenty-second wedding anniversary.

Mom refused to press charges. She wanted everything to go away quickly and quietly. Just like when Dad was arrested for public drunkenness at Pizza Inn, she acted as if nothing was wrong, as if Dad hadn't held a knife to her throat. I was outraged. I wanted to see him punished but she still needed my father. He contributed to paying bills. She reasoned that out of jail, there was the potential for him to find work and he could help deal with David. Without her cooperation, the police had no case against my father. Eventually he received probation and was freed before Rob returned from duty.

Now that things had escalated to physical violence, Mom finally came clean with me. She told me that on August 12, the Friday before the attack, my father had stolen her gun. I was alarmed to learn she had one in the first place.

"A gun? Where'd you get that?"

"Your uncle Doug gave it to me for protection." Why would her sister's husband think she needed protection? And protection from whom? Dad?

"And now Daddy has it?"

"I don't know, Kambri. He told me he threw it away. Maybe he's lying. And he went into my closet and slashed all my clothes with a knife!"

I felt sick to my stomach. It was my fault. I had let Dad in the apartment that night. Dad was banging on the door and I had just wanted to sleep.

Mom's trip to see my father's sister Cathy, after which she had come home to smoke a joint with me, had been a visit to plead for help. After discovering her clothes destroyed and gun missing, Mom was truly frightened. She finally realized she was in over her head and needed help knocking sense into Dad, to get him to move on with his life and stop harassing her. She hoped Aunt Cathy could intervene somehow, and at the very least shame him to his family. When my mom got home from that visit with Cathy, she'd been emotionally spent. That's why we'd gotten high together and gone to Six Flags. One of the best nights of my life had been her attempt to unwind from a stress so great, I couldn't imagine.

Being arrested didn't discourage my father. He continued to drop by the apartment in the early morning hours after a long night of drinking. Mom avoided him by staying at Aunt Cathy's house, leaving me alone at the apartment to deal with him. Even though his beef wasn't with me, I was still afraid. Sometimes Alexis stayed over so I had backup. Time and again, Dad hounded me for Mom's whereabouts until I threatened to call the police. Then he'd slip away. After a few failed attempts at seeing my mother, Dad resorted to phoning at all hours. When I answered, he cooed into the receiver, "Ellooooo. Luh yoooo. Kipree, luh yooo." I never turned on the TTY, so he was unable to hear whom he was talking to or if anyone had even answered.

Mom and I reacted by changing our number, but Dad knew where to find me. He came striding casually through the doors of Malibu Grand Prix as I cleaned the candy display case. He smiled and waved hello.

"I miss you," he signed. "How are you doing?"

"Fine. Busy."

"I tried calling but your number is changed."

"It was shut off," I lied.

"Is your mama dating?"

"I don't know, Daddy. I'm busy. This is my work."

"Okay, I understand." He looked dejected and hopeless. Rather than alienate me entirely he left without incident, waving goodbye with the ASL sign for "I love you."

When Rob returned from duty, I presented him with my journal that detailed everything that had happened since he left, including Mom and Dad's situation. Rob was infuriated when he read what my father had done to Mom. He adored my mother and swore that if he had been there that night he would have killed my father.

Having Rob in my life provided me with a certain amount of stability, and I smothered him with so much love that he had no choice but to love me back. I was a damsel in distress, and I looked to him as my hero and protector. What better scenario for a young man hundreds of miles from his own family to swoop in and sweep a girl off her feet, to save her?

Two weeks after my father attacked my mother, I began my senior year of high school.

The theater department buzzed as everyone swapped stories of their summer vacations. I chatted with Charity, a classmate whom I had gotten to know my junior year. When it was my turn to share, I didn't mention anything traumatic. I bragged about a small independent movie I had been starring in over the last few weeks. I had snagged the lead role and I loved the long days and nights of filming, another distraction from the drama at home.

"The movie's gonna be entered in festivals and stuff," I crowed. "I worked a lot at Malibu, too, and I met this guy Rob. He's almost twenty-three and works on Tomcats in the navy. He's gonna pick me up from school in his Trans Am. I can introduce you to him."

"Wow, that's great, Kambri." She smiled. I had gotten to know Charity during long hours of rehearsal and travel to and from competitions. She could see right through me, so I decided to confide in her. "But, then, umm . . ." I lowered my voice and said, "My dad tried to kill my mom."

"Huh?" She gave me a mystified look. I delivered a short version of the night from just a few weeks before. She looked as though she didn't believe me. She had interacted with Dad at various one-act play competitions and knew him as handsome, flirtatious, and a cutup, the deaf Elvis impersonator. It was obvious that she was straining to express concern and find the right words. "Oh, that's sad, Kambri. I'm sorry." She slid away as if my family's problems were contagious.

I worried that I had shared too much with her. We weren't that close, after all, and my explanation of Dad's attack must have seemed pretty unbelievable. Her reaction taught me to keep my mouth shut. So, for the next fourteen years, she was the only one I told.

In the first weeks of school, I landed the lead role of Bunny Watson in the fall play, *The Desk Set*. I was back to my busy schedule of school, rehearsals, homework, and shifts at Malibu. My mother and I still lived at the apartment, but she was working up to eighty hours a week to make ends meet. Rob drove me to and from school and rehearsals and, on his off nights, slept in my twin bed. Mom didn't object to his staying over. We both felt safer with him there.

On opening night, Mom and Rob greeted me in the school lobby at the end of the final curtain, each holding a single red rose. I hoped Rob would gush and be overwhelmed by my talent. Instead he shyly handed me my flower and said, "Pretty good, kiddo."

The second night of the play, Charity squealed, "Hey, Kambri! Somebody sent you roses!"

"What? Where?"

"They're in the dressing room."

I couldn't imagine who would send them. Mom and Rob had already given me flowers. I opened the card and was surprised to learn they came from Steve, a tall, handsome blue-eyed blond who was on the basketball team and ran with the popular, preppy crowd.

"You were wonderful. Break a leg tonight. Love, Steve."

My heart fluttered with excitement. After the show, I met Steve in the lobby, where he looked positively starstruck, as though I were Bernadette Peters and this was not the auditorium of Richland High School but the boards of Broadway. He gave me a long hug and congratulated me on a job well done. That was all it took—roses and a hug—and I was his.

Dad had stopped coming around. Mom worked so much that he could never find her at home and things seemed to calm down. I was finally able to focus on being a high school senior. Being wooed by a popular jock was intoxicating. While circumstances at home may have made me grow up too fast, at the end of the day I was still a typical teenage girl. I liked the idea of having two guys vying for me. It reminded me of how my mother was dating another boy when Dad relentlessly pursued her.

Rob's shifts often didn't coincide with my hours at school and rehearsal schedule, so I used that as the excuse to break up. Things at home were not as volatile, and I didn't need his protection. Too timid to tell him in person, I broke the news over the phone.

Rob was crushed, but he didn't cry or get angry. He told me that he loved me and that he would agree if it was what I wanted.

Steve, like me, was active in school and together we bounced from basketball games to assemblies, from after-school parties to variety shows. I couldn't believe someone so clean cut and popular wanted to date me. He made me feel normal, and normal was all I wanted to be.

David, however, was reaching a tipping point.

Mom thought David's troubles might be the result of his upbringing. "We should never have smoked marijuana in front of you kids. Maybe I shouldn't have let you watch so many R-rated movies when you were little."

Dad thought the downfall started around the time David was caught sniffing paint with Allen in the Kings' barn. "That ruins your mind," he signed, shaking his head in disappointment. "It kills your brain cells."

Whatever it was, it was a combustible combination. My parents tried several times to check my brother into a hospital, but unless he was deemed to be a threat to himself or the public, he was allowed to leave under his own free will.

"But he is a threat! How can they just let him walk out?" I asked.

"It's the law," Mom sighed. Even David's old friend Allen, who had been clean and sober since leaving Montgomery and was serving in the military, knew something was wrong. He had recently visited David and was so jarred by my brother's appearance and behavior that he secretly talked with my mother. He urged her to intervene, telling her that her son was likely addicted to crank and who knows what else. She followed Allen's advice, played the tough-love card, and refused to allow David to stay with us.

Dad took him in but was unequipped to deal with my brother's problems and quickly grew impatient. After just a few weeks, he ordered David to leave. It was wintertime and David was left alone to deal with the elements. One particularly cold night, during a rare snowstorm in Fort Worth, David returned to my father's doorstep begging for shelter. Dad refused. Snowfall or not, David was on his own. He became transient, disappearing for weeks only to resurface looking dazed and wild-eyed and in need of money or a ride from a bus station.

Eventually Mom's parents stepped in and took David into their home in Oklahoma, hoping the change in scenery and Grandpa Worth would knock some sense into him. Just like Mom, Dad, and me, Grandma Worth quickly became terrified of David, and Grandpa Worth couldn't reason with him. They were heartbroken and powerless. Next, Dad's sister Cathy opened her home, offering David a place to stay in Fort Worth. Another of Dad's sisters offered to enroll him in a drug rehabilitation facility in Winnsboro, Texas, about a two and a half hour car ride from Fort Worth and run by the Assembly of God ministries.

When he agreed, Mom needed to pick up some things of David's that were still at Dad's apartment to send to him. She also needed money for bills. She was uncomfortable going alone so she asked me to drive her. I had never been to Dad's apartment and didn't want to see him, but I knew I needed to be there with Mom in case trouble started.

His apartment was on the first floor of a run-down complex on a busy roadway in a seedy part of town. We rang the doorbell and waited for Dad to let us in. He greeted Mom casually and looked genuinely happy to see me. He gave me a hug and waved me in. While he and Mom signed back and forth, I remained by the front door and looked around. The apartment was dingy. It was odd seeing pieces of our furniture from the trailer at Boars Head, like the matching maroon hide-a-bed sofa to the one Mom and I had at our place. The cheap plastic blinds had clearly come with the apartment and the worn acrylic shag carpeting showed years of wear and tear. A layer of dust covered the hodgepodge of knickknacks.

Dad noticed me eyeing his things and signed, "B-A-C-H-E-L-O-R P-A-D. H-A-H-A-H-A."

I smiled and he took me by the shoulder and gave me a tour of his place. "This knife is from World War II. It used to belong to a German soldier. See the swastika? That means Nazi."

He pointed to a black-and-white framed photo of a man pinning an award on a soldier. "That's President Truman and that's my uncle—your great-uncle, John R. Crews—getting the Congressional Medal of Honor, the highest, best award a soldier can receive."

Mom was growing impatient with the wait. Dad had been doing odd jobs and was still collecting disability checks, but he still hadn't given her the money she was expecting. She wanted to leave and when she demanded that he write a check, they started bickering.

Unlike their confrontation weeks earlier, we weren't trapped in our own apartment. We didn't have to be there. My instinct was to flee. "Mom, let's just leave!" I shouted. "Stop arguing, please!"

Mom's hands were in a flurry of angry signs and Dad kept grabbing at them to stop her from signing, making her angrier.

"Please, Mom, let's go!"

She finally listened to me and gave a grand flip of her open palm and charged toward the front door. Dad was enraged that she had picked this fight and was not going to stick around to finish it. I flew out the front door with Mom closely behind me. "Go, go, go, go!" Mom screamed as Dad followed us to the parking lot.

Mom and I jumped into our car and locked our doors just as Dad grabbed at my handle on the driver's side. I started the car and threw it into reverse. Angry that we were getting away, Dad balled up his fist and slammed it into my window. The sight of his fist barreling toward my face momentarily stunned me. The punch was deafening, but to my amazement, the window didn't shatter.

My tires squealed out of the parking spot and I saw Dad running toward his own car. Worried that he would chase us back to our new apartment, I slammed the gas pedal and sped through the parking lot.

"Kambri! My God, slow down!"

"Leave me alone." I wasn't listening to her. My flight instinct was in overdrive. Without looking for traffic, I sped across four lanes of two-way traffic. Cars honked and swerved and tires squealed as drivers slammed on their brakes to avoid us.

"Kambri, you're gonna get us killed!"

"Shut up!" I screeched.

Mom held her breath as she clenched her seat. I didn't know where to go and knew I needed to calm down. I had nearly killed us in my frantic getaway. I parked the car behind a Dumpster and caught my breath. My hands trembled as irate thoughts swirled through my mind. Why did Mom go over to my father's in the first place? Why couldn't she sense when it was time to leave? And how could Dad throw a punch at me, even if there was a pane of thick glass between us?

Back at the apartment, my heart was still racing when the phone rang. I answered with a terse greeting. It was Steve calling. We'd been dating a few weeks and I really liked him. Sweet and sensitive as he was, though, I couldn't imagine putting him in the position to have a showdown with Dad. That would have been the last thing I would want kids at school to hear about. I wanted to protect him from this nightmare and myself from the embarrassment.

"Don't call me anymore," I said, curtly.

"Why? What did I do wrong?" Steve was mystified. He hadn't done anything. In fact, we were having the time of our lives. I quickly pushed away any empathy.

"You didn't do anything; just leave me alone," I snapped.

Steve was heartbroken and confused. He began crying and wailed, "Why won't you talk to me? Why are you being this way? Please just give me a chance."

I couldn't tell him the truth. "Just leave me alone!" I shouted and slammed the phone back in its cradle.

The next day after rehearsal, I came outside to meet Mom for a ride home, but saw Rob's white Trans Am idling. He hung his arm out the window with a cigarette dangling between his fingers.

"Your mom asked me to come get you." He grinned.

I raced out to greet him and slid back into the passenger seat. As much as I liked Steve, I was more comfortable with Rob. Not only was he older, but he already knew about Dad and wasn't afraid. He would be there to protect me.

I was back with Rob for only a week when Mom dropped another bombshell: "We're going to be evicted."

"Evicted? Why?"

"Excessive noise disturbance. Come on and help me pack."

My blood boiled. I had screamed and begged for help the night my father smashed our porch light, punched holes in the walls, and broke down our front door. Not only had the neighbors heard my cries for help and chosen to ignore me, but they had *complained*?

Defeated, I packed up my room for another move. I was loading up boxes of books and letters when I came across a pile of college brochures and scholarship applications. Before August 15, I had planned on attending a university to major in aeronautical engineering as homage to Mom, admiring her for her work with helicopters. Aeronautical engineering could be my backup plan in case my acting career didn't pan out. The paperwork had been overwhelming and asked detailed questions that I didn't know how to answer, like what my parents' income was. On the rare occasions Mom inquired about the process, I brushed her off. She never went to college, so she wouldn't know how to fill out the forms any more than I would. "I'm working on them," I answered and that was that. They remained incomplete.

Who am I kidding? I angrily hurled the blank applications in the trash and emptied the rest of my room. I felt hopeless and just gave up. I should have asked for help, but I didn't know how.

Mom found a two-bedroom, two-story townhouse and applied for a lease. Before the landlord would rent to us, he checked our references and found out from our previous landlord about all the trouble David and Dad had caused. But he was sympathetic and agreed to rent to us on the condition that we not disclose our new address to either of them. Mom and I made a pact not to give our address or phone number to anyone, especially now that Dad was out of jail and free to stalk us.

Our new townhouse was in a commercial part of town with at least six auto dealerships within walking distance. On the bright side, it was just a few hundred yards from Malibu, which made it easy for me to work more shifts and hitch rides from co-workers or, in a pinch, walk home along the highway.

Since Rob stayed over on his nights off, Mom gave me the master bedroom and the king-sized bed she had once shared with Dad. But most nights Rob was required to stay in the barracks. He had requested approval to live off base, but the wait list for housing pay was long.

"The only way around it is if you get married," Rob told me.

"Then what happens?"

"You get to move, but then they also give you housing money *and* dependent pay."

"Really? They *pay* you to be married?"

It sounded too good to be true.

"Why don't you wait until after you graduate from high school?" Mom asked when I approached her for permission to marry Rob. She and I were seated at a small table given to her by a friend in our new apartment building. Our old dining table was too big for the new place.

"That's only a few months from now. The navy will pay Rob more if he's married, and he'll get to move off base, which means they'll pay us housing money, too. We're gonna get married anyway but this way we can get extra money while we live here and save for dishes and a deposit and stuff."

It didn't take much persuasion for her to agree. Mom had begun to rebuild her shattered life now that she was free from the stress of living in fear. David was being taken care of. Her divorce was finalized and she filed for individual Chapter 13 bankruptcy, working out payment plans with the IRS and other creditors. Whatever Dad did to pay his half was his business; she was moving onward and upward. She was even dating again. So when I—her only responsibility other than to herself—offered her a "get out of jail free" card, she took it.

Rob and I selected wedding rings at a jewelry store in North East Mall. Until our planned wedding day, I kept the band hidden in the antique metal pitcher where Mom and Dad used to stash the spare key to their bedroom. In my excitement, I shared the secret with Charity one day after play rehearsals. Too eager to wait till the official date, I wore the ring to school, which confirmed the gossip. It wasn't long before I was questioned by one of my teachers.

As I took my seat in English class, my teacher said, "I heard a rumor, Kambri." I could sense by the concerned look on her face that I was not going to like this conversation.

"Oh really?" I feigned ignorance. "What's the rumor?"

"A little bird told me that you got married."

"Really?" I laughed.

"Is that true? Did you get married?"

"No, I just got engaged, that's all. If I did, whose business is it anyway?" I smiled and took my seat in class.

While people in my family had rallied around to help David, no one had reached out to see if I needed help—not a phone call, a letter, an offer for counseling or assistance with the college application process, nothing. I was the forgotten child. By all outward appearances, I seemed fine. I was a straight-A student, thriving at school activities and holding down a full-time job. If my own relatives didn't worry about me, why would a teacher care if I got married? Besides, my friend Charity hadn't believed me when I told her about what Dad had done. If anyone had thought I was going to get married they would have tried to talk me out of it, and then what? I had missed the window for applying to college in the fall, and even if I hadn't, how would I pay for it? Every financial aid document asked about my parents' income, which overwhelmed me. Was I supposed to count on Dad? I hadn't seen him since I saw him jumping into his car as Mom and I sped away and he disappeared in my rearview mirror.

Rob was going to take care of me and the United States Navy was going to pay him to do it.

On a cold Friday the thirteenth, in January, between school and rehearsal for *The Importance of Being Earnest,* Mom drove Rob and me to a courthouse in Fort Worth. I was gussied up in a pink long-sleeved knit dress I had worn during my senior picture shoot. I figured those could double as wedding pictures. Mom surprised me with a little white rosebud with a pink ribbon that matched my dress. The ceremony took place in a courtroom. Mom served as a witness and signed the marriage license since I, at seventeen years old, was still under the age of legal consent. As the judge gave a quick sermon about the sanctity of marriage, Mom shed a few tears and giggled at herself for being so weepy.

After a couple of quick "I do"s, a judge declared me a navy wife. Four months later I graduated from high school. My knight had rescued me and we drove off in his white Trans Am.

NEW YORK CITY

2002–2008

Chapter Sixteen

OVERBOARD

It was the spring of 2002, and I was sound asleep in my apartment when my telephone rang. My digital clock glowed 3:12 A.M.

"Hello?" I weakly answered, confused and groggy.

"Hi," said a woman with a thick southern accent and gravelly smoker's voice. "Issh thisssh Kayme-bree?"

"Yes," I croaked.

"Hi, you don't know me but my name is Helen and I'm here with your daddy," she continued with deliberate formality, unaware I'd spoken to new lady friends calling on behalf of my father dozens of times over the years. Since I didn't have a TTY, I received these early morning phone calls from various drunken women interpreting for Dad. As was usually the case, I heard his voice in the background.

I could tell Helen was signing something to him to let him know I had answered, because she whispered each word and letter, a common habit for people not skilled in ASL.

"K-A-M-B-R-I O-N telephone."

Dad grabbed the receiver and cooed into the mouthpiece, "Kipree, luh yooo. Mih yoo, Kipree. Luh yooo."

His chatter was followed by the muffled sounds of my father and the woman signing and handling the receiver before she finally slurred, "He saysshh he loves and missshhes yew."

"Okay, tell him I love him, too, but it's three in the morning and I have to go to work in a few hours."

More whispers as Helen relayed my words to my father. "It's only 'bout two o'clock here. He forgot you're in New York City."

It was true. I was in New York City. Alone.

When a seventeen-year-old gets married nobody expects it to last, but Rob and I gave it a decent try. After our courthouse ceremony, we continued living with Mom in her apartment to save money while I finished high school. When my senior prom rolled around, I begged Rob to go with me and let me use some of our savings to buy a gown. I'd been nominated for "Most Talented" senior, after all, and I had to be there to accept the trophy if I won. Needing everything from a microwave and dishes to toothpaste and toilet paper, we had no business spending money on a prom.

"Please?" I pleaded. "Prom's only a few days away. I have to get a dress now before they're all gone!"

After everything I had been through, Rob didn't have the heart to tell me we couldn't afford to go. He drove me from boutique to boutique in search of the perfect gown. When I finally found the one I simply couldn't live without, Rob balked. At almost four hundred dollars, the purple sequin dress, more suited for a drag queen than a prom queen, was more than one month's rent on the apartment we were going to lease. I grew indignant at his hesitation. Most of our meager savings came from the money I'd collected as congratulations on my upcoming graduation. Technically, it was my money, and the dress was so glitzy, I knew I'd outshine my peers.

I offered a compromise. "I'll sell it at a consignment shop and get most of the money back."

"Okay, but you promise me you will sell it."

I squealed with joy and threw my arms around his neck. "I promise, I promise, I promise. Thank you!"

Our money blown for the dress, Rob wore his dress blues instead of a tuxedo. We didn't quite match but Mom assured me that a grown man in uniform would look better than any teenage boy in a rent-a-tux. At twenty-three years old, he was far more mature than any of the other girls' dates.

That purple explosion of satin, taffeta, and sequins hangs in my bedroom closet to this day. It rests in peace next to my high school letterman jacket and dozens of cocktail dresses I've amassed over the years.

Shortly after the prom, I graduated from high school forty-sixth out of nearly seven hundred students. The ceremony was held in the same convention center where I had seen Ozzy Osbourne, AC/DC, and Metallica. This time I was the one onstage as Mom and Rob sat in the stands with Mom's parents, who had driven my brother to Fort Worth for the occasion.

David was unnaturally subdued, almost comatose. Where was the rabid dog I had come to know as my brother? I didn't know what they were doing at the Jesus detox camp but I preferred him this way. Dad wasn't there. In fact, he didn't know about the ceremony because I didn't send him an invitation. I predicted that David would be a handful enough. As I glided across the stage to receive my diploma, I was announced, "Kambri Dee Crews, summa cum laude."

"Summa!" David bellowed from the stands. "Summa girl!"

He was prouder than any father would have been. I smiled at my brother's joy before I sulked to myself. *Summa, pfft. What's that gonna get me?*

After Rob was honorably discharged from the navy in March 1991, we relocated to his hometown of Akron, Ohio. Since the Internet wasn't around, my taking his last name and moving cross-country served as a homespun Witness Protection Program. Like the time we moved from Boars Head to Fort Worth, I had another shot at reinventing myself. This time I aimed for normalcy with Rob and his close-knit family.

No longer a dashing sailor in crisp navy whites, Rob took a job cleaning carpets. As I predicted, my diploma with highest honors was worthless for landing anything other than menial jobs, so I found part-time work as a bank teller. I told my co-workers, all middle-aged women with children, that I was a year older than I really was so they wouldn't figure out I was married before the legal age of consent. That would prompt unwanted questions.

While my friends were attending college and pursuing their dreams, I was a cashier at a bank. The best I could hope for was a full-time assignment as a real teller instead of working the drive-through. Every waking moment was spent regretting what could have been. I dwelled on an elaborate fantasy life I dreamed up for my high school classmates. They must be in dorms, performing in university theater productions, rushing sororities, and going to frat parties. While they were living the American dream, I was dealing with senior citizens who smelled of mothballs and didn't trust those newfangled whatchamacallits. "ATM machines," I'd grumble. "They're as dependable as I am."

In all the years on Boars Head, Mom and Dad had prided themselves on not taking handouts when money was tight. They had taught me to endure and I suffered in silence, berating myself over my lost potential. My start-up life was adequate but far short of my dream. I didn't know where to seek out help. The only scholarship organization I'd ever heard of was the United Negro College Fund and I didn't qualify.

While Rob scoured the classifieds looking for a more stable, better-paying job, he came across an ad for "The Academy of

Court Reporting and Paralegal Studies." I had never shown any interest in the law, but it sounded interesting and, more important, it offered a program that I could complete in less than two years. The name was clumsy, but it was an accredited school. The academy offered night classes, cut out the superfluous required electives that add to tuition cost, and used practicing attorneys to serve as teachers. As an added bonus, the bank reimbursed me for selective books and courses depending on my grades. The goal of making straight A's finally had cash incentive, so I buried my nose in my studies.

Rob began driving an eighteen-wheeler and while the pay was better and the work steady, it meant he was rarely home. I juggled work, classes, and homework while taking care of our one-bedroom rental home in Rob's absence. Days blurred together, punctuated only by holidays, which were spent with Rob's family, since mine had splintered. The grueling two-year-long schedule was like counting grains of sand on a beach. It was overwhelming and tedious, but I finished, graduating with an associate's degree as a paralegal. It was no Ivy League diploma, but it meant I no longer had to skip the education section in employment applications, which had always felt like a twist of the knife.

My love of theater hadn't faded; it had merely taken a backseat to my adult responsibilities. The next week, certificate in hand and school loans abated for six months, I scoured the *Akron Beacon Journal* for audition notices. A listing for Weathervane Playhouse's production of *Noises Off!* caught my eye and reignited my dream of working in showbiz. I was used to spending every waking hour studying so I poured that effort into preparing for the tryout. It paid off when I was cast in the role of the young ingénue Brooke Ashton, who ran around in lingerie for the entirety of the play.

One taste of the stage was all it took. I was hooked. I quit smoking again (and for the final time), was cast in *A Midsummer Night's Dream,* volunteered backstage for *Annie,* and even won an acting award for my portrayal in *Noises Off!* After years of being chained to work and school with no time for socializing, I was immersed in a new circle of friends who shared my love of the arts. My independence, coupled with Rob's long absences from home, spelled the end of our lackluster six-year marriage. We rarely saw each other and when we did, we had nothing to say. We were roommates, plain and simple, and misery oozed from my every pore.

Rob had rescued me. He had been a life preserver when my family's ship was sinking and he had taken me in as a refugee. I owed him my life. I couldn't leave him. Feeling trapped, I brooded and nitpicked until Rob finally grew fed up with my complaining and asked the question I had been waiting for: "Do you think we should get a divorce?"

An audible sigh of relief escaped me. "Yes."

After six years together, I left him the house and everything in it. I hadn't wanted any of that stuff anyway. I wanted a clean slate. I had childhood dreams to reclaim.

Since my graduation from high school, Mom, Dad, David, and I had become independent satellites orbiting around the black hole that had once been our familial universe. With each of us living in a different state—me in Ohio, Mom in Texas, David in

Indiana, and Dad in Oklahoma—our paths rarely crossed one another's. Each person did the exact same thing I did, in his own unique way: built a new life far away from what had been "home." As we had done on Boars Head, where we had scorched the earth, we were waiting to see what grew.

I was disappointed when Mom remarried soon after her divorce from Dad—one year after I was betrothed to Rob at the courthouse. I felt let down. I had hoped that my marrying Rob and leaving home would have freed her up to finally take care of herself. But Mom was really happy to have someone new in her life. She met her new husband while out dancing with friends three months after her divorce from my father was final. He didn't smoke or do drugs and rarely drank, which made him a keeper in her eyes.

Together they bought a large three-bedroom, two-story home in the southwestern suburbs of Fort Worth. It was bigger and nicer than any home we had dreamed of back in Montgomery. She also distanced herself from the Deaf community, possibly out of embarrassment or to avoid running into Dad. Besides, her new husband didn't know ASL, so my mother would have to serve as his personal interpreter when they attended social events at the Deaf club rather than relax and enjoy time with friends. Instead Mom preferred spending her free time on adventurous road trips with her husband in a travel trailer. Over the years they would explore forty-eight of the fifty United States. She also spent most holidays visiting with his family, who all lived much closer than our own. But what was "our own" family anymore, really?

Since rehabilitating himself, David had replaced his drug habit with a feverish addiction to Jesus Christ. He proselytized to anyone and became a counselor at Teen Challenge, the facility that helped him get clean. Eventually he settled in Indiana and his preaching tapered to a modest level where I wasn't afraid to sneeze in his presence, lest I be barraged with a slew of scriptures.

Defeating his addictions is something he is proud of. He even spoke at churches testifying about what God's mercy had done for him. Now he had earned his GED, was attending college, and worked with troubled boys who were like he had once been as a youth.

He hadn't witnessed the violent end of our parents' marriage. He couldn't understand why I was reluctant to write or visit Dad. "He misses you," David told me time and time again. "Why won't you talk to him?"

I tried to tell him about what our father had done, but he refused to listen. He acted just like Mom did when it came to my father's misdeeds: He pretended it never happened. "I don't wanna hear it, Kambri," he'd say as he walked away.

Killing his demons had been battle enough. David didn't seem to want to acknowledge that our dad was far from perfect. He had idolized our father like I had, maybe even more. He was a boy, after all, and had been Dad's sidekick. He had triumphed over his demons and was not looking back. I respected his decision. I also feared the truth might have made him relapse, so I dropped the matter.

My relationship with my dad was complicated. While my life had been tough at times, it was generally good, wasn't it? Everyone had done the best they could under the circumstances. I always had a roof over my head, even if it was made of sheet metal. It's not like my parents *wanted* their lives to turn out this way. What kind of bitter, unforgiving daughter was I? Wasn't it better for me to have a cordial relationship with him than hold a grudge? Dad had never intended to hurt me anyway; he barely raised a finger to me my whole life. I was the collateral damage in his fallout with Mom.

Time and distance helped me forget the wounds. Besides, there was one law Dad couldn't escape: Murphy's. He'd send me letters with news consisting of another broken-down vehicle, car wreck, failed relationship, and just overall bad luck. Dad shrugged off the misfortunes and said if it had tits or tires it was bound to cause him trouble.

His money woes and lack of steady work forced him to live on his parents' farm in Oklahoma in a cast-off dilapidated and moldy Airstream trailer. It was decorated with stolen road signs and had a shower so small he had to bend at the knees to fit in it. We kept our relationship superficial through sporadic phone calls from his drunken lady friends and a handful of brief face-to-face visits.

If Mom or David or the state of Texas didn't condemn him, why should I?

After six years of marriage, I said goodbye to Rob and I was free. Sort of. I had worked my way up the corporate ladder. Quickly rising through the ranks at the bank, I went from being a teller to a legal secretary to a paralegal. The board of directors appointed me an officer, then, two years later, an assistant vice president of the Credit Quality Department, where I dealt with delinquent commercial loans valued over fifty thousand dollars.

Once I was divorced I wanted to see the world. Here I was, twenty-six years old, still working at the bank and demanding money from people who were more than double my age. I loathed bill collectors. They had stripped me of my trailer that was nothing more than scrap metal to them, but a world to me.

Oh, sure, I wasn't collecting against the average mom-and-pop debtor; they were usually distinguished middle-aged men on entrepreneurial missions building their own businesses, securing patents for environmentally safe packaging, or restoring historical landmarks. They had one thing in common: They had defaulted on large commercial loans. Sometimes I seized their personal assets to offset their business debt. I repossessed yachts and even helped uncover a stash of more than twenty thousand dollars in cash stuffed into the door panels of a DeLorean. But these high-flying debtors were still people. They had hopes and dreams not unlike my own father's plans for Boars Head. I rebuilt their loans with payment plans so lenient they had no excuse not to pay on time, and pay on time they did. I watched over them like they were books in my long-forgotten library. Each was worth putting back on track instead of tossing into the trash pile to be set ablaze.

I didn't want to slave away another day behind a desk. I confided my dissatisfaction in a journal. "Being young is feeling the pull of unlimited possibility. As long as there are books unread, seas uncharted, mountains unscaled, lands untouched, there remains endless opportunity. Therein lies the secret of youth. I will drink from her fountain."

I just needed a shove off the dock.

Events in my life just seemed to happen *to me*. Now, however, I wanted to make life *happen*. I composed a list of things to do before I died. Included were grand plans of scaling mountainsides and sailing the seven seas, along with dozens of mundane things I never tried, like riding a train or eating sushi.

I wrote letters to Dad highlighting efforts to cross things off that list. Having my father as my pen pal helped us reconnect. I got to know him and vice versa. I wrote about my escapades attending parties and sporting events, foreign travels to Mexico and the Virgin Islands, and aversion to being tied down to a job or relationship. "You are just like your daddy," he wrote back. I learned I had a lot more in common with Dad than I had realized. Both our childhoods had been spent in a kind of prison: his in the form of a dorm at deaf school; me isolated in the woods on Boars Head. We both had a "wild and free" spirit and deep wanderlust.

Dad's letters made it seem that life was good. He may not have been walking the straight and narrow, but he didn't seem to be the dangerous man I had seen in our apartment some years before. Oh, sure, now and again his exploits included a run-in with the law, like the time he took a road trip to Houston and his truck broke down, forcing him to ride a Greyhound bus back to Dallas. On the way home, he snuck a few puffs on a cigarette in the restroom. When the bus made a pit stop, cops were waiting to arrest him for smoking. Dad spent twenty-four hours in jail before they let him go, which he laughed off as part of life's adventure.

Growing up, he had lived with strict rules governing his day-to-day activities at Deaf school. As an adult, he was rid of housemothers, cherry tree switches, and razor straps and wanted the spontaneity that freedom granted. He was living by the principle that it was easier to beg for forgiveness than ask for permission. Walking that fine line and taking risks was part of his charm. I had been such a serious student and hard worker that I missed out on a lot of fun. I crack a smile whenever I think of him "singing" and writhing around on the stage as Elvis. His antics were the most memorable moments of those theater trips. Maybe I could learn a thing or two from Dad's impetuous ways. Focusing on his charming side allowed me to minimize his faults.

While I was antsy in Ohio and searching for a way out, Dad married an older woman nicknamed JB. She worked for a bail bonds company and possessed the traits my father loved: big breasts and long fingernails that she accentuated with tight clothes and lots of jewelry. I only met her once during their three-odd-year union. Like most events in my father's life, I never knew the exact details of his relationship. I discovered they divorced when I received a letter from Dad. JB had shot a pistol at him during an argument. He claimed she was schizophrenic and, as luck would have it, a bad aim. Her shot barely missed, whizzing by his ear. Corresponding in longhand lends itself to truncated reports and I was left wondering what he was leaving out. Namely, *why* would she shoot at him? Whatever the facts were, I never knew. His letter moved on to more routine topics like car troubles, construction projects, and travel plans, as if dodging a bullet was no more or less interesting than the weather.

After almost two years of complaining that Bowlegs, Oklahoma, was a dead town, Dad was done with his childhood home and moved back to Texas. He was holed up in a room at Motel 183, a dingy inn that let him pay by the week, which he paid for using his disability benefits. It was located in the suburbs of Fort

Worth, not far from where we'd lived on Grove Street and Weyland Drive. There he became a regular at dive bars. During a trip back to Texas for my twenty-year high school reunion, I drove to his favorite haunt, called the Cobra Club. I thought I'd slip in, have an ice-cold beer, and maybe even meet someone who knew Dad from his days in the Free World. The place was a sleazy dump with a handwritten sign taped to the door that warned "Member's Only!!!" I was too afraid to go in, sure that the "members" were carrying weapons they were not afraid to use.

Dad embraced the swinging bachelor lifestyle, but from reading his letters it seemed he was unlucky in love. Years of late nights, excessive drinking and drug use, and a two-pack-a-day smoking habit were stealing his good looks quickly. His itinerant ways and lack of steady work made it that much harder for him to snag a woman and, if he did, it never lasted for long. He blew through a few failed romances in quick succession, one with a woman he said looked like Xena, the Warrior Princess. "She has an inseam of thirty-six inches as long as me W-O-W!" But Xena didn't last after Dad "found out she had too many men in seven days." Dad didn't say how many was too many. No rest for the wicked, however, because in the same letter he wrote about his latest love, a woman he described as a never-married, big-boned forty-five-year-old with dirty blond hair and bright blue eyes. After they broke up, Dad chalked it up to her jealousy and wanting him to pay her bills.

Then he met Helen.

Dad gushed about Helen, calling her kind and sweet. They had been dating for a few months and decided to move in together into a cheap one-bedroom apartment. Now that he was settling down, he ached to be a family again. Every letter asked when I would visit them in Texas or what my holiday plans were, and had him wishing I lived closer so we could visit more, "as much as once monthly."

It had been more than twelve years since Mom and Dad's divorce, and I was thankful to be hundreds of miles away. I had been so studious and dependable, growing up too fast, handling adult tasks for my deaf family, being married so young. Now I just wanted to keep it light, to have *fun*, finally.

While I still worked at the bank during the day, I ensconced myself in a frivolous life at night. I took side jobs in event marketing. Sometimes I was a model, a title that made me uncomfortable. Others complimented me on my beauty, but I still saw myself as an ugly, freckled tomboy. I wanted to be respected for my intelligence, perhaps overly sensitive that I had been denied my dream of a college degree.

I preferred being in charge of an event, hiring the models, and organizing the affair. We promoted everything from Pepsi and Lipton Iced Tea to Winston and Camel cigarettes to liquor like Stolichnaya vodka and Jose Cuervo tequila. Our on-site projects took us to fabulous locations. One weekend, I'd be in the Cleveland Indians dugout during a home game, another I'd be in a race car at a NASCAR tour stop, yet another I'd be in a private jet returning home from the Kentucky Derby. Knowing how much Dad and Helen liked to drink and smoke, I sent them care packages of free swag like T-shirts, hats, pens, and photos from the events.

In just a few years, I was recruited for better-paying banking jobs that moved me from Akron to Columbus, and then Cincinnati. I was making enough money to rent a penthouse apartment with a rooftop pool overlooking the Ohio River and Paul Brown Stadium, home of the Cincinnati Bengals, and drive a VW Cabrio convertible. To some, it may seem extravagant, but I was careful to live within my means. I carried little to no debt and paid cash for everything I could. I even had a savings account and a 401(k).

Then Dad dropped a bombshell. Helen was pregnant, due on Christmas Day. "Are you in shock?" he asked in his letter. "We have a baby because I can't wait for you and David to make me a grandpa."

My reactive emotion was jealousy. When Mom remarried so soon after her divorce to Dad, I felt ditched. She had rebuilt a new life with a different family. Dad having a baby with Helen meant he would do the same. Even though I wanted my distance, I wondered where my brother and I would belong.

Soon jealousy was replaced with fear for the future of my unborn sibling. Dad had no business bringing a kid into the world. I had a fleeting fantasy that social workers would rescue the infant and give me custody. Not long after Dad broke the news, I received a letter from Helen.

Dear Kambri,

Things have been a little crazy around here and I have been real bad about getting in touch with people, but more on that later. . . .

On the 29th I started bleeding & on the 30th I lost our baby. Oh, by the way, if he doesn't kill me (just kidding), we want to get married. We hope you will be able to be there.

We love you.

I felt sad for Helen and worried about her health. I knew her loss was devastating, but I still couldn't help but be relieved. Now things could get back to usual, with occasional inebriated phone calls or letters filled with their latest hardship.

In the summer of 2000, I was hired as a marketer for Jose Cuervo for a promotional tour that was stopping in Cincinnati. There I met a man from New York who was also on the tour. He sensed I was ready for a change and raved to me about opportunities in New York City, where he lived. I had been to Manhattan a few times with friends of mine from the theater. We'd rent a van, share a hotel room in the theater district, and attend as many as five plays in four days, making the most of our visit. The Broadway excursions inspired me, but New York was extremely expensive.

For the first time, especially with my friend's encouragement, I considered my East Coast options. I was bored with Ohio and tired of banking. I had even begun the application process to join the Peace Corps. My assignment was to be in the Fiji Islands to teach business management, but the United States was forced to scuttle the project after an unexpected coup d'état. My friend assured me that I would be able to find work in New York and I gave my resignation to the bank via email, packed up my apartment, broke my lease, and made my big move, filling my Cabrio with my belongings and unloading it at my new two-bedroom shared apartment in Queens.

I was filled with anxiety about moving without job security, after my childhood of deprivation. I quickly found work as a legal assistant to ease my fear. My new office was posh, and located in the British Empire Building in Rockefeller Center. Every day I walked through the throngs of tourists in Times Square, passed the *Today* show, 30 Rock, St. Patrick's Cathedral, and other iconic sites that I had visited as a tourist with my Ohio theater friends.

I missed acting, but I still worked nights and weekends in event marketing and promotions. I also worked as a party wrangler at private events, in charge of making sure people were dancing, interacting with one another, and having fun. Just three weeks after relocating, I worked at a bar mitzvah held at the posh Pierre hotel, on Fifth Avenue overlooking Central Park. The decadent, multimillion-dollar bash featured performances by Mandy Moore, Jessica Simpson, the Village People, and Barry White and his entire orchestra. It also landed the father of the bar mitzvah boy in the *New York Post*'s Page Six a few years later when it was revealed that the party was paid for with embezzled funds.

I was approaching my one-year anniversary of living in New York City when, on September 11, 2001, terrorists flew planes into the twin towers of the World Trade Center. Some new residents were spooked by the calculated evil attack and fled to the perceived safety of their hometowns. My reaction was the opposite. I dug in my heels. I had finally found a place where I belonged and I was staying.

I set forth to work harder, faster, longer than anyone else so I could make it. I wasn't quite sure what that meant, but I wasn't going to let the grass grow under my feet mulling it over. I had broken free and was carving out a life for myself. I went out to events every night, and watched the latest plays both off and on Broadway.

After a year of living in the city, I started my own party production business, and handed out my card to hundreds of people in hopes something would stick. It was starting to pay off, too. Over the years I would attend red carpet parties, premieres, and other only-in-my-wildest-dreams events where I would often find myself in the ladies' room marveling at my reflection in the mirror. I'd smile broadly, shake my head, and say aloud without caring who might hear me, "Can you believe this is your life?"

Many times, I didn't believe it. The juxtaposition from my old life to this fantasy I was leading filled me with an intoxicating sense of relief. I had escaped from Dad's downward spiral and violent outbursts, the scariness of David's self-destruction, and Mom's devastation at her son's disease of addiction and the obliteration of her marriage. I had run away and kept running until finally finding a place that I could call home. I felt for the first time that maybe, just *maybe*, I'd never be that girl again. The one who worried that one day she would wake up and find herself back in a tin shed.

I had just celebrated my thirty-first birthday when, on a hot summer night in June 2002, I found myself at an underground comedy show at Don't Tell Mama. Rumor had it that Mark Cuban, a famous billionaire who often invested in new business enterprises, would be present.

"He's a *bil*lionaire?" I asked, doubting the plausibility that anyone so well-to-do would be caught dead in that seedy little cabaret. In the off chance the buzz was true, my business partners and I wrote a note about an entrepreneurial venture that might hold special interest for him. Lo and behold, Mark was in the audience. My friends and I strode up to him after the show and introduced ourselves. Thinking that this encounter on the streets marked our only chance to make conversation, I gave him the letter.

To my horror, he ripped it open and read it right there on the sidewalk in front of the performers from the show. Part of me wanted to tear off running for the subway, but everyone else stood by, lingering expectantly. He shoved the note in his pocket, grinned at all of us—an eclectic group of comedy nerds—gathered in front of the nightclub, and said, "Let's go grab a drink!"

Many hours and many more beers, bottles of champagne, and shots of tequila later, and the night became a blur. As we walked into one nightclub, Mark sailed past the maître d' without checking in.

"You're not allowed to do that," I said playfully.

He patted my hand with a sly grin and whispered in my ear, "Kambri, when you live in my world, you can do *anything* you want."

I could get used to a world like his.

That same night, 1,542 miles away, Dad was stabbing Helen.

I stumbled out of the dark bar and blinked my eyes at the bright lights of Times Square. Was that the sun rising? Mark piled the holdouts of the group into the back of his limo. "Come on, where you wanna go now?"

"Man, some of us have to work!" I raised my arm in the air to hail a cab to take me home. The impromptu night out with a famous billionaire had proven memorable and, who knew, maybe it would lead to bigger things.

I had become used to this thrilling, opportunity-filled, unpredictable life I was living in New York City. The brush with fame would make for an interesting blog entry or just an anecdote I told my friends. Meanwhile, I had a real fish to fry. In a matter of hours, I was flying to Marina Cay, a five-acre island in the British Virgin Islands dubbed "the Cuervo Nation," a playground for the rich and famous, where I was going to orchestrate more all-expenses-paid depravity.

As part of their promotional marketing plan, Jose Cuervo hired "brand ambassadors" to spread the good word of all things tequila. In Cincinnati, I had toured bars in a double-decker bus with a full bar and DJ booth. My friend was one of the select few sent to live on the island several weeks each year and host small groups of contest winners. The tour was over but since I had been a brand ambassador, I was able to travel to the British Virgin Islands as an unofficial co-host. The company paid my way to essentially eat, drink, and be merry.

John Hodgman once told a story on *This American Life* about meeting another host of the Cuervo Nation, and described him as a person "whose job it is to force us to interact . . . because apparently this is something we've forgotten how to do. A job that seems so intuitive and skill-free that you initially think anyone can do it. It's only when you are trying and failing to get someone to drink a shot of tequila off your head that you realize how hard it is to be 'Cuervo Man'" (or, in my case, "Cuervo Woman").

Listening to Hodgman's account, I was both proud and grossly embarrassed. I was being paid to party, but it was a gig with no merit, morals, or thought required. It was a lifestyle of debauchery in a bikini doing tequila body shots, dropping poker chips out of my butt crack into a beer stein, and jumping from the upper deck of a boat into a pool of anacondas swimming in the deep blue awaiting discarded burgers and buns and me.

I was tan, young, happy, fearless, and free. Then the phone rang.

"Hey, Kambri, telephone!" the bartender yelled. I sat frozen, confused as to how anyone could track me down. The Cuervo Nation isn't exactly listed in the phone book. It has no air-conditioning, no television, no radio.

The bartender smacked the table a few times and repeated, "Kambri! The telephone, it's for you."

I snapped out of my trance. "Telephone?" I looked at the guests seated around me. Empty bottles and glasses littered the dinner table. "I didn't even know they *had* a telephone here."

I walked to the bar in a surprisingly straight line and took the receiver. "Hello?"

"Hey, Kambri." It was David. I hadn't seen him since he stayed with me in Columbus to ring in the year 1999. With our busy schedules and my abrupt relocation to New York, I couldn't remember the last time we had spoken. I was dumbstruck wondering how he had found me. "How's it going?"

It is strange, in that brief static moment of anticipation when gaining unwanted news, how clear the message is before a word is ever exchanged.

This is about Dad.

"David, I know you didn't track me down just to make small talk."

"Yeah . . ." His voice sounded heavy and tired.

I looked back at the table of prizewinners, their faces red and shiny from our day in the sun. They looked curious and some-what anxious. I interrupted David from saying another word.

"Whatever it is, I don't want to know right now." I spoke delib-erately, cautioning him to not go any further. I didn't want any of the tourists to know something was wrong. "I'm stuck on this island for a few more days and there's nothing I can do or change from here."

I knew when I returned home I would be saddled with the re-sponsibility of dealing with the fallout of whatever had prompted this call. My gut told me that Dad had a more serious run-in with the law, something on par with JB nearly shooting him in the head. Whatever it was, David needed to handle it for now. I was being paid to be the life of the party, and I couldn't fulfill that role if I were drowning in Dad's sorrows.

"Okay, have fun." He was forlorn and added with poignancy, "I love you, Kambri."

"I love you, too."

I climbed out of the vacuum of my thoughts and tried to focus on something else: the reggae music, the pattern of the wood-grain table, and the sounds of waves lapping against the dock. I walked back to the table of the last holdouts of the twelve visiting prizewinners.

"Hey, where's my Cuervo?" I took a swig and added, "Who wants to go for a swim?" I skipped out to the end of the pier, stripped down to my bathing suit, and dove headfirst into the dark water.

The anacondas were waiting.

~

A few days later, after the last ferry of Cuervo prizewinners was shoved off the dock, I hitched a ride in a dinghy to the main island of Tortola and took a taxi into town, where I borrowed a computer from a friendly shopkeeper. Knowing there was some sort of message looming in the universe addressed to me, I scoured the Web not knowing what exactly I was searching for.

Was Dad dead or in the hospital? My leg bounced, and I chewed my fingernails. My father's given name appeared in the *Fort Worth Star-Telegram* with the grim headline "Boyfriend Jailed in Knife Attack." The blood drained from my face. I clicked the link and read the brief report.

> *BEDFORD—A man was arrested on suspicion of stabbing his girlfriend Thursday night. A 45-year-old woman, who suffered cuts to her neck and upper chest, was in critical condition Friday at John Peter Smith Hospital in Fort Worth. Her boyfriend, Theodore Crews, 55, was in Bedford Jail on Friday with bail set at $100,000 on suspicion of attempted murder.*

I thought back to Thursday night. I was partying with a charismatic billionaire in *his* world, while *my* world was falling apart.

My heart sank, but there were no tears. I was stoic and contemplative. My mind didn't race to wonder what happened, why or how. I knew he was capable. It was wishful thinking that what Dad had done to Mom was a fluke. I had pushed aside any worries that his troubles with women were beyond what he described in his letters, choosing to believe that he wasn't dangerous. But I was wrong. The only thing missing was the gruesome details.

When I flew home to New York, I returned to my full-time job at the law office. Arriving at my desk that first day, I acted as though everything were business as usual. Growing up, I was taught to keep quiet about family matters. This was how I was raised, but I was also shell-shocked and the routine kept me from collapsing. Throughout the day, my mind flashed images of a bloody attack on Helen or replayed the scene of Dad attacking Mom. When I slept, my sleep was fitful.

For years after Dad had attacked Mom, I had nightmares of murderous rampages. My dreams were a horror movie, where an unknown villain would stalk and butcher people. I would be the sole survivor, on the run, hiding in terror of being slaughtered. Other times I dreamed I had killed someone years before and hidden the body. Now the cops knew about my dark secret and were following me. I woke up feeling consumed with guilt and fear.

Both nightmares haunted me on a regular basis. It had been thirteen years, ten months, and twenty-six days since Dad had snapped. The repressed trauma was as alive as if my memories had gotten a stiff snort of smelling salts. My subconscious was screaming for help because I seemingly could not.

I was overwhelmed with anxiety and concern for Helen. I needed to know more than what the article in the paper had told me. What exactly had Dad done to Helen and, more important, was she okay? I hoped that finding out the details would allow me to move on. Nervous, I called the Bedford police station and introduced myself.

"Hi, I'm calling about a case I read in the *Star-Telegram*." My voice shook as I gave the officer Dad's name and listened to the click, click, clicks of his keyboard as he brought up the case on his computer.

"Oh, yeah, this one. The officer on scene busted down the door and found him on top of her stabbin' her."

Just like when I interrupted Dad straddling Mom that night.

"So what can I do you for?"

"Um, well." I cleared my throat. "I, uh, what about Helen? Is she okay?"

I rubbed my neck and tried to loosen my shirt, which felt uncomfortably close to my skin.

"What's yer relationshee-ip?"

"Oh, um, well, Theodore . . . ," I said, awkwardly repeating Dad's formal name as it was written in the article. "The man who did it . . . Theodore . . . he's my father."

"I see," he paused, weighing the situation presenting itself to him. "Well, last I heard she was in the hospital and might not make it. She pretty much lost all her blood." He spoke bluntly, clearly someone who had seen more than his fair share of crime scenes and had lost the ability to buffer the brutal truth. "If the officers didn't get there when they did, we'd be lookin' at a murder case."

Unable to muster enough air behind my voice to make a word, I squeaked, "Oh." I rubbed my lips together in a poor attempt to press away the trembling tension that was building up.

"He damn near decapitated her."

The disturbing news surged through me, but the angry tone in the sergeant's voice caught me off guard. *Did he think I was calling to defend my father?* He made me feel as though by being related to Dad, I had helped plunge the knife into Helen's neck. The judgment I perceived in the officer's voice made me want to set him straight. I fought back the swelling emotions. "It wasn't the first time."

"What's that? Yer gonna have to speak up, ma'am."

"He did it before. Back in August 1988 . . . in North Richland Hills. Look it up."

I didn't want my father to slip through the legal system's cracks unpunished. If they knew a case existed with a similar modus operandi, they would realize they were dealing with a repeat offender and sentence him accordingly.

The embedded splinter of anger and betrayal had risen to the surface. Ratting out Dad's past brutality against women to an officer extracted the anger altogether. A sense of clarity and calm blanketed me, soon followed by guilt. I knew Dad would finally be punished, but at what cost? Helen's life was in the balance and I, his own daughter, wanted him to pay not only for what he had done to Helen, but for what he had done to our family.

I wanted justice.

Chapter Seventeen

WITNESS FOR THE PROSECUTION

I entered the office of Greg Mason, the attorney I worked for, just as he yelled into the phone, "Do you see the words 'Charitable Contribution' after my name? Fuck no! Call me when you're ready to negotiate." He brought down the receiver with a satisfying slam.

"Hey, I have two things for you," I said, dropping mail on his desk.

Greg grinned. "I know you do, darling, and they're beautiful."

Greg was an attorney from Brooklyn who, as a partner at the law office where I worked in Rockefeller Center, dealt mostly with high-profile sports figures. His name was engraved on brass plaques in various restaurants. Maître d's knew him by name and for his reputation as a tough customer. As a lawyer, he was known for being hard as nails and, among his past assistants, as virtually impossible to work with. In fact, he hadn't had one stay more than six months before I moved to New York City and got the job.

With his slicked-back hair, custom-tailored suits, and the designer sunglasses he wore indoors and out, rain or shine, Greg was hard to ignore. He reminded me of the Looney Tunes rooster Foghorn Leghorn. When he walked into a room he demanded attention, strutting with his chest puffed out. I loved his twisted sense of humor and impish insistence to not play by anyone's rules. Incorrigible as he might have been, he was equally charming. Essentially, he was a sharper, more successful, and non-imprisoned version of Dad.

I didn't take offense at Greg's temper or inappropriate office banter. After years in the staid banking industry, I had had my fill of sexual harassment seminars and dignified protocol. Working with Greg was delightfully unpredictable, an added bonus to the already thrilling location of our offices in Rockefeller Center. Besides, Greg's demands of me weren't unreasonable: Show up on time, stay at my desk, and answer his phone on the first ring. As long as that was happening, Greg overlooked my use of his time to run my production company.

"Listen," Greg continued. "I need you to find me a hotel in Santa Monica. Yahoo has all kinds of directories and stuff like that."

This was the same man I had instructed on the complexities of copying and pasting text . . . five times.

I smirked at the irony. "Um, yeah, I'm well versed on the Internet, but thanks anyway."

I was still laughing as I reached my desk and saw my phone was ringing. I raced to answer it, singing into the receiver, "Hello, this is Kambri!"

I heard a deep wheezing breath before someone exhaled in a gurgling rasp, "Kambri?" Another hissing sound came before the voice wheezed, "Hi, it's Helen."

I collapsed into my chair.

My body was shaking. I tried to pretend we were old friends catching up and asked warmly, "Hi, Helen, how are you feeling?" *Did my voice betray me and reveal my horror? I hoped not.*

"I'm all right, I guess," she croaked, her Texas drawl unaltered by Dad's knife. "I got to go to therapy all the time, and I still have a lot of surgeries ahead of me." Her speech was labored. She explained the extent of her injuries and after every third word I heard a whistling hiss as she sucked in air.

"Are you going to be okay? Are you still in the hospital?" I asked, wondering how she had gotten my work number.

"I'm so sorry, Kambri."

"Sorry"? Had I heard her right?

"What are you sorry for, Helen?"

Why would she feel the urge to apologize to me, the daughter of the man who had brutally attacked her? "My *God*, Helen, you don't need to apologize. You just take care of yourself."

"But I don't want you to hate me."

"Hate you? How could I hate you?"

"I don't want you to blame me."

"My God, Helen! I wouldn't blame you. Why would I?"

"He's saying it's my fault." Helen started to cry. "I still love him." She choked on her words, the tears making it that much harder for her to speak.

"I do too, but don't worry about him. You should just take care of yourself right now." I sensed that Joan, a secretary who sat within earshot of my desk, was eavesdropping. "Helen," I whispered, fighting back the welling tears, "you focus on getting better."

"My throat hurts, so I can't talk for very long. I'd better go now, but can I call you again?"

"Of course, Helen. Anytime you need to talk, I'm here."

As the receiver returned to its cradle, I let out an uncontrollable, guttural groan. My hands trembled as I sat in a daze.

"Is everything okay?" Joan asked. "Was there an accident?"

"Worse," I said in a barely articulate gasp, before breathing in heavy gulps of air.

Like my recurring nightmares, Helen's voice continued to echo in my head. "I don't want you to blame me." Knowing what Dad had done to Mom there was no way I could fault Helen, but I knew her fear was real. When I was a teenager and newlywed, Dad's family never reached out to me or offered to help me sort through the trauma of seeing him assault my mother.

They had assisted David through his detox and continued to embrace him. Why hadn't they helped me? If I had been a drug-addled lunatic and created problems for everyone, would that have made a difference? Medical diagnoses like post-traumatic stress disorder didn't apply to everyday citizens; it was the stuff of war veterans, not teenage girls. I guessed that because I was a good girl, I was written off as perfectly fine. For a while, I kept in touch via a regular update that I formatted like a newspaper and dubbed "Crews News." I mailed it to relatives on both sides of my family. Dad's kin never wrote back or even acknowledged receipt, so I stopped sending it. Why waste the postage?

Since then, I had rarely been in touch with them. There didn't seem to be any point in trying. I felt Mom and I had been abandoned in our greatest time of need. Their ignoring me wouldn't have stung as much had they not been so active in church. It seemed to me the height of hypocrisy for them to preach the gospel and help random strangers around the world, yet not lift a finger, pick up a phone, or write a letter to their own teenage relative who was in desperate need of family support.

Two months after Dad was jailed, David married a woman he had been dating for some time. They had a small wedding near their home in Indiana. Mom and I attended, but Dad was in custody and couldn't go. Despite our father's recent incarceration, the event was like any ordinary family's celebration. At the reception, David and I shared a dance, laughing as he twirled and dipped me. He had worked so hard to conquer the mistakes of his youth and always seemed so somber. It was nice to see him let loose. The subject of Dad was never mentioned.

Soon after, David shared his momentous news that he and his wife were expecting their first baby. I knew how overwhelmed he was with working full-time and pursuing his master's degree. His new bride was sweet and came from a close family. Her parents were still married and lived down the street from them in a very small, tight-knit community. Now they were experiencing one of life's greatest joys; I didn't want to burden them with Dad's ugly situation.

So, soon after I returned from the Cuervo Nation, I decided to ask Dad's brother and sisters for their assistance in selling his truck and putting his personal belongings into storage. I emailed my uncle and a few aunts and implored, "When my father did this before, you didn't help. Well, I'm asking you to help me now."

I wasn't sure what to expect. I had never been taught to ask for help. Part of me thought they would ignore me again. Instead they rallied and responded immediately with heartfelt sentiment. They were hurting, too, after all. They still loved their brother Teddy. I even received a remorseful email from one of Dad's siblings. "You are right, I didn't help. I blamed your mother and for that, I'm ashamed. Forgive me."

And there it was written. Acknowledgment was all I needed. I no longer wondered if my dad's family spurning Mom and me had been real. She had married and enabled him, and had to live with the consequences. Placing blame on Mom absolved them from admitting their own flesh and blood was capable of such great sin and protected their good name from being soiled. Now, over fourteen years of Dad's troubled life later, it was clear that rebuking the victim had been the easy way.

His family's new responsiveness may have been aided because society's views on domestic violence had substantially changed, too, most notably when Congress passed the Violence Against Women Act (VAWA) in 1994. As Catherine Pierce, acting director of the Justice Department's Office on Violence Against

Women, said on September 15, 2009, "VAWA recognized the devastating consequences that violence has on women, families, and society as a whole. VAWA also acknowledged that violence against women requires specialized responses to address unique barriers that prevent victims from seeking assistance from the justice system."

Since Dad's attack on Mom, laws had been enacted placing stricter punishment on abusers and increasing the amount of support given to victims. High-profile cases like O. J. Simpson's alleged murder of his ex-wife Nicole Brown and his record of abusing her helped bring the issue to the forefront. Seeing rich, beautiful people associated with domestic violence on the nightly news changed the perception of a stereotypical victim or abuser and people were talking about it openly.

The violence against Mom hadn't been her fault; she didn't ask to get choked or to have a knife pulled on her and have her own daughter witness the assault. Mom was a good woman and hadn't done anything to deserve being attacked. No matter what Helen felt she might have done to be worthy of *any* blame, I was not going to allow history to repeat itself: a crime against a woman having no consequence. There would be no burying of heads in the sand this time. There would be no embracing the attacker as if nothing had happened. The facts were undeniable. The only one at fault was Dad, plain and simple.

The autumn air was thick and clouds formed in the night sky poised to burst with rain. I was standing outside Michiko Studios on Forty-sixth Street, missing a rehearsal of an off-Broadway musical I was co-producing. I had just gotten a call from the district attorney in Fort Worth, who had dug up Dad's 1988 conviction for aggravated assault with a deadly weapon against Mom. As the sole witness listed on the police report, she was prepared to call me to testify for the prosecution at Dad's trial. "Well, Ms. Crews, it's either you or your mother. We don't care which one of you it is, but we will subpoena you if it comes down to it."

Everything from fourteen years earlier was abruptly in my life again. I had spent the last decade and a half distancing myself from my family's drama. My hopes of college and an acting career had been dashed back then, and now I felt like my dreams were being threatened again. I was in New York City on the cusp of *something*. I was not going to miss my first real off-Broadway production for their drama. In a panic, I raced downstairs so no one at the rehearsal would overhear me.

When Mom answered her phone she was caught off guard to hear me frantic and gulping back tears. "They want me to testify against Dad."

"What? Testify? Why? What for?"

"For what he did to you," I sobbed. "I'm listed as a witness on the police report so they want me to testify."

"Kambri, calm down and tell me what happened."

I recounted my brief conversation with the DA and how they pulled the old case file. For the first time ever she and I talked about August 15, 1988. Mom had little recollection of that night. I was baffled. How could anyone forget the details of an attack at the hands of her own husband? I presumed that she had moved on in a way that allowed her to wipe clean any remembrance.

For me, the memory was vivid. In the middle of the Manhattan sidewalk I erupted into a flurry of words. I reminded her of the holes in the walls, the hours of interrogation, the choking, the knife to her throat, my frantic 911 calls, and me pleading with Dad to spare her life. As the details emerged, the fog was lifted and she began to remember, piecing together the fragments. We were sobbing hysterically when I noticed a group of fanny-packed tourists headed straight for me. Tears streamed down my cheeks, and I hid behind a street sign pole in a pathetic attempt to avoid eye contact with the ladies, who couldn't help their voyeuristic curiosity.

Baring the resurrected pain left me exposed and outraged, and opened old wounds. "You let me get married in high school and fend for myself. Why didn't it dawn on you that 'Hey, maybe it's illegal for seventeen-year-old girls to get married for a reason? Maybe Kambri deserves to go to college!' Well, you failed me then and I am asking you to not fail me now. Please do *not* make me testify against my own father!"

Mom took a deep breath and sighed. "I'm sorry, Kambri," she said. "I'll make it up to you."

And she did. She called the district attorney and volunteered to go in my place. She would confront her past face-to-face and protect me from having to do the same.

A few weeks passed and I was at my desk at the law office when my phone rang.

"Hi, Kambri," Mom said grimly, her voice trembling. "Twenty years."

I knew Dad would be found guilty. I knew he deserved whatever punishment he got, but, still, the breath was knocked out of me. My head spun.

My daddy is going to spend the next twenty years in jail.

Throughout the trial it was revealed that not only had Dad nearly killed Helen, but he had a history of abusing her. Prior to assaulting her with the knife, Dad had broken her ribs during an incident in Dallas. He had received probation and an order of protection was put in place against him. But he violated that directive from the court during another altercation. To evade repercussions for that assault, he used his twin brother's name and Social Security number as an alias, something he had apparently done before. He used his brother's ID to earn money on a job while he was collecting disability payments from the government via his own Social Security number, which was illegal as well as damaging to his brother. They were on to that scam now, too, and he potentially faced federal charges for the fraud.

By the time Mom was called to the stand, the jury had already found Dad guilty. She was meant to be a character witness for the prosecution during the punishment phase. Their goal of putting her on the stand was to ensure that my father received the harshest sentence allowable under the law. Seeing Dad looking so old and frail, convicted of attempted murder and without a single friend or family member present in support, tugged at her heartstrings.

"When they called me to the stand I was nervous but I felt like I could do it. They asked me questions about where I lived, how I met your daddy, our marriage. I gave all good, positive statements. Then they asked me about the 1988 incident, and I said that . . ." She stopped.

"That what?" I pressed.

Mom swallowed and sniffled before squeaking out her next words. "I said that you were traumatized. I started to cry, so they had to stop for a minute while I tried to catch my breath." Mom gulped and gasped as though she was in a live-action role play of the trial.

"It's okay, Mom, take your time." I wished I had gone after all. It was selfish of me to ask her to do this alone. She and I had been through it together then. Why not now? I felt like my family had abandoned me, and now I was doing the same to her.

Mom inhaled deeply several times before continuing, and I forced back the golf-ball-sized lump in my throat. "I said you were traumatized, and your daddy covered his mouth like he was trying to control his emotions, so I know it bothered him to hear it. I told them he was a good father and a good provider and real talented at construction. I ended up crying and crying after I got off the stand, but not in front of the jury—outside the courtroom. Do you think he'll have to go to a regular jail?"

"What do you mean?"

"Because he's deaf, do you think he'll go to a regular prison?"

"He tried to kill someone."

"I hope not," she said, preoccupied with her own train of thought. "There are too many predators in there."

Dad won't even hear them coming.

I shuddered. The thought was too much to bear.

I heard Greg barreling down the hallway, snapping me out of my spiraling self-pity. His voice got closer as he asked an equally sharp-dressed, high-priced attorney, "Can you make a meeting at four o'clock?"

"Can't. My son is starting a T-ball league today."

"Good," Greg quickly retorted. "Now you'll find out if he's gay."

Greg could always count on me for a reaction to one of his zingers. Instead I kept my head down and scribbled on my shopping list: Kleenex for desk. A napkin from the deli does not make a good tissue.

"What's wrong with you?" Greg asked, slightly annoyed that I was ignoring him.

I put on a blasé face and shuffled papers as I told him, "My dad was just sentenced." Greg was one of the few people I had confided in about my father.

"Oh," he said as he sized up my grim look. "Come on, I'm hungry; let's get lunch." I was a regular lunch companion for Greg. I always joined him and his two partners or a client. He headed to the elevator without asking them, but I didn't balk; I grabbed my purse and trailed after him. We weaved through the horde of tourists in the Channel Gardens and passed the gleaming golden Prometheus statue that lorded over the iconic skating rink outside our offices. I blinked back tears, which became easier with the fresh air and sunshine, but that damned lump in my throat was lingering.

We arrived at Joseph's Citarella, a fancy restaurant next to Radio City Music Hall. "I've been meaning to check this place out," Greg stated, and quickly secured us a table for two by a window. The menu was mostly seafood, prepared with words I couldn't decipher or pronounce, all listed at exorbitant prices; my eyes crossed. Growing up, the only fish I ever ate we had caught by ourselves or was prepared by Long John Silver's and doused in malt vinegar. Catfish and perch deep-fried over a campfire I can handle, but what the heck is kanpachi or skate or fluke? My mind wandered. I thought about how Dad showed me how to eat fish without choking on a bone and used his favorite pocketknife to deftly shave corn off the cob in a way that kept the kernels attached in perfect little rows.

I wonder if that's the knife he used to stab Helen?

I sighed pitifully and Greg swooped in to take over. He was not opposed to a scene; he just wasn't used to not being the center of it.

"I'm going to order for you. She'll have the tuna steak medium rare," he instructed the waitress. He looked back at me and said, "You like meat, so I know you'll like this. You should order it rare, but since you've never had it before we'll start you out gently." He rolled up his pant leg and jabbed himself in the thigh with a shot of insulin.

I was skeptical. Mom used to make a tuna casserole with cans of Starkist tuna and the smell of it baking made our trailer reek and my gag reflex go into overdrive. Now somebody wants to charge thirty dollars for a lunch of cooked tuna? At least Greg was paying, and I was grown-up enough to know how to pretend to enjoy something.

Greg was right about the fish. I really liked tuna steak and it was nothing like baked Starkist. We ate in relative silence. The silence may have made Greg uncomfortable, but I was too busy thinking about Dad and wishing I were Greg's daughter instead. He had put his girls through college, helped pay their rent, and had gotten them out of jams. Maybe Greg would adopt me.

I'm a good daughter.

"So, how long did he get?"

"The maximum," I muttered. "Twenty years."

"That long, huh? How old is he?"

"Fifty-five. He's gonna die in there." I chewed on the inside corner of my lip to stop myself from crying and stared at a sesame seed I rolled between my fingers. If I didn't look Greg in the eye, none of this would be real.

"Yeah, maybe or maybe not."

"He drank and smoked pot his whole life, he snorted crank; he's not exactly the picture of good health. Let's be real. My *dad* . . . is gonna *die* . . . in *jail*."

Greg took a big bite of tuna and smacked, "Yeah, well, he's not dead yet. And, hey, at least now you'll know where to find him." Greg shoved another forkful of meat into his mouth and tacked on matter-of-factly, "He's lucky he's got you."

Chapter Eighteen

NOTHING BUT THE TRUTH

On a beautiful summer day in 2002, not long after Dad's assault on Helen, I sat perched on Greg's window ledge peer-
ing down to the street below. The bagpipes wailed in front of St.
Patrick's Cathedral, but they weren't part of any annual parade.
Instead, countless men and women in dress blues filled the

street paying respect to someone who had died on September 11. This had become a near daily occurrence over the last year, a constant, palpable reminder of the attack. I remembered walking alone across the 59th Street Bridge that day in 2001. The acrid smoke rose from the heap that loomed to the south.

For every funeral service, I found myself drawn to the same window ledge and leaned my head against the glass. As I listened to the sad strains of "Going Home," I wondered which person was finally being honored.

I wished I could swap Dad with the stranger in the casket.

Dad will grow old and die in jail and nothing good will ever come of his life. No one would know him as he was or care to know him as he is. He will always be flawed in a stranger's eyes; not worth anyone's compassion or pity or love; earning his dank cell devoid of warmth and filled with pain and suffering.

The heralded stranger may have been flawed; hell, maybe he was even a convict who had served his time, but he was now a victim. Innocent, unsuspecting, and undeserving of what lay ahead that September day. His family deserved great sympathy for their loss.

If Dad could switch places with someone who died that day, that someone could go on and lead their life as flawed as they wanted it to be. I fantasized that they were young and vibrant and would be able to hear music and sing the way Dad always wanted; they were loved unconditionally instead of disowned by their whole family and they had a future and life worth living. Then, if anyone asked about Dad, they would not care about his flaws; they would only hear that I had sacrificed him unwillingly. Dad would somehow be worthy of their respect without reservation and I wouldn't reject their sympathy.

"Thank you," I'd say. "He was a lot of fun. I'm sure he's listening to Elvis in Heaven right now, where they say the Deaf shall hear again."

The day I received word of Dad's twenty-year sentence, I returned to my apartment after work, ran to the bathroom, stripped off my clothes, and collapsed into a heap in the bathtub. I lay there as scorching hot water pelted me, hoping it could burn each layer of shame and grief from my skin. I sobbed and gasped for air, anguished at the thought of my father behind bars alone and loathed, his life wasted and reviled.

I grieved, I presume, as one might for a father who had unexpectedly died without saying goodbye. A father who had been unnaturally stripped away in a swift, deadly blow, leaving his family to wonder what had been the last words said. When was the last "I love you" and had they meant it?

This was my father's due, but I was devastated. Despite everything, I loved him. Then I received a letter. It was from Dad and was filled with rage. Dad described fighting with other inmates. He was bitter with the system, asserting his innocence and complaining about everything. He didn't think he should be in jail. I thought back to my lunch with Greg and his take on things as he munched on tuna. "Hey, at least now you'll know where to find him."

So, I wrote back. Other than an infrequent note from David, I was the only one who did. I thought that maybe by writing to him, he wouldn't be so angry or fighting so much. But his letters weren't cutting to the heart of the matter: Why couldn't he take responsibility for his violence? How did one child of ten become the blackest of sheep? I asked myself over and over. Just how could someone with so much charm and talent fall so far?

Over the course of several phone calls with Mom, I grilled her for the uncensored answers. I knew that with Dad in jail she no longer had to worry about breaking social mores by bashing her ex-husband to their daughter. There was no more reputation to protect; nothing more to fear. It was time for the truth.

"Do you remember the time Dad threw your necklace into the bonfire and we had to sift through the dirt like we were panning for gold?"

"Yes." Mom seemed leery of where this conversation was headed.

"What were y'all fighting about? What made him throw it?"

"Oh, I don't remember, Kambri. It was usually the same thing over and over. Your daddy would drink too much and start accusing me of cheating on him. He was so suspicious."

From Dad's letters, I knew what she meant without her needing to elaborate. His insecurity about being born deaf exacerbated his paranoia. He always feared that people were talking about him or keeping secrets.

"If we were at an event," Mom continued, "he might come by and squeeze my arm so tight to let me know, 'I'm watching. Be careful what you do.' I always had bruises that were hidden. There was another time when my mother and father, the Sloans, Aunt Carly and Uncle Doug, and your cousins were all visiting from Oklahoma. We used the leftover logs from the cabin to make big bonfires. We would sit around and talk and have such a good time. This year everything went berserk.

"We had a few drinks, then all of a sudden your daddy just went crazy. He accused me of cheating on him and grabbed me by my neck and broke my necklace. All hell broke loose.

"My daddy and your uncle Doug tried to stop him but he was

too strong. I fell to the ground to look for my chain. I didn't know this until afterward but your uncle saw your daddy was aiming to stomp my head with his cowboy boot. Just as he swung his leg, Doug intervened and stopped your father's boot with his own foot. Doug actually saved my life!"

My grandparents were there? My aunt and uncle, too? They witnessed something as frightening as the heel of a cowboy boot coming within an inch of Mom's skull, and yet I never knew a thing about it.

"My God, Mom! Why didn't anyone do anything?"

"Everyone was upset. Carly and Doug left for home the next day. Carly said she never wanted to be around if your father was there. He was always mean to her and she was tired of it! The next day he told everyone how sorry he was and he really meant it. You could see that he was really ashamed of himself. My parents stayed to make sure things had cooled down. I should have left and gone home with my parents, but I didn't. Why didn't I? I don't know."

So he just got away with it.

I thought about my grandfather and how he had convinced my mother she didn't need to go to college. Getting married, raising children, and helping her family were her purpose in life. I wonder if he carried guilt or if he figured working through these family issues was just a fact of life.

"That time you had a black eye, you told me you slipped and fell on the ice: I'm guessing that was a lie."

"Yep," Mom said matter-of-factly. "Your daddy did that to me, too."

I had known Mom's excuse sounded odd, but I was just a ten-year-old girl. When she said she slipped on the ice, I had wanted to believe her.

"I went to work and people asked me what had happened," Mom recalled. "I told them I fell and hit my face on the steps. Some came right out and asked, 'Are you sure it wasn't your husband?'"

She had told them the same lie as me, but they weren't naïve like I was. What's more, they had witnessed Dad's predatory behavior before.

"There was a time a few of us were working late. Your daddy came strolling in, acting like he was Mr. Big Shot. When I think back, he was alerting the guys there that I was his and to stay away from me. Later a few people would ask me, 'Are you okay? Everything good at home?' I never let anyone know what was happening in my marriage, but I guess they could tell."

After years of keeping up appearances, Mom was skilled in self-delusion.

"When your father and I first got divorced, he started dating a cute young blond deaf girl that I always saw him teasing and flirting with at the Deaf club in Dallas. One night at the Deaf club she came up to me with a very distressed look on her face. She asked me if your daddy had ever hurt me. I told her, 'No. Never.' She was really upset and asked again, 'Really? He never threatened you or anything?' She said your daddy had been hurting her. That he would grab her by her hair and shove her around. He was really scaring her, but I told her, 'No, he never did anything like that to me before.' I didn't want the Deaf to know. I was too proud, I guess.

"But I also lied out of fear because I just knew that your father would come after me and threaten me again. I hoped the girl knew I wasn't being honest. After that he only dated hearing women because the Deaf knew what kind of a man he was and wanted no part of him."

After hearing about Mom's volatile marriage, I began searching through public records for Dad's name. The list of discoveries of his past offenses grew so long that I stopped being
surprised. My father was a felon, a petty criminal, and a predatory domestic abuser.

He was also a serial adulterer. Mom said the first time Dad
cheated on her, David was only six months old. Forty years later,
she still got so choked up thinking about it that she was barely
able to tell me the story. They were newlyweds with a baby. It was
the late 1960s, and failed marriages were stigmatized, symbols of
shame and failure. She didn't want to be a divorced, single mom,
so she took him back.

"I knew your daddy was still messing around, so when I found
a woman's coat in the back of our car I took it inside. I went
through the pockets and—hey, do you remember my jade ring?"

"Sure I do," I said. I had always loved Mom's jewelry. While
she and Dad were out dancing, I rooted through her closet and
played dress-up with her clothes, high heels, and rings. Mom
was allergic to anything but real gold, so I knew everything I was
touching was genuine, not to be trifled with. The jade ring was
always one of my favorites. It was bold. Its oversized green face
demanded attention. "Look at me!"

"Well, I rifled through the coat and that jade ring was in one
of the pockets, so I snatched it."

*That beautiful jade ring I had admired all those years was stolen
from one of Dad's tramps?*

"Your daddy came home and asked if I knew what happened
to the coat that had been in the car. I smiled and said it was hanging in the closet. He disappeared for a second, then came back
looking real anxious and asked, 'Where is the ring?' I told him I

took it and he said, 'No, it's not yours. I need to give it back.' I told him, 'No! It's *my* ring now!'"

She had challenged Dad's audacity at wondering about his lover's coat and she had won. The jade ring was her trophy.

"I should have made him buy me something for every woman he had an affair with. Wow, the jewelry I could have had!"

Mom and I cried and laughed and cried again as we recounted old stories about life with Dad on Boars Head, focusing on the good times. We recalled fond memories of movie nights at the Sloans', trips to Galveston, developing our land on Boars Head from scratch, building that bridge, how he could tell a story so funny your sides ached from laughing.

I was feeling better about the situation, that my dad wasn't pure evil. Even Mom, who had every right to string him up by his balls, could still see some good in him. I joked, "At least Dad only *tried* to kill you and Helen and didn't *actually* kill somebody."

"Well," Mom said. "That we *know* of . . ."

My heart stopped. "Ummm, what do you mean 'that we know of'?"

"Well . . ." Mom sighed. "There was the time he wrecked the Thunderbird. He had disappeared for a week and came home with the Thunderbird stinking to high heaven."

"I hit a deer," he had explained. I remembered the incident. I had used the accident in my excuse to keep Ken, my co-worker at Showbiz, from seeing our dreadfully ugly car. Mom hadn't bought it. We were in the city by then and the stench of death on the car wasn't like anything she had gotten a whiff of before. "That smell. I'll never forget it.

"Just a few weeks later, he went out drinking at the Deaf club and I stayed home. I was asleep in bed when I felt the vibration of the garage door opening and shutting, but your father didn't come to bed, so I went to check on him. I opened the garage door and your dad was just covered in blood, scrubbing the car clean. I said, 'Oh my God! Are you okay? What happened?'

"He said he broadsided the whole left side of the Thunderbird on a concrete divider on Airport Freeway while trying to avoid an accident on his way home from the Deaf club. A woman in another car was hurt and he stopped to help her. That's how he explained why he had blood all over him and the car was wrecked."

"If his accident wasn't his fault, why didn't we ever get the Thunderbird fixed? Didn't we have insurance? What happened to the woman? Was she okay after the ambulance got there?"

"I have no idea. It's one of the many stories he told. We bought the Thunderbird from a used car dealer, the type where you might not have good credit so they charge you an arm and a leg. We let it get repossessed and never heard from the dealership again.

"Imagine what they must have thought when they saw the car!" At this, Mom laughed. "But really, who knows how many other wrecks he caused? What if he was killed? What if he killed someone?"

"I wonder if that's why that cop pulled us over when Dad drove me to work at Malibu?" I recounted the scenario where my father and I had been pulled over by a policeman. The officer supposedly stopped us for missing a front license plate, but that hadn't seemed genuine. "Maybe our Thunderbird had been reported as being involved in a hit-and-run."

"Yeah, maybe . . ." Mom's voice trailed off. We sat quietly, each mulling over the possibility. After a minute, Mom broke the silence. "Do you remember Donna?"

Oh no, there's more?

"Yeah, of course, I do. I worked at her fireworks stand and she had that foxy son, Cash."

"Well, she was your daddy's mistress."

I had no idea my father was such a cad. Over the years, different friends in the Deaf community had told her about Dad's catting around. Stealing the jade ring from one of his trollops had been her one defiant act. She finally got fed up and packed our things in storage. That was days before we made the trip to Oklahoma for the National Deaf Bowling Tournament, which I thought was an ordinary trip. Our move to the woods was Dad's opportunity to refocus his wandering eye on Mom, and it had worked, for a while at least. Then he fell back into his old ways and met Donna at Johnny B. Dalton's, one of the two bars she managed.

"So all those times he was gone for days . . ."

"He was with Donna." By then, Mom and Dad were having serious money troubles and she was planning on leaving Dad. "Then one day Donna calls me to ask me if I know Cigo Crews." (Dad had begun using the nickname Cigo in the mid-1980s, saying he no longer wanted to have his father's name. He preferred the unusual moniker, which Mom said stood for "Can I Go Out.") "I told her, 'Yes I do. I'm his wife.' She apologized and said she did not know he was married and we talked for a while about how your daddy seemed to be a nice man. He had never said anything about a wife and family."

My hours of pacing the driveway wondering about Dad were unnecessary. Mom had known where he was. She could have allayed my fears.

Mom continued. "I worried the entire time he was out," she said. "He was always drinking and driving. I would stay awake worrying until he came home, then get up early and go to work the next day. I was tired. I thought if Dad had to confront *you*, his baby girl, seeing how upset you were, he would know firsthand what his gallivanting was doing to the family."

I was dumbfounded that not only had my mother agreed to let my father carry on this way, but that she ended up working for Donna at her fireworks stand.

"Why didn't you care that he had a mistress?"

"I told her that he and I were not getting along anyway and that she could have him if she wanted him. I was hoping that if he got involved with another woman, he wouldn't mind if I left. I would finally have a way out.

"Well, when your daddy wanted to be with Donna, they used to hang out at her other bar Cooter's. There was this pretty, young blond bartender that your dad was infatuated with. He used to flirt and tease her. You know how he is. Well one day her body was found dumped under a bridge on Highway 2854 over the San Jacinto River. She had been raped and strangled with her own nylon stocking. I thought maybe your daddy did it, but I didn't ask. I didn't want to know the answer."

My blood ran cold. It was jarring to learn that my mother could suspect Dad of such a thing. "How could you *not* want to know?"

"I was afraid, Kambri. He had hurt me and threatened me too

many times, that he would cut me up all over my face, body, and crotch so that no man would want me."

My father had Mom so intimidated that she didn't voice her suspicions and feared for her own life. I wondered aloud if that was why she never took my claims of abuse at David's hands seriously; it was child's play compared to what she was dealing with.

"I used to complain to you that David was beating me up but you never did anything. He sat on top of me and tormented me, dangling long strings of spit and thumping my forehead or sternum with his index finger."

"Hmm, is that so?" Mom seemed intrigued. "Interesting . . ."

"What? *Interesting?* What's interesting?"

"That's what your daddy would do to me. If I confronted him about driving home drunk late at night, then he'd fight with me till dawn. I remember having a lot of fights in our master bathroom because I didn't want you kids to know what was going on, but then I guess I forgot that you both can hear.

"He would grab and push me to let me know that I can't tell him what to do. Once I fell backwards in the tub. That could have killed me. I knew he would never hurt me in front of you kids, so when he would get angry and start to act out, I ran to David's bedroom. Your dad would sit on top of my chest and interrogate me for hours, calling me names, accusing me of fucking this guy or that, and blowing cigarette smoke in my face."

The revelation was potent. I hadn't done anything to make David turn on me. David had just been treating me the way Dad did Mom. My heart ached for my brother witnessing what he had and not knowing how to help.

I couldn't stop wondering about the barmaid. I speculated that Mom may have been so consumed by her abusive relationship that she was being histrionic. It's one thing to be in love with a man prone to domestic violence. It's entirely another to suspect him of murder. But the story nagged at me. Everything else my mother had shared with me corresponded with my memories. Using the little information I had, I searched online for old articles using keywords from Mom's story. I didn't expect to find anything. But my first query yielded an article from the *Houston Chronicle* detailing a crime almost exactly how my mother described it. Only now, I had a name.

The body of Brenda Maureen Hackett, 25, was found under a railroad trestle near FM 2854 by a train conductor. Hackett had been sexually assaulted before she was strangled with a stocking.

The murder was in the summer of 1985, just when our lives on Boars Head were falling apart. Jerry Michael Ward had been suspected but committed suicide before he could be questioned. I asked a friend who is a police officer in Texas to investigate. He made a call to the Montgomery County Sheriff's Office, which revealed that my father had also been a person of interest.

After his arrest for the attack on Helen, Dad was required to submit a DNA sample. During a routine check of cold cases, my father was cleared of Hackett's murder. It was a relief to know he was absolved for that crime, but it was no comfort to know that more than one person believed he was capable of it.

The mystery was finally unfolding. Mom was helping me

piece together the clues I had been too young to understand. She had been a good wife and had protected me from ever seeing this side of my father, a jack-in-the-box crouched and waiting for a turn of the crank to set him off.

Her only mistake was that she was afraid to leave. The one time she tried—during the move from Grove Street to our apartment on Weyland Drive—Dad had caught her in the act. He discovered her new address and pressured her into giving him one more chance. She needed help and didn't know how to ask for it. Even if she did, then what? The whole Deaf community would know her dirty laundry. She was too proud for that. Or worse, Dad wouldn't be punished and his fury would be fueled by Mom's disloyalty and she would have no protection.

Dad hadn't just woken up one day and turned into a criminal. Society, our family, and the criminal justice system had colluded to give Dad the keys to a warship. His life hadn't spiraled out of control; it was on a steady downhill course from day one.

Just like in Oz, the curtain was pulled back. The Wizard was a fraud.

After Mom left Dad, many of her friends said how free and re-laxed she looked. "Before, I always had to be careful who I talked to. I can't talk to him, or him, or him, and if a guy approaches me just for friendly talk, I need to have an excuse to move away or your dad might think I was flirting.

"Your dad would show up at the helicopter company I worked for in Fort Worth to check on me. One time, after you and I got evicted and were living in the townhouse apartments, I was driving home from work when I saw his car following me. I thought,

'Oh no! I can't let him know where Kambri and I have moved to!' So I sped up, but he sped up and was not going to stop. I now think about how reckless this act was, but I was speeding over forty miles an hour in a residential area. Think what could have happened? I could have hit and killed someone, a kid playing in the street, someone's beloved pet. I was crazy with fear.

"One time, out of the blue, your daddy showed up at my place of work. Several people lingered close by just in case. He said he didn't mean to be so mean and hurtful to me. He was there to say he was sorry."

This came as a great surprise to me. Dad has always denied any responsibility for anything. Learning that at one point he felt compelled to make amends with Mom gave me hope. My father is capable of admitting his wrongs and healing rifts. This awareness also irritated me. Dad has never once told *me* he was sorry.

"Really? He told you he was sorry?"

"Uh-huh, and he returned my jewelry he stole the night he slashed my clothes and took the gun your uncle Doug gave me. Remember the jade ring I told you I found in a woman's coat? I still have it. Now it's yours! A keepsake of your daddy's cheatin'!"

A floozy's trinket and a sliver of the truth aren't much of an inheritance, but I'll take it.

~

"*Thirty minutes,*" a guard mouths to Dad while tapping his watch. Dad's demeanor shifts.

"*I need you to help me write a letter for an appeal. I'm tired of staying in prison so long. I should be walking free because of the lack of evidence in my case.*"

Since his incarceration, Dad declares his innocence in every letter to me. Now that we're face-to-face, he wants to tell me his side of the story.

He launches into a dramatic reenactment of events the night Helen was nearly killed. "*She was mad because we didn't have money for more beer. She was already drunk and wanted to pick a fight with me.*"

His signs are big; his hands strike each other with force. The smacks are loud enough to cause his neighboring inmates to shoot us worried glances.

"*She grabbed my knife, held it up to her neck, and said she would kill herself. I tried to get the knife away from her but it was too late: She cut her own throat. I grabbed her hand with the knife and when we struggled she got stabbed a few times.*

"*I'm still angry at the cops for spraying me and holding pistols to my forehead. Dammit. I wish they shot and killed me so you could sue them.*"

I had wished him dead, too. I hear Greg's words echo, "*He's lucky he's got you.*" Yeah, some luck Dad has.

His story, while swallowed up as the truth by a prisoner like his child-molesting friend Larry, doesn't ring true with me. In addition to all that Mom told me about Dad's criminal past, I ordered the trial transcript, retrieved police reports, and read written statements from witnesses to Helen's attack, ranging from a fourteen-year-old neighbor to the arresting officers.

Everyone's accounts support the devastating picture. My father's version was full of lies. It only took the jury one hour to decide Dad was guilty, and I've never once questioned their decision. But Dad is grasping for the hope that I believe him; that I won't leave him to die alone in jail. Rather than ask him why the facts are against him, I just nod along as Dad signs. He interprets this as support, which seems to spur him on. His anger and paranoia kick into overdrive. "Helen planned this. She wanted me to go to jail so she could take my things."

Helen had not wanted Dad to go to jail. Her desire to protect him had almost gotten her killed. Mom had acted the exact same way. And both of them defended him on the stand.

"He was the most loving man I've ever been around," Helen testified when asked how Dad behaved when he wasn't drinking. My father insisted he didn't have a drinking problem or see a need to seek counseling for the addiction. His public defender noted, however, that every time Dad got into trouble, alcohol was a factor. I thought of Mom's testimony and, even after all he had done to her, how she tried to lessen the blow by talking about what a good father and provider Dad had been.

As if he can read my mind, Dad says, "Your mother lied on the stand about the 1988 case. See, I was mad that she let Rob stay at the apartment and left you alone with him. I never had a knife at her throat. I just punched holes in the wall, only five. I don't know why your mama lied. Maybe she wants to see me in jail."

You're forgetting one thing, Dad: I was there.

We can sort the details out later. The one thing we have now is time.

Dad must serve ten years of his twenty-year sentence before he is eligible for parole—something he has little chance of getting with his record of fighting and unwillingness to accept responsibility.

"Twenty years? Why me? Why me? Why me?" He shakes his head slowly in disbelief. His chin wrinkles and his pursed lips turn downward. "I will tie sheets around my neck and hang myself," he signs with defiance.

"No," I scoff. I scan his face for a sign that he won't do it.

He stares back, scanning my face; perhaps his only reason not to.

I left the prison at peace. He is my father, for better or worse. I accept him as he is. And my bad dreams? I don't have them anymore. Dad and I write to each other now. I send him postcards and photos, and tell him about my life in New York City. I buy him writing supplies and subscriptions to magazines, and deposit money into his inmate trust fund. I hope he will use it to purchase strawberry ice cream. "Don't worry," he tells me. "I will pay you back when I'm in the Free World."

I research things for him on the Internet—mostly sports trivia and history—to help settle intellectual disputes with other prisoners. And lately, Dad has channeled his anger and time in a more productive way by researching the Americans with Disabilities Act and how it applies to inmates. Dad has even anointed himself "Warrior for the Deaf." I'm encouraged by his investing his intellect and time toward a greater good. Sure, he might be motivated to help himself, but isn't there usually a selfish reason for being unselfish?

He sends me drawings and gives me fatherly advice "to not commit adultery, take dope, or drink heavily." If anyone would know, he would. Sometimes Dad's cards just say, "Send money. Love, Daddy."

I had wanted justice, and had gotten it. Now I just wanted my daddy, the one I chose to remember. The man who rescued my flip-flop because he thought it meant something to me; the father who danced better than John Travolta; the dad who let me drive the Toyota. The father who was my Daniel Boone, Frank Lloyd Wright, Ben Franklin, and Elvis Presley all rolled into one.

So when his notes are a brief demand to "send money," well, I will. After all, I'm in the Free World. My cross to bear isn't a heavy load. I'll humbly carry it as a reminder of where I came from and how far one can fall.

EPILOGUE

During a trip to Texas, I find myself compelled to revisit Boars Head some ten years after we left it behind. The two-lane country route that takes me to Honea Egypt Road is now a four-lane thoroughfare. I see that Webb's Grocery is gone, replaced by a bank; and the old horse auction where I first met Charlie Brown is now a Wal-Mart. I had perfectly preserved a memory of the place I called home and the expansion has wiped away all things quaint and unique and replaced them with homogenized conglomerates. I am nervous. I don't know if I should go farther and see our old land. *What if it's a Wal-Mart, too?*

I am comforted to see that Honea Egypt Road isn't much different, though all the real estate signs with looming threats of "Coming Soon" don't bode well for its continued preservation. The road seems wider, the blacktop is smoother, and the signs for roads and subdivisions that never existed throw me off, but I am close. I feel it. A turn down Circle Drive brings more familiarity as the road narrows and the trees outnumber the trailers by a few thousand to one.

As I round the hairpin turn onto Boars Head, my heart quickens. I feel like a dozen butterflies have hatched in my belly. The road is now paved, though there are still no traffic signs, curbs, or lane dividers painted on the asphalt. Passing over a dry creek bed, I realize this must be the bridge Dad constructed. At least I think it is. It seems dwarfed in size, and with the layers of asphalt covering it, there's no way for me to check for his inscription carved into the concrete. With the authentication paved over, I wonder if there is anyone left in these parts who knew how my father salvaged this stretch of back road with his design and changed the lives of the schoolkids who rode Bus #9.

I approach what used to be the driveway we cleared and notice the gate is gone. But that's okay. Nothing much left to keep in, is there? Some posts have rotted and collapsed and the barbed wire is caked with rust, but to my surprise the fence Dad and David built for my horse, Charlie Brown, remains mostly intact.

I park the car off to the side of the road, open the door, and take a deep breath of thick, humid air before I step out onto the pavement. *Pavement?* This patch of earth is familiar and foreign all at once. Our mailbox is gone and the land is overgrown with trees and brush. If it weren't for the empty space where the gate used to be, there would be no way of telling where the driveway once was. Since leaving Boars Head I haven't spent time in the wilderness and my nerves are on edge looking for snakes. Dusk is fast approaching and the deeper into the woods I get, the less the sun lights the way.

My eyes adjust to the darkness, and I realize I am surrounded by nothing but dense forest. My heart sinks. This trek was in hopes of seeing something, anything that reminds me of the home my family and I once made with our love, sweat, and tears. Time has taken it all back. I sigh in resignation and breathe in the pine-scented evening air. I turn in place, looking up at the trees and whispers of darkening sky in awe. *How on earth did we ever manage to turn this place into a home?*

Then the shed comes into focus. The rusted tin and dim light serve as camouflage, but there it is just as we left it. The woods seem to swirl around me and disappear, revealing the bones of our past lives.

With the shed serving as a point on my compass of memories, I get my bearings.

If that's the shed, then I'm standing near where our basketball hoop was.

I look around on the ground, kicking back layers of growth to see if I can find the basket. I don't find it, so I look up and see the red ring still nailed to the tree that has now grown several feet. Bits and pieces of net dangle and chunks of the backboard's edges have rotted away. Seeing the formerly slight tree as thick and sturdy as one of the logs from the old cabin makes me laugh out loud in amazement. My basketball tree is all grown-up.

One of the two trees that held our swing hasn't fared as well.

It is bent in half and when it fell, however many months or years before, it took the metal pole and swing down with it. The two-by-fours of the swing are soggy splinters eaten away by termites and carpenter ants. I think about Mom's beautiful landscaping and how disappointed she would have been when the tree gave way. Dad would have had to rebuild the swing for her somewhere else.

The outhouse has succumbed to Mother Nature. Not a speck of it is visible. The rusted-out Bug sits nearby in shambles, stripped of anything worth taking; the red paint is faded, revealing a metal skeleton. The roof, still dented from the time David flipped it three times, is covered in leaves and dried pinecones and needles. Weeds, bushes, and tree branches sprout through the holey floorboard and busted back windshield. The Bug is so lushly covered that it almost seems intentional, like a quirky piece of lawn decoration.

It really is beautiful down here. No wonder Mom and Dad loved this place.

The lock on the door to the shed is broken and I walk inside the carcass of where our fantasy home was supposed to be. Inside nothing remains except a musty smell and memories. It is smaller than I remember, and I had remembered it as being small.

We sure didn't have much, just each other.

I step back outside into the evening air, which is dripping with humidity. Darkness has taken over almost without warning. It is nearly pitch black and the sounds of the forest spook me. I don't want to be in these woods without light so I hustle back to Boars Head. Safely back beside the car, I stand on the blacktop and stare through the wall of trees at the old fence that surrounded my little universe, built by Theodore R. Crews, Jr.

A breeze blows through the leaves, and I swear I hear the spirits of our laughter and our tears in the swaying treetops. The flame of our lost dreams is rekindled inside me.

I could burn down the ground and clear the snakes and try again. I could.

ACKNOWLEDGMENTS

When a book is about one's life, where do the thanks begin? The beginning of the book's inception, I suppose. So, thank you to Rachel Kramer Bussel for encouraging me to submit my story to Hillary Carlip of FreshYarn.com and to Hillary for editing and publishing my piece. Thank you to Kara Welker for reading that essay and introducing me to Peter McGuigan of Foundry Literary & Media without recompense, and to Peter for giving me a chance and his continued friendship. And, of course, thank you to Bruce Tracy for ushering me into the Big Time.

Very special thanks to my agent Chris Park for the patience, understanding, and gentle but firm counsel she showed me, which educated and kept me sane; and to my editor, Ryan Doherty, for answering my innumerable questions and helping me sculpt my pile of words into something readable.

Sincerest thanks for the numerous readings, comments, questions, and edits by Lisa Pulitzer, without which this book would not have been possible. She taught me loads with her expertise.

My appreciation also goes to performing arts programs in schools, local theaters, and comedy communities, without which so many freaks, geeks, and at-risk kids and adults might find themselves in heaps of trouble or, at the very least, lonely and inert. The arts (and, yes, stand-up comedy is an art form) are important, as significant as organized sports. These groups helped me find my voice to tell my story and gave me peace knowing that my family has nothing to be ashamed of. Without them, I would not have the pleasure of friendships with Scott Ramsey, Liam McEneaney, Sara Benincasa, Jenn Dodd, Sue Funke, Eddie Gutierrez, Rachel Kempster, Carolyn Castiglia, and Chuck Wills, who never fail in their enthusiasm and willingness to listen to my chatter.

To my first husband, Rob, and his family, I express my deepest gratitude. They took me in when no one else did and loved me as one of their own. I'm so happy that our friendships have endured and thankful for their irreverent senses of humor.

Love and thanks to my brother for understanding that the truth really can set you free and that it was time for me to tell my truth. He is rightly proud of conquering the enormous odds that were stacked against him. I admire him for all that he has accomplished. He's a survivor, too.

I'm eternally grateful to my dynamo mama for her willingness to shed her fear and field my relentless interrogations that opened her long-forgotten wounds. She carried a lot of guilt from some of her choices, but what mother doesn't? She did right by us. She once cracked, "We may not have put you through college, but we sure did give you an interesting life." That they did, and I love them for it. I hold her in high esteem for her courage, tenacity, and work ethic and adore her puckish wit. I also appreciate that she passed on to me her passion for reading.

And, finally, there are not enough ways to thank my husband, Christian. The care and patience he bestows on me make me wonder if he isn't harboring some horrid secret. Why else would someone be so kind and encourage me with such ardent passion? He is my biggest champion and best friend. His undying support, thoughtful advice, compassion, and devotion go unmatched. He is amazing, and I am so lucky he said, "I do."

ABOUT THE AUTHOR

KAMBRI CREWS owns a PR and production company specializing in comedy. A renowned storyteller and public speaker, she has appeared at The Moth, Upright Citizen's Brigade, and SXSW Interactive. She splits her time between Astoria, Queens, and Cochecton, New York, with her husband, comedian Christian Finnegan.

www.kambricrews.com

ABOUT THE TYPE

This book was set in Scala, a typeface designed by Martin Majoor in 1991. It was originally designed for a music company in the Netherlands and then was published by the international type house FSI FontShop. Its distinctive extended serifs add to the articulation of the letterforms to make it a very readable typeface.